Immigration and American Democracy

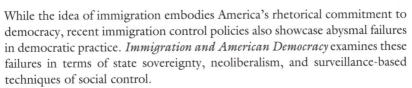

D0223624

While the idea of immigration embodies America's rhetorical commitment to democracy, recent immigration control policies also showcase abysmal failures in democratic practice. *Immigration and American Democracy* examines these failures in terms of state sovereignty, neoliberalism, and surveillance-based techniques of social control.

The ideological argument for privatization is not new. But immigration has provided a laboratory for replicating on American soil the sorts of outsourcing travesties that have occurred in America's war in Iraq. As an outcome, abusive executive powers—many delegated to state and local governments and private actors—are manifested every day in data collection, spying, detention, and deportation hearings, and in many cases bypassing the Constitution. The practice of privatization extends this leviathan immigration state by clamping down on civil liberties without having to oblige the courts.

Ultimately, Koulish examines the contested terrain between democratic and undemocratic forces in the immigration policy domain and concludes with recommendations for how democratic forces might well still win out.

Robert Koulish is Associate Professor of Law & Society at Philadelphia University.

Immigration and American Democracy

Subverting the Rule of Law

Robert Koulish

Routledge
Taylor & Francis Group

NEW YORK AND LONDON

First published 2010
by Routledge
270 Madison Ave, New York, NY 10016

Simultaneously published in the UK
by Routledge
2 Park Square, Milton Park, Abingdon, Oxon OX14 4RN

Routledge is an imprint of the Taylor & Francis Group, an informa business

Typeset in Galliard by
Florence Production Ltd, Stoodleigh, Devon
Printed and bound in the United States of America on acid-free paper by
Edwards Brothers, Inc.

Library of Congress Cataloging in Publication Data
Koulish, Robert E. (Robert Edwin).
  Immigration and American democracy: subverting the rule of law/
  Robert Koulish.
     p. cm.
  1. United States—Emigration and immigration—Government policy.
  2. Rule of law—United States.   3. Privatization—United States.
  4. Contracting out—United States.   I. Title.
  JV6483.K68 2009
  325.73—dc22   2009027873

ISBN 10: 0–415–99617–1 (hbk)
ISBN 10: 0–415–99618–X (pbk)
ISBN 10: 0–203–88322–5 (ebk)

ISBN 13: 978–0–415–99617–4 (hbk)
ISBN 13: 978–0–415–99618–1 (pbk)
ISBN 13: 978–0–203–88322–8 (ebk)

To Olivia and Julian

Contents

Preface

I decided to write this book well before the midterm elections in 2006 when it felt to me that the Bush-era abuses of executive power and government outsourcing might endure indefinitely into the future. In part, the act of writing this book was my own plaintiff wail against the Bush administration's efforts to domesticate and privatize the war on terror at the U.S.–Mexico border. I lived at the border for several years, taught there and used to enjoy hearing my students tell stories about crossing the bridge to get to class, or visiting aunts and grandparents across the River. More recently, when I brought students from a college class in Baltimore to the border at El Paso–Juarez the signs of border militarization were quite obvious. We observed surveillance towers peering over border fences and symbolically gazing down upon the flags of five nations at a historic site by the fence. Perhaps the most disconcerting part of that trip for me occurred when we visited the border patrol station and a border patrol officer asked me if I was interested in seeing what they can see through the cameras. As I walked over to the monitors, he proudly focused the camera in on the living room window of somebody's house in Juarez. It was cool and mortifying at the same time.

I also worked with refugees at the border, and conducted research about human rights abuses and about refugees moving through the administrative process to apply for political asylum. From my experiences and findings, I believed that America's treatment of immigrants at its border was shameful.

Still, I was surprised to see the post-9/11 Bush administration unveil plans to seal the border with a 2,000 mile wall and electronic fence. The absurdity of building a wall across desert, national wildlife preserves, through the private property of Texas land grant families, and American Indian reservations was magnified by the absence of democratic deliberation. Decisions were being made behind closed doors and were released to the public as final. Nobody, it seems, could question the sovereign!

When I started this project, I never imagined the outcome of the 2006 midterm elections would ultimately lead to Barack Obama's election. And so, when I was about half way done writing the manuscript and Obama was elected President, I reexamined the project's relevance, and after a couple months of the Obama Presidency became convinced that this project was more relevant than ever. President Obama has double downed on some of Bush's most egregious mistakes and his embrace of executive power and willingness to deploy risk management technologies during his early months in office increases the salience of this discussion. It strengthened my conviction that the deep structures of immigration control and the government's commitment to using sovereign powers over immigration continue to guide government practices.

Let me position myself within the terms of this book. I am a radical progressive, a civil libertarian and an immigrant rights advocate. I am a fan of privacy rights and having constitutional rights applied to immigrants at the border and wherever else they reside. However, I do not believe the struggle for immigrant justice ends with the recognition of constitutional rights. Quite the contrary, I believe this is where it begins. Besides recognizing the relevance of constitutional norms in immigration decision-making, dramatic changes must be made in the culture surrounding immigration politics. This means reframing the terms of the immigration control debate that go beyond rights discourse to include immigrants as subjects within their communities and workplaces. It also means settling on terms that depict immigrants as assets and as eligible for justice and fairness in immigration courts and in federal courts. It would recognize that fourth amendment rights to privacy apply to risk technologies, and that immigrants have rights to justice and democratic accountability. Currently the debate is framed in terms of a security discourse that perceives immigrants as a threat to domestic security. And in the absence of constitutional norms, that is, when the logics of sovereignty and risk rather than the rule of law provide the basis for decision-making, the immigrant struggle itself barely even registers among policy makers.

And so like any author's work, my book comes with a point of view, which will indeed inform my presentation. In part I would like to see my two cents added to the political discussion, and briefly here's the argument: the immigration control debate is currently framed in terms of security rather than in terms of law. This is a mistake. I shall argue that the current Hobbesian version of sovereign powers and security logic as the basis for immigration policy must be replaced with one that recognizes the rule of law, constitutional norms, and the assets that immigrants bring to their communities. I do not oppose the internal and external realities of sovereignty related to the US as a nation state. I do oppose the existing discourse that denies immigrants' human subjectivity and diminishes the contributions they make as workers, members of communities and families. The rule of law and a rights-based discourse belongs in the process of including and excluding immigrants.

I also believe the book contributes to the academic debate about the role that immigration plays in America's national identity. Immigration is the Id of American politics, more precisely, of nativist and racist zeal and of uncontrolled executive power. It shows what politicians, administrators, and bureaucrats are prone to doing if many of their decisions and actions go unchecked by such democratic processes as pluralist politics, popular opinion, or the courts. Following David Cole, I also believe that excesses in the immigration field easily bleed over into other domestic policy fields affecting citizens. I believe such was the Bush administration intent, to use immigration control as a policy lab for the purpose of experimenting with executive power, risk management, and social control technologies.

Early drafts of chapters referring to privatization were published in *Journal Migration and Refugee Issues* (Koulish, 2007); *Saint Thomas Law Review* (Koulish, 2008); and *MR-zine* (Koulish, 2008). In addition, early ideas were published as op-ed pieces in the *Baltimore Sun*, in "Making Real ID real" (2008); "Facing Manipulation on Immigration" (2007); and "A Corporate Takeover of American Borders" (2006).

I would like to thank Stephanie Flores-Koulish, my loving wife and best friend, whose encouragement and patience supported me throughout the process; to Olivia and Julian, my heart and soul, who keep me grinning; to my parents Joan and Sasha whose stories about their own parents' journeys, and their gift of my grandparents' and great grandparents' immigration documents, helped inspire my interest in immigration; to all the participants at the immigration panels for the 2008 and 2009 Law and Society Annual Meetings in Montreal (2008) and Denver (2009), particularly the Immigration and Citizenship CRN; the 2007 LatCrit conference meetings in Miami, Florida; and Philadelphia University; to Joel Grossman, a mentor and friend, who read a *Baltimore Sun* op-ed I wrote about privatizing the border and told me it was time to write a book; to the editors at Routledge, Michael Kerns and Mary Altman; to Sue Davis; Daniel Levin; Jeremy Koulish; Jon Goldberg-Hiller; Michael Cross-Barnet; Sonya Borton; Andrea Giampetro-Meyer; Tim Dunn; and to my students.

Abbreviations

ACLU	American Civil Liberties Union
AEDPA	Antiterrorism and Effective Death Penalty Act
APA	Administrative Procedures Act
ARRA	American Recovery and Reinvestment Act
BCIS	Border Crossing Information System
BIA	Board of Immigration Appeals
CAP	Center for American Progress
CBP	Customs and Border Protection
CCA	Corrections Corporation of America
CCR	Center for Constitutional Rights
CIS	Center for Immigration Studies
COP	Common Operating Picture
DHS	Department of Homeland Security
DMV	Department of Motor Vehicles
DOJ	Department of Justice
DRO	Detention and Removal Operation
DTA	Declaration of Taking Act
EAGLE	Enterprise Gateway for Leading Edge Technology
EDLs	Enhanced Drivers' Licenses
EFF	Electronic Frontier Foundation
EOP	Executive Office of the President
FAIR	Federation of American Immigration Reform
FBI	Federal Bureau of Investigation
FIAC	Human Rights Watch and the Florida Immigrant Advocacy Center
FOSS	Free and Open Source Software
FOTs	Fugitive Operations Teams
GATS	General Agreement on Trade in Services
HSAC	Homeland Security Advisory Council
HSIN	Homeland Security Information Network
ICE	Immigration and Customs Enforcement
IIRIRA	Illegal Immigration Reform and Immigrant Responsibility Act

INS	Immigration and Naturalization Service
IRCA	Immigration Reform and Control Act
IRTPA	Intelligence Reform and Terrorism Prevention Act
ITECC	International Technology, Education and Commerce campus
LIC	low-intensity conflict
LSI	lead system integrator
MOU	memorandum of understanding
NFOP	National Fugitive Operations Program
NSA	National Security Agency
NSEERS	National Security Entry-Exit Registration System
OIG	Office of the Inspector General
OLC	Office of Legal Counsel
PFLP	Popular Front for the Liberation of Palestine
PMO	Program Management Office
PVTSAC	private sector advisory committee
RFID	radio frequency identification
SBI	Secure Border Initiative
SBODAC	Secure Borders and Open Doors Advisory Committee
SEIU	Service Employees International Union
SPP	Security and Prosperity Partnership
TBC	Texas Border Commission
TSA	Transportation Security Administration
UFCW	United Food and Commercial Workers Union
US-VISIT	U.S. Visitor and Immigrant Status Indicator Technology
WHTI	Western Hemisphere Travel Initiative
WTO	World Trade Organization

Chapter 1

Introduction

Immigration Politics within a Post-9/11 Frame

In September 2001, almost immediately following the tragic plane attack on the Twin Towers and Pentagon on 9/11, the Federal Bureau of Investigation (FBI) initiated a massive investigation, called PENTTBOM,[1] to "identify the terrorists who hijacked the airplanes and anyone who aided their efforts." In the days following 9/11, Michael Chertoff, then Assistant Attorney General for the Criminal Division, led an ungrounded campaign of racial and religious profiling against Muslim, Arab, and South Asian immigrants across the country. In the two months following 9/11 about 1,200 persons were detained and questioned. The names of 762 of those immigrants were added to the Immigration and Naturalization Service (INS) Custody List (OIG, 2003).[2]

Chertoff had primary authority over this part of the PENTTBOM Investigation, to "make all decisions on who was released and even who was held in solitary"[3] (DHS, 2003). He made sure that once on the INS Custody List, immigrants were held indefinitely until the FBI could clear them of connections to terrorism and were seemingly guilty until proven innocent (Dew & Pape, 2004, p. 187). Few detained immigrants ever faced criminal charges or a trial, and no immigrants placed on the INS Custody List were convicted of crimes related to 9/11 or terrorism (Cole, 2003; Janofsky, 2004). Immigrants were held as material witnesses or charged with minor immigration violations that do not normally warrant detention (Brill, 2003; Cole, 2003; Janofsky, 2004). They were denied access to attorneys and family, and were detained under abusive conditions; many were denied access to basic hygiene and medical treatment.

Chertoff was bothered by none of this ethnic and religious profiling. Nor was he perturbed that the Office of Inspector General harshly criticized these arrests and detentions as "indiscriminate and haphazard" (DHS, 2003). Quite the opposite; he "later told Congress that he would have done the same thing all over again" (Whitney, 2005). When choosing between the rule of law (due process) and the arbitrary use of state power, Chertoff chose the latter. Chertoff made the same choice again in October 2001 when he co-authored the Patriot Act, and then again in summer 2002, when he told the CIA that its members would not be prosecuted for waterboarding prisoners.[4] On Chertoff's advice, several people were tortured. Rather than acting as a rogue agent, however, Chertoff was merely applying the Bush administration's policy to immigration. All was fair game in the Bush administration's "war on terror," as long as any act that ran roughshod over the constitution could be justified in terms of securing the homeland. Indeed, Chertoff's activities earned him recognition as a "key leader in the War on Terror,"[5] for which he was rewarded with the appointment as head of Department of Homeland Security (DHS) in January 2005.[6]

After Chertoff had monitored the racial profiling of immigrants and advised the CIA about torture, he was appointed to the U.S. Court of Appeals for the Third Circuit,[7] a lifetime appointment that removed him from the line of political fire that might have eventually held him responsible for mishandling these crucial human rights issues.[8]

Just before Chertoff was nominated to the federal bench, Tom Ridge became the first head of the DHS.[9] As first head of the DHS, Tom Ridge established a revolving door culture for private defense contracting firms where outsourcing and future employment opportunities informed policy (Klein, 2007). Ridge himself owned stock in several of the companies lobbying the Bush administration for defense contracts.[10] One such firm, Unisys, would soon join the Boeing team in soliciting and receiving a several billion dollars SBInet contract, which gave the company the responsibility for designing and implementing a virtual fence at the Mexico border. Thus, Ridge was implying more than dialogue when he told these firms, "You can count on regular contact . . . We welcome your input" (Theimer, 2002). Regular contact was further institutionalized in a private sector advisory committee (PVTSAC), which Ridge established to solicit advice from "leaders in the private sector on homeland security" (DHS, 2003). Rick Stephens, Executive Vice President at Boeing, was an early member at PVTSAC and this social network helped bring about the Boeing deal. When Ridge left his post at DHS, he quickly secured employment in the IT/security sector (Klein, 2007).

The combination of ideas that informed the Ridge and Chertoff tenures at DHS became popularized as a neoconservative approach to sovereignty and neoliberalism. These ideas germinated in the Nixon "Imperial" White House[11] and developed over the quarter century that followed the Church Committee investigations that documented executive branch abuse of power during the Watergate era. Nixon's demise was a formative moment in the political development of Nixon disciples Donald Rumsfeld and Dick Cheney[12] (Klein, 2007; Hayes, 2007). Regrettably for the nation and world, however, both men spent the next 25 years plotting in both the public and private sectors to recoup the power they decried as lost. In 2001, they returned to the executive branch as evil archetypes of neoconservatism and neoliberalism. In the years following 9/11, no one and no institution dared rein in their efforts to restore and extend the "imperial" excesses first experienced a quarter century before.

The Rumsfeld/Cheney team set the tone for DHS as it began to deploy risk management technologies in the war on terror against immigrants. Risk technologies were a Bush era add-on to Nixonian power politics.[13] Bush actors extended the notion of sovereignty onto subunits of government and the private sector, largely for the purpose of managing risk, or more precisely as Louise Amoore notes, to make sure "the appearance of securability and manageability is sustained" (Amoore & de Goede, 2008, p. 9). Judith Butler refers to the subunits as "petty-sovereignties," which denote the immigration officials, mid-level bureaucrats and private actors who render unilateral and unaccountable preemptive security decisions (Amoore & de Goede, 2008, p. 13). As Butler notes, "Petty sovereigns abound, reigning in the midst of bureaucratic ... institutions mobilized by aims and tactics of power they do not inaugurate or fully control" (2004, p. 56). As I will argue, such petty-sovereigns were given a mandate to manage risk, and thereby unleashed risk management technologies in the immigration control field.

As Secretary of DHS, Chertoff quickly gained a reputation for extending executive power, mismanaging the federal bureaucracy and hollowing out DHS in a manner similar to the way Donald Rumsfeld managed the Pentagon.[14] Perhaps nothing is more indicative of Chertoff's belief in arbitrary executive power than the arrogant power grab of April 2008 in which he declared that the DHS would ignore more than 30 laws enacted by Congress.[15] On June 22, 2008, the Supreme Court refused to stop Chertoff from circumventing these laws, which led Oliver Bernstein, Sierra Club spokesperson to say:

> This decision leaves one man—the Secretary of the Department of Homeland Security—with the extraordinary power to ignore any and all of the laws designed to protect the American people, our lands, and our natural resources.
>
> (Stout, 2008)

With this decision, Chertoff also smoothed the way for Boeing Inc. to fulfill its obligations under the boondoggle SBInet contract and meet its timeline in constructing the virtual and concrete border fence along the Mexico border.[16]

Starting almost immediately after 9/11, as the INS Custody List suggests, immigration became a laboratory for Cheney, Rumsfeld, and their neoconservative acolyte demi-sovereigns—Ridge and Chertoff—to experiment with a distorted version of sovereign power and free-market enterprise in domestic policy. Once the DHS was created in 2003, and the immigration control agencies placed within it, Tom Ridge and then Michael Chertoff had the task of replicating the neoconservative/neoliberal template that Cheney and Rumsfeld had already created in Baghdad.

Why a laboratory? The search for undocumented immigrants is conducive to preemptive risk management strategies. DHS, and immigration more specifically, was a perfect laboratory for experimentation with risk management, an awkward concept that disdains the rule of law, because of its secrecy and office holders' lack of concern. Consider that immigrants, and the immigration process, politics and bureaucracy have always held a marginal status in the democratic polity (Koulish, 1996). Immigrant interests are more easily ignored and immigrant abuses are more easily shrugged off when few resources and rights and fewer votes are at risk, and when the courts have been stripped of the review authority.

Because immigrants cannot vote[17] in national elections and are excluded by most locals from voting in local elections, they do not matter to election-minded politicians.[18] Neither have immigrants been known for writing checks to political candidates (it's illegal if they're not permanent legal residents), or volunteering in political campaigns. Finally, since immigrant populations have been undercounted in the census, their contributions to the economy in terms of social security, and property taxes have also been under-represented.

Before 2003, the immigration agency had been neglected for more than a century, by every one of its host bureaucracies—Treasury, Commerce, Commerce and Labor, Labor and then Justice—ever since federal immigration controls began in the late nineteenth century. Invariably last in line to receive funding, quality staff and other resources, the immigration agency was a bottom feeder in the federal bureaucracy. If an applicant did not score high enough on an aptitude test to join the DEA or become a U.S. Marshall, for example, she might still join the border patrol (Harwood, 1986).

In addition, due process is more diluted in immigration court than in other administrative hearings, in part because immigration courts are neither Article I nor Article III courts,[19] and meet only sketchy approximations of an administrative hearing (Juceam & Jacobs, 1980; Roberts, 1980). For example, the immigration judge has a great deal of discretion to decide how to prepare a case record; determine what is proper court etiquette; to decide what evidence she will hear.[20] Unlike judges in other courts, immigration judges may permit hearsay[21] and exclude from the record arguments in connection with motions, applications, requests, or objections (Koulish, 1992). The immigration judge is technically not even an administrative law judge and holds no contempt powers. As a result, immigration hearings tend to be ad hoc and arbitrary, and when it comes to immigrants "almost all procedural errors are considered harmless" (Koulish, 1992, p. 552).

One recent intervention that helped weaken due process in immigration proceedings is court stripping, a phenomenon of Congress that removes a great deal of the courts' review authority, starting with the Illegal Immigration Reform and Immigrant Responsibility Act, 1996 (IIRIRA) (Kanstroom, 2006/2007). The IIRIRA eliminated judicial review of non-final orders or rulings primarily involving aliens in removal proceedings, and retroactively rendered permanent residents deportable based on prior criminal convictions.[22]

It also contained provisions that expedited the removal of prospective asylum seekers without affording them the opportunity for judicial review. Only final removal orders directed at aliens were reviewable. Further, Section 1252(a)(s)(B)(ii), entitled "Judicial Review of Orders of Removal," provided:

> Notwithstanding any provision of law, no court shall have jurisdiction to review . . . (ii) any other decision or action of the Attorney General the authority for which is specified under this subchapter to be in the discretion of the Attorney General, other than the granting of relief under section 1158(a) of this title.

The Anti-Terrorism and Effective Death Penalty Act of 1996 (AEDPA) further diminished the government's commitment to due process for aliens by eliminating judicial review for criminal aliens. According to the AEDPA, "Notwithstanding any other provision of law, no court shall have jurisdiction to review any final order of removal against any alien who is removable by reason of having committed a criminal offense . . ." The Act also deleted the law that permitted habeas corpus review of claims by aliens who were held in custody pursuant to deportation orders.

In 1997, the Supreme Court reviewed the IIRIRA provisions.[23] Speaking for the court, Justice Scalia upheld Sec. 1252(g), which prohibited the courts from reviewing decisions by the Attorney General to "commence proceedings, adjudicate cases, or execute removal orders against aliens under this Act." According to the Court,

> [t]he Executive should not have to disclose its "real" reasons for deeming nationals of a particular country a special threat—or indeed for simply wishing to antagonize a particular foreign country by focusing on that country's nationals—and even if it did disclose them a court would be ill equipped to determine their authenticity and utterly unable to assess their adequacy.

By suggesting that immigration adjudicators did not need to state the reasons for ruling against nationals of a particular country, Scalia discounted the role that facts play in adjudication and instead justified the "kangaroo court" character of many immigration hearings. The Court further noted, "Congress has the power to determine the terms and conditions of a non-citizen's presence in the United States and has vested in the Attorney General the power to enforce such provisions; therefore it is not for the Court to second guess the other branches' actions in the typical deportation case . . ." Once Congress vests power in the Attorney General, it rarely reviews that delegation of power, leaving it to immigration authorities to interpret and enforce the law per whim.

In 2005, Congress enacted the Real ID Act, which precluded judicial review of all discretionary decisions, and removed an entire level of review for immigrants in removal proceedings. Since a huge amount of immigration decisions are discretionary, a great many legal and factual issues now exist beyond the scope of judicial review (Kanstroom, 2006/07, p. 165), which suggests political and ostensibly legal actors may ignore legal norms with impunity. The Act removed the jurisdiction of federal trial courts to review BIA decisions, which is where the judge typically reexamines facts as well as law. Instead, cases are directed into the federal court of appeals, which reviews only matters of law.

In sum, the immigration regime functions in the absence of several important legal standards that are designed to provide checks on executive power. An even stronger interpretation suggests the creation of a "counter law" regime that provides the government with an alternative rationale to bypass legal constraints in its effort to secure the homeland. The regime was solidified in 2003 when immigration was removed from the Department of Justice and placed within the DHS, which has as its mission to "prevent and deter terrorist attacks and protect against and respond to threats and hazards to the nation" (DHS, 2004). By transferring immigration to DHS, the administration furthered the securitization of immigration (Walters, 2008).[24] Migrants would henceforth be defined through the lens of security, rather than labor markets or law enforcement.

Immigrants are susceptible to such securitization because as a group they are politically impotent (cannot vote) and have few rights. Further, the regulating agency is susceptible to such top-down change in mandate because of its own structural weaknesses. The immigration agency has a reputation for gross incompetence, broad discretion and loose procedures; and the judiciary is prevented from scrutinizing a great many decisions that are made by immigration actors that ostensibly deal with life and death issues. The absence of such constitutional checks on power encouraged the Bush power elite to make a game of immigration control.

Because of their low status within the federal bureaucracy and such weak claims to fair process, immigration agencies and officials working for them never receive peer-to-peer or top-down accountability, much less the public review that has kept other federal agencies in line over the years. To the immigration elite, these factors help make immigration a perfect vehicle for securitization and neoliberalization. Thus with few people watching, Ridge and then Chertoff enlisted private firms and local governments to help extend executive power along market rationales into the nooks and crannies of different immigration control policies and programs[25] (Simon, 2001).

Ridge and Chertoff were able to reconcile disparate social forces in ways that create serious problems for democratic accountability. The disparate social forces consist of neoliberalism, a phenomenon that when applied to immigration urges border-softening measures (facilitating guest worker provisions), and neoconservative sovereignty, the idea that urges harder and more secure borders (border walls and mandatory detention and removal).

Chertoff's and Ridge's response to 9/11 provides a "parable" for how the Bush administration brought the "war on terror" home and secured it on domestic soil through immigration control policy. Their actions while at DHS and in Chertoff's case, including those before he arrived, serve as an introduction to the dominant immigration control discourse, which is the focus of this book. In this book, I examine a highly charged racialized/political space where discussions, policies and practices encourage unchecked executive power, free market capitalism, and the use of criminal and surveillance techniques. Three broad concepts help shape the discourse: neoliberalism, sovereignty, and risk management. These concepts frame the immigration control discourse in such ways that encourage racist and denigrating depictions of immigrants so as to legitimize official responses, however harsh and however contrary to the rule of law.

Neoliberalism

The term neoliberalism has different meanings and is used in a variety of ways.[26] It is an approach to government that reshuffles the relationship between individuals and the market. Neoliberal policies include free trade, privatization, financial deregulation, and fiscal austerity. As applied to immigration it is the social force that has people imagining soft borders that open to trade and facilitate temporary immigrant labor. In 2001, this imagining of soft borders framed the policy negotiations between President Bush and Mexican President Vicente Fox. On September 10, 2001, *Business Week* reported that the United States was about to adopt a sea change in immigration policy. President Bush, along with Fox, was preparing to propose changes in immigration policy that would consider "regularization" of status for unauthorized Mexicans, and facilitate the entrance of Mexican temporary workers into the United States:

> It is now clear that without the biggest immigration wave in its history, the U.S. would not have been able to achieve the high growth rates of the '90s. The Bush-Fox meeting promises to open a dialogue that could lead to reform of American immigration policy, shifting it away from a system based on quotas, family, and policing toward one aimed at international negotiations that meet the labor needs of the U.S. and other countries. This could be a welcome breakthrough.

Immigration policy that focuses on the labor needs of the United States reinforces neoliberal values associated with flexibility, personal responsibility, and efficiency in the labor market, and results from the structural connection between markets and immigrant labor.

The immigration control regime was developed in part to codify conditions that facilitate the interests of capital and persons who possess human capital within the market, and the exploitation of immigrant labor. This market logic is embedded within two prongs of many immigration laws. For example, it is embedded in the "mentalities and technologies associated with audits, performance assessments, benchmarking, and risk ratings" (Sparke, 2006, p. 16). Like the court stripping provision of the IIRIRA, such micro-political reforms streamline bureaucratic procedures and endeavor to efficiently produce outcomes at less cost. Court stripping is a neoliberal strategy that endeavors to expedite the legal process; it also sacrifices individual rights and fair process along the way at the altar of personal responsibility. In summer 2008, the government overstepped its assumption of personal responsibility when it introduced a pilot program that encouraged "illegal immigrants to come forward and schedule their own deportation" (Gaynor, 2008).

Perhaps more important in terms of democratic culture is how the neoliberal approach threatens to downgrade traditional conceptions of citizenship (political entitlements and claims) to more closely approximate the rights and entitlements currently assigned to immigrants. Neoliberalism draws upon metaphors that derive from a vision of capitalism that equates markets with democracy. It imagines a system of markets where individuals are free to participate according to their own interests and abilities (Aman, 2007, p. 8). This becomes the kind of participation that is favored by new citizenship. One's citizenship status is determined by one's status in the market. As Aihwa Ong notes, ". . . [S]trict discriminations between citizens and foreigners are dropped in favor of the pursuit of human capital" (Ong, 2006, p. 409).

Along these lines, membership in a society would be reconstructed along the lines of human capital attainment and boundaries separating new citizens and non-citizens would now be hardened between such haves and have-nots. Americans who do not have human capital, like society's business class, could expect to see their rights and privileges downgraded to approximate those currently made available to immigrants (Ong, 2006). New surveillance and policing technologies would enforce the demarcation. The benefits of 'citizenship' for the haves are transferable from one country to the next, while the have-nots would have few rights anywhere. This is the somewhat exclusive and apocalyptic vision of neoliberal citizenship. Whether they are born on U.S. territory, persons who lack human capital would be reduced to what Georgio Agamben refers to as "bare life" (Agamben, 1998), by which he means those individuals lacking legal and cultural forms of recognition.

While neoliberals imagine some law[27] as the enemy of markets, I am interested in how law and legal process is perceived as the enemy of a particular *governmentality* that unfairly criminalizes immigrants and preemptively subjects them to policing and surveillance technologies that comprise the authoritarian underbelly of neoliberal politics. This authoritarian side of neoliberalism is justified in terms of sovereignty and risk, terms that represent efforts to harden boundaries between citizen and non-citizen that I examine below.

The criminalization of immigration is part of the larger risk strategy that redefines immigration in terms of crime and punishment (Simon, 1997). This approach also describes the risk scenarios that Chertoff orchestrated at DHS. In this approach the government criminalizes subjects for whom it previously provided care. Economic migrants who seek a better life in the US, for example, find that they are being charged with felonies and subjected to mandatory detention and removal (Monahan, 2006). They are monitored and surveilled through SBI-net, US-VISIT, E-Verify and Real ID although they are not suspected of wrongdoing. Such preemption intends to catch visa holders, for example, before they overstay their visas and break the law.

As Valverde and Mopas suggest, "neoliberal authorities couple widespread surveillance with 'targeted government' to identify and manage risk" (2004, p. 232). The risk of a possible civil infraction at a later date justifies deployment of the dataveillance strategies. Along the way everyone who crosses the border, enters or leaves the country or applies for a driver's license is caught in the web. Such endeavors are also where the apocryphal claims of personal responsibility become most obvious (Nadesan, 2008). As Nadesan notes:

> In a sense, neoliberal government presupposes an impossibility—the rational, self-governing neoliberal agents who always act (or learn to act) responsibly in accord with neoliberal value orientations—and the ruptures that point to the impossibility of the neoliberal fantasy result in ever more invasive efforts to properly produce, manage, and discipline neoliberal subjects.
>
> (p. 34)

Sovereignty

Like neoliberalism, the term sovereignty is somewhat amorphous and has been used in different ways to advance various political agendas. A consensus exists, however, on several features of sovereignty: it refers to a supreme authority over territory, and has an internal and external dimension that is coexistent and omnipresent, with each dimension having to do with territoriality. The internal dimension of sovereign authority is exercised within borders and separates citizens from non-citizens, but as the external dimension suggests, sovereignty also has to do with outsiders who may not interfere with the sovereign's governance.[28] Internal sovereignty defines the state's political and legal supremacy with respect to affairs within its nation-state borders. External sovereignty has to do with the state's status as equal to and independent of other sovereign states, as expressed in its ability to enter into treaties, economic agreements, and military alliances.

Immigration represents the tension between different facets of sovereignty and between different political agendas. For example, the idea of immigrating or border crossing forces one to examine the state's power relationships with individuals and entities on both sides of its borders. It raises questions about the sort of power that is deployed, who deploys it, and how it is deployed. In the United States this tension is embedded in the notion of E pluribus Unum (out of many, one). The contested terrain is comprised of the debate over origins: does sovereignty reside in the hands of the people, the President and legislature, or the Constitution? Another set of questions has to do with how sovereign power is deployed: is it deployed through the rule of law or is it a political force that opposes and supersedes the rule of law? And finally, questions of sovereignty have to do with national identity formation and the construction of the political community within sovereign borders. In America, the contested terrain is comprised of an amalgam of restrictionist and xenophobic forces, which adheres to an exclusionist politics, and the forces of a more inclusivist cultural pluralism (Aleinikoff, 2002).

In American history, the concept of sovereignty draws upon two images: the birth of liberty and its prospective demise. The first image centers on July 4, 1776 when American sovereignty was declared and ushered in American independence and freedom against British tyrants. Section Three of the Declaration of Independence states that the former colonies of Great Britain are now to be considered sovereign states. The Articles of Confederation were established with every intention of implementing the Declaration's vision, but the experiment failed. Sovereignty was soon redefined and interpreted through the lens of the Constitution, which since 1787 has placed separation of powers and checks and balances at the center of American governance. The nation was sovereign but the meaning of American sovereignty would be interpreted in terms of limited government and commitment to constitutional norms. The coercive force of the sovereign would be mediated through the rule of law.

Immigration policy remained an anomaly to the U.S. legacy of constitutional governance. It remained one of this country's few policies that drew its authority from the sovereignty that preceded the Constitution rather than from the document itself. Thus, decisions were made without appeal to constitutional norms, and institutional actors were limited by their own conscience, but certainly not by constitutional constraint. If sovereignty is the enemy of law, sovereignty may be defined as government power with its monopoly over coercive force—military and police—to contend with the lone individual who tries to cross the external border.

Since the Supreme Court (discussed in the next chapter) first referred to sovereignty as the source for the government's power over immigration in the Chinese Exclusion cases, sovereignty has also been deployed to advance perhaps the most exclusionist, racist, and xenophobic policy agenda in American politics.

The Bush administration experimented with legal processes that reconcile the hard borders and racist politics of immigration sovereignty with the soft albeit exclusionary consumer capitalism of neoliberalism. It softened the hard borders with Mexico by advancing a virtual fence along with more draconian border walls, and hardened the soft borders inside the United States by criminalizing immigrants, establishing mandatory detention and removal programs, and deploying dataveillance,[29] biometric and state of the art policing technologies in immigrant communities and against individuals from Middle Eastern countries as well as all persons entering and exiting the country.

In the months following 9/11, immigrant rights advocates were virtually silenced by the shock of 9/11 and the culture of fear that quickly developed. During this period, criticism of the government, particularly as its actions pertained to immigrants, was attacked as treason. As a result, neoliberal and executive power elites were able to connect Bush's war on terror to domestic politics, and extend the sovereignty-neoliberal-risk narrative. Immigration control provides a ready-made government bureaucracy to implement the war on terror at the border and within the country. Domestically, the war on terror has played out as a war against immigrants. This war doomed any chance of comprehensive immigration reform during the Bush administration. Stories about alien terrorists, identity-fraud rings, border fences, rampant factory raids, surveillance, data bases, expedited deportations, and mass detentions still comprise the subtext for discussions about opening borders for migrants and trade. Conversations about guest workers, for example, are accompanied by talk insisting that a wall between the United States and Mexico must precede any effort to open the border. The reason is simple: walls inspire intimidating fear of the unknown and foster images of the alien-other. These are just some of the myriad ways that the Bush administration has appealed to nativist and racist metaphors to whip up anti-immigrant hostility and created even more obstacles for immigrants trying to enter the United States and reside in communities after they arrive.

As treacherous as border crossing has been for hundreds of thousands of undocumented immigrants, and as ugly as angry anti-immigrant rhetoric sounds, such travails do not so much reveal the well-worn tropes of racism, nativism, and xenophobia, as they demonstrate a new kind of commodifying activity. This activity turns anti-immigrant fear into a product for defense and security contractors, and displays the profits to be gained by creating and then maintaining a new risk society at the border that includes a new industry of border and immigration control. This industry brings together two warring sides of the immigration debate around a common project.

Risk Management

The privatization of risk started well before George W. Bush stepped into the Oval Office, but as Jacob Hacker suggests, Bush's government privatized risk more than any administration in history (Hacker, 2006). This strategy shifts risk on important matters of security from society to private individuals. As a strategy of governance, risk management weaves threads of sovereignty and neoliberalism into preemptive law enforcement and surveillance. It starts with the idea of "individuals managing economic uncertainties on their own with limited government help but of all of us providing the common foundation for economic prosperity, and advancement through smarter and broader sharing of risk" (Hacker, 2006). The availability of public services depends upon the willingness to pay for them, which means, among other things, that private police patrol local communities and criminals are held in private jails. Those of us who cannot pay for such social imperatives as law enforcement are denied all but the bare minimum that society can accept. Thus, rather than insuring subjects against misfortune, this new system subjugates subjects as prospective security risks, and endeavors to minimize risk though preemptive surveillance technologies.

Whereas in the previous era, society socialized risk against discrete threats to health or safety, during the Bush administration it socializes suspicion and individualizes risk (Garland, 2001).[30] Thus, as Deborah Lupton has suggested, this new paradigm holds that "more and more risk avoiding practices are required of the 'good' citizen"[31] (Lupton, 2006, p. 14).

Such new expectations of the good citizen coincide with a new economy of power that perceives security as the objective of government, and subjects a good deal of social behavior to surveillance. The idea of risk establishes a set of government objectives that endeavor to manage risk through tactics and strategies that are dispersed among public and private actors and that endeavor to mitigate uncertainty. Private actors who gain authority under this regime include private risk assessment firms, biometrics companies, homeland security consulting, financial data mining firms, and so forth (Amoore & de Goede, 2008). Among these strategies are ones that encourage citizens to relinquish rights in favor of security. The idea here is that in a risk society, the greatest fear is of the unknown and its real world embodiments such as "illegal aliens," who are by definition, undocumented and hence unknown. The term "alien" is such a loaded bit of jargon that children grow up in fear of alien monsters from outer space. Thus it is only a couple of small steps to consider "aliens" as "illegal," which suggests human beings as opposed to human behavior is illegal, and for "illegal aliens" to be dehumanized. Thus undocumented immigrants are easy prey for this risk management regime.

With "good citizens" and private actors playing integral roles, sovereignty is dispersed. It is no longer embodied only in the head of state. Rather, this is a regime "whereby sovereignty rules through 'strategies of security,' while simultaneously rendering citizens individually accountable" (Amoore & de Goede, 2008, p. 13).

The dominant strategy in a risk management regime is preemption. How to spot terrorists before they commit the terrorist act? How to stop the criminal before the crime is committed? This fundamental strategy runs counter to a common sense understanding of law, which is reactive, not proactive and is based on evidence, not conjecture or some risk formulae based on probabilities of some future act. Strategies of preemption are run through risk management techniques that assign blame to people on the basis of "risk factors" that include lifestyle choices, demographics, and racial profiling (Suskind, 2006). Examples of specific risk management techniques include the immigration ATS program, which screens international travelers,[32] and "deep packet inspection," which screens Internet information.[33] By relying on such surveillance technologies to assess risk, the security regime intrudes on the individual liberty of all, rather than on the liberties of discrete individuals (Simon, 2001).

The immigration controls that I examine in this book are part of this story of identifying, monitoring, and criminalizing people who are perceived as a risk. They include the surveillance and data base technologies that since 9/11 have been turned against immigrants, and that along with mandatory detention and exclusion policies, have led to the widespread development of an immigrant control regime.

The regime is run by "petty-sovereigns," immigration officers, local police and private actors, who instill fear and docility among immigrants in part by advertising surveillance in the immigrant community and enriching firms that had been supporters of the Bush family (Butler, 2004). The fear and docility serves two purposes: first, it deters immigrants from becoming proactive members of their communities and workplaces and perhaps softens them for more extreme punitive measures. Second, it supports the growth of the risk management industry, which provides jobs to many former DHS officials.

With all its structural and procedural weaknesses, immigration was particularly susceptible to a risk overhaul. With risk technologies in place immigrants could be "virtually detained" wherever they were in the country, monitored almost as if they were wearing ankle bracelets, and detained psychologically by virtue of the fear imposed on them by the regime. In terms of being detained within harder borders of sovereignty, you need only consider the specter of border walls, neighborhood and workplace raids, and mandatory detention and exclusion policies.

How Immigration Authorities Frame "Illegal Aliens"

Within the discourse of immigration control, *free market* and *sovereignty* memes coalesce into an anti-immigrant risk narrative that perceives immigrants as a risk to the nation's security. This narrative constructs meanings about immigrants that legitimate treating them as if they really were a threat to national security. This discourse helps create a political imagination that drives the immigration control debate, showing how, among other things, the "suspension" of the rule of law becomes normal.

In large part, suspending the rule of law endures because as non-members of political society, immigrants have always been society's "the other"[34]

(Ngai, 2004). The American version of the "alien other" gets its resonance from a legacy of nativism,[35] xenophobia, and practices of counter-subversive state repression that have occurred too frequently throughout the American experience.[36] America's legacy of nativism[37] and counter-subversion (predecessor of counter-terrorism) provide the deep cultural underpinnings of the anti-immigrant risk strategies since 9/11, and the public's acceptance of them.

It helps explain the public's tepid response to government actions against immigrants throughout history that have been justified with rhetoric pointing to crisis but with few facts. This explains, as William Walters suggests, why the public was predisposed to accepting 9/11 as an immigration problem, and when the planes hit, an almost instantaneous response was to suspect almost all immigrants in the US, particularly those from the Middle East[38] as being potential threats to security (Walters, 2008, p. 169). Also blamed in the post-9/11 narrative is a "broken immigration system" which allowed "perpetrators slipping through its net to commit their crime" (Walters, 2008, p. 170). Thus immigrants are elusive perpetrators capable of slipping through the net of existing immigration control technologies. With a problem defined in such terms, three things become evident: first, immigrants are elusive perpetrators; second, they place the nation at risk; and third, no expense is to be spared repairing the broken system. This prepares the way for punitive preemptive policies, overzealous enforcement and militarization of the border to be depicted as acts of patriotism, rather than inappropriate and illegal policies and practices.

Age of Surveillance author Frank Donner notes that "America's obsession with such conspiracies is deeply rooted in our history." Donner reminds us that the "othering" of immigrants is part of a strong American conspiratorial tradition. According to Donner:

> The American obsession with subversive conspiracies of all kinds is deeply rooted in our history. Especially in times of stress, exaggerated febrile explanations of unwelcome reality come to the surface of American life and attract support. These recurrent counter-subversive movements illuminate a striking contrast between our claims to superiority, indeed our mission as a redeemer nation to bring a new world order, and the extraordinary fragility of our confidence in our institutions. This contrast has led some observers to conclude that we are, subconsciously, quite insecure about the value and permanence of our society. More specifically, that American mobility detaches individuals from traditional sources of strength and identity-family, class, private associations—and leaves only economic status as a measure of worth. A resultant isolation and insecurity force a quest for selfhood in the national state, anxiety about imperiled heritage, and an aggression against those who reject or question it.
>
> (Donner, 1981, p. 10)

This combination of "exaggerated febrile explanations," the government's post-9/11 mission as "a redeemer nation" (in Iraq, Afghanistan), and the extraordinary fragility of our confidence in our democratic institutions that followed the 9/11 attacks, aptly describes the "paranoid style" of right-wing decision-making that has always been part of this legacy. As Richard Hofstadter once said:

> National security and independence have been destroyed by treasonous plots, having as their most powerful agents not merely outsiders and foreigners as of old but major statesmen who are at the very centers of American power. Their predecessors had discovered conspiracies; the modern radical right finds conspiracy to be betrayal from on high.
>
> (Hofstadter, 1964)

With right-wing groups tapping into a nativist discourse that has existed since the days of Benjamin Franklin, and government dipping into its own legacy of counter-subversion that dates to the Alien Acts of 1798 and more recently CointelPro,[39] there is little that seems extraordinary about the post-9/11 discourse that reconfigures immigration as a security issue. Thus as the narrative instructs, immigrants = security risk.

Still, Walters notes a different meaning to the security meme before and after 9/11. Pre-9/11 the security meme was defined in terms of poverty and economic insecurity. Since most immigrants were poor, and came to this country for jobs and higher salaries, it was useful to address undocumented immigration in terms of social (anti-poverty) policy. Once the planes hit, the security meme changed dramatically from economic insecurity to national insecurity. As Walters says, "Instead there is a new political imagination preoccupied with the play of mobilities and populated by elusive persons (terrorists, asylum seekers, smugglers) and mercurial things (contraband, drugs, weapons) that are able to move around almost undetected, exploiting the smooth, networked spaces of national societies, but also the seemingly ungoverned borderlands of the "global world" (2008, p. 170). Walters continues, whereas before insecurity was to be addressed by attempts to restore economic equilibrium, "under the paradigm of homeland security, it is much more a game of government governing access, targeting weak points and risk factors, preventing intrusion, tracking movement, verifying identity and detecting the undetected" (Walters, 2008, p. 170). In other words, the discourse shifted so that the problem was no longer about being poor, it was about being undocumented; anyone undocumented, unidentified, was now perceived as a potential terrorist.

This new narrative thus also served as a catalyst for an anything goes approach to government contracts with surveillance technologies firms. Risk management technologies were now en vogue as necessary to manage the risk presented by the undocumented immigrant. In other words, the domestication of the war on terror = war on undocumented immigrants.

This shift in narrative also unleashed the unchecked powers of the sovereign against immigrants. The immigration discourse has always contained an obvious foreign policy element, which would now be unleashed: immigrant = foreign. This is important because the executive wields greater power over foreign policy than domestic policy. As Justice Sutherland suggested in Curtiss-Wright, executive prerogative is exaggerated in foreign affairs (Scheuerman, 2004). By domesticating the war on terror and focusing attention on undocumented immigrants as potential terrorists, these exaggerated foreign policy powers would now be turned inward. Thus following 9/11, these monarchial tendencies have been prominent in American immigration policy. Along the way, as the master narrative of immigration = security is delegated down into the practices of "petty sovereigns," immigrants have been reimagined as potential "enemy aliens" (terrorists) by small-town sheriffs and their posses, who suddenly morph into the persona of anti-immigrant sovereigns protecting the homeland.

The security and foreign policy memes that help legitimate the use of monarchial powers and the deployment of state of the art technologies would be understandable were the United States really at war with Mexico or even with the people crossing the border. Terror at the border, however, is imaginary. There is no enemy at the border, nor are battles being waged there. Thus, the "war on terror" is fighting a phantom foe. Its metaphors are misleading.[40] Researchers at Syracuse University recently examined millions of "detailed records obtained from the Immigration Courts (EOIR) as well as from the Executive Office for U.S. Attorneys (EOUSA)". They found that despite the Bush administration's protests that fighting terrorism is the main reason for militarizing the border and creating an immigration control industry, a claim of terrorism was made against only 12 (0.0015%) of the 814,073 individuals "against whom the DHS filed charges in the immigration courts" (Transactional Records Access Clearinghouse (TRAC), 2009).

The Syracuse study also found that only a fraction of the relatively small number (620) of terrorism-related federal prosecutions filed in FY 2004–2006 were immigration related (28). Of the 28, only 18 were found guilty, of whom, eight received no prison time, and only two were sentenced to five years or more (TRAC, 2009). Put a slightly different way, only two individuals out of 814,073 received terrorism-related sentences of up to five years in prison. Only one of the small number of individuals charged with a terrorism-related offense "appeared to have entered the country illegally." Even Dick Cheney's 1% Doctrine, which means the government could act without the need for evidence or extensive analysis, would not justify the exorbitant resources expended at the border as part of Bush's war on terror (Suskind, 2006).[41]

There is a gaping hole between the government's rhetoric about fighting a war on terror at the border and the exorbitant resources it has spent there, and the reality of no criminal prosecutions for terrorist-related crimes. The obvious question is how is to justify the war against undocumented immigrants?

The obvious answer is that it cannot be justified, at least when the problem is perceived through the meme of the rule of law.

In a March 25, 2007 column in the *Washington Post*, Zbigniew Brezinzski, former national security advisor to Jimmy Carter, said that the Bush administration's elevation of the words "war on terror" to what he called "a national mantra" "undermined our ability to effectively confront the real challenges we face from fanatics who may use terrorism against us." Brezinski contended that the heavy use of this language "stimulated the emergence of a culture of fear (that) obscures reason, intensifies emotions and makes it easier for demagogic politicians to mobilize the public on behalf of the policies they want to pursue."[42] According to noted linguist George Lakoff, the "war on terror" meme escalates fear by appealing to "a general state" that is internal to a person. "Terror is not the person we're fighting . . . The word terror activates your fear . . . The war on terror is not about stopping you from being afraid, it's about making you afraid" (Lakoff, 2004). When people are afraid, Lakoff continues, they turn to a strongman leader (a sovereign) who promises to safeguard their security, hence the connection between the war on terror and sovereignty.[43]

Linking the war on terror to immigration, already linked institutionally by the government having transferred immigration into the DHS (Tirman, 2004; Walters, 2008), presents the image of a nation state mobilizing against the perceived alien threat. This goes well beyond earlier anti-immigrant memes that created the image of criminal immigrants. The difference is one between calling out the police and calling out the military.[44] In war, there is little concern for the rule of law and due process. The war on immigrants connotes this different approach.

However, the reality of immigration law is twice removed from the realities of military pursuit and once removed from the realities of the criminal law's hot pursuit. "Illegal immigration" is largely a civil offense, as defined by Congress, but more importantly the civil heading for immigration offenses impedes upon a discourse that is determined to equate immigrants with violent criminals and terrorists. The anti-immigrant meme conflates civil and criminal law. It constructs the apocryphal perception that unauthorized immigrants are criminals, whereas in reality they are likely to be charged with a civil offense. Lakoff's framing analysis captures the sleight of hand at work. Imagine a criminal. It is likely you just imagined a murderer, rapist or thief, someone doing intentional harm to a person and/or property. Now consider the reality of economic migrants who seek a job: different image, different response (Lakoff, 2004).

The term "illegal alien" criminalizes both the act of crossing the border and the person committing it. When you unpack the term, the word "illegal" connotes criminality. The person crossing the border without papers personifies the "illegal." You would never see someone who jaywalks called an "illegal walker," or someone who speeds called an "illegal driver." Usually there is a clear demarcation between the act and the person committing the act (the sin and the sinner). In immigration law, however, no such demarcation exists. Rather, the illegal alien is portrayed as a criminal who, by definition, has intentionally harmed someone or something. As Lakoff reminds us, since the failure to punish a criminal act is itself perceived as threatening the system itself, "all law and order would break down," were the "illegal alien not apprehended and punished."

By law, undocumented immigrants are not the same as "criminal aliens." "Illegal entry" is a violation of civil immigration law, not criminal immigration law. However, were you to adhere to the meme rather than the law, and take seriously the idea, as Lakoff puts it, that the moral universe might collapse were the illegal alien not punished, then you could more easily imagine the connection between crossing the border and criminal acts. It is no longer a stretch to also imagine that undocumented entries might morph into potential terrorists endangering the homeland.

The scenario of making war against undocumented immigrants makes sense when viewed through the prism of risk management, which puts in play almost any technique intended to surveil society and protect the homeland. In the risk narrative, security is "assumed to be a universal value and a good beyond question," (Monahan, 2006) which thus limits resistance to and inspires huge investments in deploying militaristic, policing and surveillance technologies. The risk discourse also blurs differences between criminal and civil law.

When discussing "illegal aliens," the risk discourse imagines "illegal aliens" are "criminal aliens," bearing criminal intent or "enemy aliens." The technical differences among these terms are irrelevant. Regardless of the text of a legal provision like 287(g), state and local law enforcement imagine that there is no difference between criminal and civil law, and interpret a right to enforce civil law within the mandate to enforce criminal law. As some local sheriffs see it, they have permission to apprehend criminal aliens. If all illegal aliens are criminal aliens, they have the right to stop, apprehend and detain all persons they suspect of being "illegal aliens." They fail to recognize that aliens are human beings, immigrants, like you or someone in your family or who lives down the street. They also fail to consider that these immigrants crossed the border with little more than the intent to enhance the quality of their own lives. Again, the earlier economic interpretation of security has given way to this new interpretation of security as risk.

Politicians who rely on the term "illegal alien" for political gain demonize not only immigrant scapegoats, but also all people in the political opposition who might support immigrant rights. Immigrant rights supporters are portrayed and dismissed as people favoring "open borders." Once you are tagged with the label of being pro- "open borders," you are perceived as having an ideology that helps "the enemy" who is bent on invading and destroying America. As a result, the lines between civil infractions, criminal laws, and military maneuvers become blurred (Edelman, 1985, p. 74).

Such rhetoric creates an alternative universe that acknowledges the inherent sovereign powers of local sheriffs, who also can name the enemy and demonize their political opponents.[45] Why else would federal officials suggest that local sheriffs needed inherent sovereign powers, were it not for some perceived life and death battle against "aliens?" But such demonizing comes at a price. After 9/11, the architects of anti-immigrant ordinances took over a system already teetering on the brink of unconstitutionality, and pushed it into an abyss of lawlessness. Local law officials enforce 287(g) (and pitch anti-immigrant ordinances) as if it gave them these inherent powers. These individuals are likely to fail to distinguish between civil and criminal law violations, and thus their enforcement actions are likely to go beyond their own limited powers to enforce federal immigration law. In other words, law enforcement officers follow the security meme, not the law.

Through the 287(g) program, the federal government outsourced its immigration authority to state and local officials. Once in state and local hands, such authority can then be further outsourced to private detention centers, where gulag-like conditions help create and perpetuate an anti-constitutional regime. Even if it isn't outsourced, the presumption of sovereign enforcement over immigrants perpetuates the reign of unaccountability and irresponsibility when it comes to immigration control.

These approaches coalesced during the Bush administration. The 9/11 attacks shocked America into relinquishing important civil liberties. They also created an opportunity for the Bush administration to move quickly on its own neoliberal agenda domestically, not unlike how the Pentagon helped Augusto Pinochet to impose such policies following the Pentagon-inspired coup in 1973. Neoliberalism after 9/11 thus turned into a game of "securitization." The Bush administration could get away with almost anything as long as the proposal contained rhetoric about national and homeland security and terrorism. This allowed Bush's friends and cronies to profit by devising and implementing spectacles—border walls and virtual fences—of control at the border.

Because immigration is a racialized space the lines between nonracist profit motives and racism blur. Over the course of United States history, immigration has been one of this country's most racist federal policies. Immigration racism, nativism, and xenophobia are a big part of an immigration control system that is not accountable to constitutional norms of due process and equal protection.[46] We need look no further than the history of immigration control in America, from Chinese Exclusion, to National Origins Quotas, to "Operation Wetback," Operation Blockade, and recent efforts by such xenophobic right wing organizations as the Minutemen,[47] FAIR,[48] and CIS,[49] to mobilize opposition to comprehensive immigration reform proposals. But racism is not the driving force behind post-9/11 immigration control politics. Rather, the Bush administration wielded racist tropes as strategies in the larger war. The idea that racism could be a technique of immigration control helps explain how nativist groups seem always at the ready to mobilize massive numbers of volunteers against immigrants, whether at the border, in Maricopa County, Arizona, or in Hazleton, Pennsylvania.

The tactic of using race and demonizing immigrants and other minorities sold well in Bush's America, and provided a rationale for unfolding the theory of the unitary executive in the immigration sphere, and for rationalizing private profit on the backs of immigrants (Lovato, 2008). The business of immigrant demonization doesn't care one whit about racism and xenophobia, but at the same time is not reticent about deploying such cynical technologies of power for the purpose of gaining contracts and concentrating control. In other words racists are not the only ones who create racialized spaces. By criminalizing immigration and immigrants, the immigration control complex has sold billions of dollars worth of social control technologies to taxpayers whose government gains power from such techniques.

In this book, I contend that a dominant immigration control discourse exists. This narrative justifies immigration control as well as media representations of it. The narrative translates into policy and practice in terms of three overlapping concepts: sovereignty, neoliberalism, and risk management. These concepts outline the racialized/political space of immigration control where discussions, policies, and practices are laced with such metaphors that encourage unchecked executive power, free market capitalism, and the use of criminal and surveillance techniques. Within this discourse, immigrants are depicted in racist and denigrating ways so as to legitimize official responses, however harsh and however contrary to the rule of law. Nowhere in this space do metaphors about the rule of law, constitutional or human rights or exploitation hold much sway.

Book Outline

This book examines how immigration embodies a post-9/11 era system of neoliberal social control, and as such has led the way for the U.S. government's recent assault on democracy. While immigration embodies America's rhetorical commitment to democracy as a land of liberty and asylum, it also showcases abysmal failures in our democratic practice. I examine these failures in terms of three broad categories: 1) excessive executive powers circumventing the constitution; 2) privatization and social control technologies; 3) risk management technologies of social control.

I show the relevance of sovereign power to immigration control, and how the Bush administration's adherence to the unitary theory of executive power was substantially inspired by the plenary powers doctrine of immigration control. As a result, executive powers—many delegated to private actors—are abused every day in and around data collection, spying, detention, and exclusion/deportation hearings. The key questions have to do with how the executive branch exploits a loophole in constitutional jurisdiction that connects immigration control to the doctrine of sovereignty rather than to the

Constitution.[50] The loophole is that there is no mention of immigration in the constitution. The outcome has been "leviathan state"-like domination over immigrants, using near-absolute executive power.

This introductory chapter introduces the immigration control discourse that flows between three central concepts: sovereignty, neoliberalism, and risk management. It also discusses how anti-immigrant rhetoric reinforces the hegemony of these concepts by supplicating immigrants and diminishing their humanity. Although civil libertarians and immigrant rights activists comprise an extremely important voice in immigration matters, their say is not heard in the echo chamber constructed by the sovereignty advocates and neoliberals.

In the second chapter, I rely upon the recent work of Georgio Agamben to introduce the theory of sovereignty, and address concrete problems for democracy that arise from having immigration come under sovereign as opposed to constitutional control. Among these problems are the State's failure to protect basic civil and human rights of immigrants who pass through administrative processes that are controlled by the doctrine of plenary powers, which is legitimized by sovereignty. Although the court flirted with the idea of softening its reliance on sovereignty and plenary powers towards the end of the twentieth century, since 9/11 it has deferred to the unchecked authority of the political branches.

I examine the criminalization of immigration in Chapter 3. "Criminalization" is a term that helps explain how the sovereign creates exceptional administrative processes for immigrants, which would not be considered legitimate or even credible were they applied to other groups. The criminalization of immigration consists of the sovereign using civil processes to inflict punishment on immigrants, and how immigrants who have committed civil offenses are instead put through the criminal process.

Chapter 4 is about neoliberalism as well as corresponding risk management and surveillance technologies. In this chapter I discuss how the immigration control industry makes use of such newfound technologies of control as RFID (radio frequency identification),[51] biometrics[52] and surveillance to justify the privatization of immigration control. I discuss how privatization expands executive powers by shifting them into yet another extra-constitutional realm. The chapter also features a section about the "incredible shrinking state action doctrine," which opens the door for pro-business justices on the Supreme Court to deregulate corporate control over immigrants.

I also examine the industrial complex, which threatens to privatize immigration policy, providing yet another mechanism for the executive branch to clamp down on civil liberties without having to oblige the courts.

In Chapter 5, I examine the geography of the immigrant industrial complex, which consists of the virtual fence at the border that monitors undocumented immigrants; the US-VISIT program, which monitors legal travelers as they enter and exit at borders and their functional equivalents; and the Real ID Program, which collects immigration data for all driver's in the country.

Under this program anybody of age and without a driver's license will be under suspicion for being an undocumented immigrant. Finally, I look at the private immigrant detention centers scattered around the country.

I examine the border fence fiasco in Chapter 6, which highlights how sovereign powers were wielded over states, local governments and individual property owners for the purpose of designing and constructing a brick and mortar border fence along the 2,000 mile border with Mexico. Each claim of plenary power came, it seems, with an equal amount of incompetence, which would be funny were it not so destructive of human and cultural life along the border.

In Chapter 7, I examine the federalization of immigration control. The concept of federalization helps explain the extension of sovereign power through the decentralized tentacles of state and local governments. The travesty of federalization was that local sheriffs were granted sovereign power, which was never limited by the guiding light of good judgment or even of risk management or other neoliberal guidelines. The federalization of immigration control helps highlight one of the more egregious paradoxes of this system: the more sovereign control was extended into the nooks and crannies of the criminal justice system (local sheriffs and their deputies), the less safe and secure the citizenry actually became. As local officials took on federal immigration enforcement responsibilities, they ignored their own anti-crime mission, leaving their community's most dangerous criminals walking the streets. The country's most celebrated culprit in this instance is Maricopa County Sheriff Joe Arpaio, whose shenanigans are discussed in this chapter.

In Chapter 8, I examine the prospect for democratization of the immigration control narrative in terms of immigrant resistance. Immigrant resistance as a movement became prominent during President Bush's second term, in 2006. Enough time had elapsed since the 9/11 tragedy to allow people to come back to their senses and begin to make sense of the immigration control industry that was controlling populations throughout the country. In the spring of 2006, largely in response to proposals in Congress to turn all undocumented immigrants into felons, pro-immigrant rights groups began to mobilize. Making full use of Web 2.0 technologies, the "day without" movement was born, which culminated in protests around the country on May 1, 2006, that involved several million people. Of course such acts of resistance also inspired the hegemon to respond with even more insidious forms of direct and indirect social control.

The focus of Chapter 9 is on President Obama and his approach to immigration control. Although he promised new priorities, the new president instead has doubled-down on some of Bush's most egregious abuses, particularly at the border. In addition to examining the issues and problems that Obama must tackle, I endeavor to assess the chances for real reform as Obama's tenure unfolds, and whether the country might expect a reversal away from the dominant immigration control discourse.

Finally, in Chapter 10, I summarize the book's major arguments and suggest what the future might hold in terms of immigration control politics. The contested terrain between democratic and undemocratic forces is summarized, with recommendations for how democratic forces might still win out in the battle over immigration. I suggest shifting the terms of debate from sovereignity and risk to homeland security, to terms that embrace human rights. With such a change, a language would be available that could embrace the humanity of immigrants.

Chapter 2

Framing "Illegal Aliens"

Sovereignty, Plenary Powers, and Discretion

Sovereignty and Enforcement Focus

Outsourcing immigration control to "petty sovereigns" pits the unchecked sovereign powers of the State against the most vulnerable of persons in society. Sovereignty is a good and necessary part of any nation-state. With it the U.S. colonies could declare independence from Great Britain. Without sovereignty, there is no rule of the law. But in the immigration context the existence of sovereignty has been used as an excuse to avoid the role of law. The norm in American politics is a national government with limited powers, based on the constitution, and subject to such constitutional constraints as due process, separation of powers and federalism, enforced by judicial review. Such fragmented powers provide for oversight, checks and balances, and accountability, and comprise the basis for demarcating democratic from authoritarian regimes and democratic regimes from their subjects.

In the immigration context, however, sovereignty serves as the basis for decisions by congress to strip the courts of judicial review authority, and by the executive and the petty sovereigns to whom they delegate their authority, to act with impunity. In this chapter I examine sovereign practices over immigrants that exist in the gray area beyond the rule of law, separation of powers, and due process. I am interested in the unaccountable state practices that force individuals—without cause—to pop their trunk for a car search (Bloom, 2008) or hand over a laptop at the border or any of its functional equivalents (Singel, 2008).[1] Sovereignty and the plenary powers doctrine that accompanies it justify these practices in a way that the rule of law cannot. They were also pointed to when Michael Chertoff waged the racist campaign against Muslims, Arabs, and South Asians in late 2001 and 2002, and when he decided to disregard dozens of federal laws that may well have impeded his efforts to build the border fence.[2]

In this chapter I follow threads in political theorist Georgio Agamben's important work on sovereignty to help make sense of the sovereign basis for immigration control. I examine the sovereign basis for immigration law and endeavor to show how its tentacles extend throughout the immigration control regime, and into border communities, detention centers, expedited removal hearings, and airports, and other places where petty sovereigns can act with impunity over immigrants. In these spaces, immigrants have few rights; instead, "petty sovereigns" wield plenary powers and prosecutorial discretion over the immigrants' "bare life," which is unprotected by rights. Next, I examine the history of sovereignty and plenary powers as they pertain to the development of immigration control law.

Sovereignty and the Suspension of the Rule of Law

Georgio Agamben usefully compares sovereignty with the rule of law and concludes that sovereignty both precedes the rule of law and extends beyond it. He also suggests that sovereignty and law exist as polar opposites in relation to individuals. The former engages in biopolitics with "homo sacer," a person stripped of rights and thus cannot temper the potential brutality of the state; the latter interacts with a juridical subject who has rights and thus some safeguard against abuse. His focus is on the space where sovereignty extends beyond law, and functions as an exception to law. Within the field of law, the juridical subject can appeal to norms of justice and fairness, but within the space of the exception, obedience to the sovereign is the objective.[3]

As Agamben views it, the rule of law exists so as to create self-regulating—obedient—subjects.[4] Sovereignty intervenes when the law fails in this regard. The purpose of sovereignty, then, is "the radical purge of those entities—people—who belie the liberal fantasy although they are constituted in relation to it" (Nadesan, 2008, p. 35). "By radical purge," according to Agamben, the sovereign gets to strip people of all citizenship rights, as well as political and social capital. As a result, the *homo sacer* stands before the sovereign's absolute power, a "life of unrelieved insignificance,"[5] figuratively naked and sans the protection of law, society, or institutions.

It is quite easy to imagine this sovereign relationship in the immigration context. Consider Ellen Knauff, a German wife of her citizen husband who had performed "excellent" work for the U.S. State Department attempting in vain to be reunited with her husband; or Mariel Cubans who sought asylum but instead were detained indefinitely; or the Muslims, Arabs, and South Asians who found themselves in the INS Custody List following 9/11. Such is the instance wherein the individual has no means of addressing a grievance against the state.

Such is the disparity of power that confronts an undocumented immigrant at the bank of the Rio Grande; or during "secondary inspections," in an expedited removal hearing; or when an immigrant stands pro se in an immigration court and wants to request asylum but cannot. In such scenarios, sovereignty is embodied within the petty sovereign (CBP or ICE official, or IJ) who decides on the exception. The finality of such interactions is amplified by their secrecy and discrete nature.

The secrecy and finality of such ad hoc processes strip human beings of their dignity, a theme that resonates in Agamben's book, *Homo Sacer* (1998). Agamben recognizes the humiliation embedded in Bush's post-9/11 America, where politics is reduced to rituals of expanded power that destroy the Bill of Rights. The most extreme series of events that Agamben points to in post-9/11 America starts with the Patriot Act, and include the Bush military order dated November 13, 2001, which provided for the detention, treatment, and trial of those who assisted the terrorist attacks of 9/11, and led to the pattern of mistreatment of prisoners at Guantanamo Bay (Gitmo) (White House Press Release, November 13, 2001). The military order established military commissions and indefinite detention for non-citizens suspected of involvement in terrorist activities (Agamben, 2005, p. 3), which in one fell swoop abandoned the country's commitment to human rights in times of crisis. Of the November 13 Order, Agamben says:

> What is new about President Bush's order is that it radically erases any legal status of the individual, thus producing a legally unnamable and unclassifiable being. Not only do the Taliban captured in Afghanistan not enjoy the status of POW's as defined by the Geneva Convention, they do not even have the status of people charged with a crime according to American laws.
>
> (Agamben, 2005, p. 3)

Such is the power of the sovereign, or, as Carl Schmitt says, "he who decides on the exception."[6] The exception is "a situation in which the existence of the state is under threat and a sovereign decision is required for the return to normality" (Fitzpatrick & Joyce, 2007). Austin Sarat refers to it as "lawful lawlessness," or "actions that are legally authorized but not legally regulated" (Sarat & Clarke, 2008). According to John Parry, "[t]he sovereign . . . determines what constitutes public order and security, and when they are disturbed" (Parry, 2007, p. 72).

Although Agamben takes to heart the extreme nature of Bush's assault on the Constitution, he also finds examples of the exercise of sovereignty in less severe processes of immigration control. In the everyday degradation of border crossing, the individual is stripped of human dignity, without cause. Consider Agamben's own protest against the US-VISIT program, which ostensibly takes and stores unique identifying information about every person that enters the country. In January 2004, Agamben was scheduled to spend the semester at NYU, but he cancelled his visit because he refused to be subjected to the US-VISIT program's biometric fingerprinting. In an article written for *Le Monde*, Agamben said, "I have no intention of submitting myself to such procedures"

(Arenson, January 17, 2004). Agamben said he was deeply opposed to the use of biological methods to track citizens, to procedures like finger and retina prints, and subcutaneous tattooing:

> By applying these techniques and these devices invented for the dangerous classes to a citizen [governments] have made the person the ideal suspect, to the point that it's humanity itself that has become the dangerous class.
>
> (Arenson, January 17, 2004)

In this quote, Agamben also sums up a dominant theme of this book. Immigration control, which includes US-VISIT, is premised upon the logic of sovereignty that since 9/11 has been used ostensibly for the State's hot pursuit of terrorists, but in fact has instead turned humanity itself into a suspect class. The grand irony of immigration control is that it collects, stores, and transmits data on everyone except undocumented immigrants. They manage to sneak through without the digital paper trail. But everyone has become suspect. The US-VISIT program is only one of many such immigration control measures that have been designed and implemented since 9/11. Such concerns also apply to the January 2009 DOJ regulations that require DNA samples be taken from arrested immigrants, as well as to NSEERS,[7] Real ID,[8] E-Verify,[9] and several other information-gathering technologies and databases that comprise a big part of the immigration control regime (Gorman, January 9, 2009).

Agamben's theory of the exception describes how the State gets away with making almost all humanity into a dangerous class. The rhetoric focuses on criminalizing and defeating immigrants, but the technologies can be deployed against anyone.[10] The State has established an industrial complex that has the technological capacity to engage in virtual exclusion, detention and obliteration as a human subject, all punishments that in some instances are as dangerous as their real, non-virtual equivalent.

Perhaps more than any other field of law, immigration practices occur in this exceptional space where petty sovereigns assert their will upon the bare life of individual immigrants, specifically, undocumented immigrants. In this space there is no accountability, and no other entity gets the final word. Immigration officials are the quintessential petty sovereigns who in their interaction with immigrants get to "decide on the exception," an abstract idea that means only that the sovereign is the one who gets to decide when the law does not apply.

In the immigration system, sovereignty is exercised in the many dark crevices of border patrol stations, and on riverbanks where individual decisions are not subject to review. Sovereign power is exercised any time an ICE agent chooses between removing an undocumented immigrant from her home and keeping the family together, or whenever an immigration judge orders deported an undocumented immigrant who is then whisked away for removal by ICE.

Cox and Rodriguez suggest such power is most prevalent at "the back end of the (immigration) system through its enforcement decisions" (2009). They refer to these executive enforcement powers as "prosecutorial discretion," wherein no second-guessing is allowed of the executive's decisions (Sarat & Clarke, 2008).[11]

Such powers exist where the law has been suspended outright, and where discretionary authority becomes an excuse for subjective whim (Sarat & Clarke, 2008). These dark crevices include public and private detention centers for political refugees and immigrants; the zone between the border fence and the sovereign border; such functional equivalents of the border as airports and the zone stretching 60 miles inside any international border; and the enforcement zone in Maricopa County where Sheriff Arpaio says he can stop, question, and detain residents without any individual suspicion of illegal activity.

Here, the mantle of sovereignty is assumed by an assortment of petty sovereigns including detention officers, customs and border patrol agents, airline check-in clerks, DMV officials, sheriff's deputies, and members of their voluntary "posse." In such instances, sovereignty trickles down from the State into the hands of individuals who are neither professionally trained in immigration law, democratically accountable, nor responsible for the incredible power they wield. Instances of sovereignty exist, of course, even when well-trained professionals wield sovereign power. The key is that the reasons for their decisions have no basis in legal norms. The decision is allowed by law but not constrained by it. When the decision-maker appeals to securing obedience rather than due process, the resulting decision is likely to strip the individual of her dignity.

The scale of sovereign decisions can be either small or large. The immigration system is replete with both. Consider decisions to detain an individual at the border or to let them go. The immigrant typically gets two bites at the apple here, both by the CBP officer and then perhaps later by an immigration judge. In each instant, the decision-maker's reasons need not be based in law. It is more likely that decisions are made for bureaucratic reasons—available beds—or policy reasons—detain Salvadorans and not Nicaraguans, Haitians and not Cubans, rather than on an evaluation of the individual's flight risk. Sovereignty also exists at those moments when despite suspicion a suspected undocumented alien is allowed to pass, or when an immigration judge denies asylum even though a well-founded fear of persecution has been presented and supported by evidence.

Broad-scale instances of the exercise of sovereignty take place, for example, when federal laws are ignored and private property is condemned because the administration wants to complete the border fence before it leaves office. Other examples are decisions about expedited removals; factory raids; a detainee's access to medical assistance; family visits and counsel; determining bonds; changes of venue; and relief from deportations. Were it not for such sovereignty, the Immigration and Customs Enforcement (ICE) would not have been able to so cavalierly raid Agriprocessors in May 2008, prosecuting workers who may have committed the civil offense of illegal entry while overlooking the employer's criminal offenses.

Sovereignty

Unlike most other public policy fields, immigration finds its core in the non-rational, illiberal ground of sovereignty, which in turn has justified the executive branch to use plenary powers over immigrants. Sovereignty deals with a nation's primal concerns of survival or national security. When such constitutional principles as separation of powers or due process get in the way, they fall by the wayside. According to the Supreme Court:

> ... the jurisdiction of the nation within its own territory is necessarily exclusive and absolute. It is susceptible of no limitation not imposed by itself. Any restriction upon it, deriving validity from an external source, would imply a diminution of its sovereignty to the extent of the restriction, and an investment of that sovereignty to the same extent in that power which could impose such restrictions.
>
> (*Schooner Exchange v. McFadden*)[12]

As it pertains to immigration, a nation's self-proclaimed, absolute right over its own citizenship, a right believed to inhere in the nation state's very existence, precedes the Constitution and transcends its authority. All this is to suggest that immigration is intrinsically and unusually undemocratic. Its foundation in sovereignty creates a monarchial bias in some aspects of immigration law. Immigration control has no constituents who are political subjects and it abides by no rule of law. The sovereignty narrative instead imagines some decision-maker drawing upon primordial powers to deal with exceptional situations, emergencies. Indeed nothing in American history was quite so exceptional as the revolution, which followed the (former) colonies' declaration of sovereignty. Since then, however, there have been no (or extremely few) situation(s) when circumstances dictated suspension of the rule of law.

Immigration has provided the enduring exception to legal norms since the early days of the republic. During the early days of the republic, sovereignty was perceived as piecemeal, and was highly fragmented among the states, people, and federal government. Nevertheless, the 1798 Alien Act established broad executive power to expel aliens, which led some supporters of this Act to allege sovereign authority beyond the text of the constitution because, it was alleged, aliens were not entitled to constitutional protections (Cleveland, 2002, p. 9).

In 1862 (*the Prize Cases*), the Supreme Court recognized that in times of war, particularly when self-preservation is at stake, "this Court must be governed by the decisions and acts of the Political Department of the government to which this power was entrusted."[13] In this case the notion of sovereignty intended to describe government power as outside the constitution but not incompatible with it.[14] It also recognized sovereignty as the basis of such power.[15] By the end of the nineteenth century, sovereignty was viewed through the lens of a nation feeling its oats and seeking to compete internationally with European powers (Cleveland, 2002). To compete with the authoritative decision-making power of overseas competitors, the United States reimagined sovereignty so as to encompass the totality of the nation's powers when dealing abroad.

In the late nineteenth century, the court asserted there existed inherent powers to uphold federal authority over immigrants in entry and exclusion proceedings. Since the Chinese Exclusion Acts of 1882, and since the court's *Ekiu* decision in 1891, the federal government has allowed its executive branch colleagues to treat immigrants with visceral abandon, with some constraint along the way.

Although sovereignty has undergone a great deal of shape-shifting since the Exclusionary Act cases, treating immigrants with abandon remains the norm—as opposed to the exception—for immigration control policies. Since then, the sovereign has ruled over immigration with impunity, which has created many awkward moments for the adherents of the rule of law and constitutional norms. The 1937 *Curtiss-Wright* decision solidified the notion of absolute sovereignty as it packed the totality of sovereign powers into the executive's foreign policy arsenal.[16] During the Cold War, the *Knauff* case caused scholar Milton Konvitz to say, "The alien, when he reaches an American port of entry, lives under a government of men, not a government of laws, in so far as Congress has subjected the alien to the absolute discretion of certain officers. The alien can find practically no protection under the Constitution" (Konvitz, 1953, p. 50).

As *Knauff* implied, immigration reveals a Freudian Id story of American politics. Political branches could act with near impunity as far as immigrants were concerned. How the government treats immigrants informs how it might treat other vulnerable minorities among us, if only it could get away with it. The Id curses separation of powers and due process of law, which keep getting in the way with how "deciders" would like to see immigrants handled; that is, until a polity were constructed that grounded its politics in sovereignty rather than in the constitution.

After the end of the Cold War, sovereignty shape shifted to accommodate the international community's growing interest in international human rights. Soviet repression in Hungary and Prague were bygone memories, allowing the international community—east and west—to take stock of this recent but bygone era. The sense of unilateral and absolute sovereignty ebbed as nation states took liberties in holding others accountable to international human rights standards.

Although absolute sovereignty was now out of step with prevailing international norms, which had become the guidepost for international policy, it returned to the fore in the political agenda of the post-9/11 Bush administration. It has been noted that the Supreme Court's deference to Congress and the Executive Branch in combating "terrorism" is reminiscent of its reaction to anti-Chinese and anti-communist sentiment in previous eras. In fact, plenary powers have had even more play in the Bush version of sovereignty than in the late nineteenth century's absolute sovereignty. During the late nineteenth century, plenary powers were limited to a defensive role. With the Bush doctrine, plenary powers would be deployed offensively and preemptively.

Plenary Powers

The existence of reserves of sovereignty power for political branches, their "plenary powers," was first recognized in the immigration context in the late nineteenth century *Chinese Exclusion Cases*,[17] which recognized it in terms of legislative power (Cleveland, 2002; Saito, 2003).[18] The key here is that plenary powers cases recognize the sovereign powers of an increasing number of authorities over immigration, from Congress, to the executive, to bureaucratic officials in immigration offices. Plenary powers are the legal technique that the Supreme Court uses to invoke sovereignty. In the immigration context, plenary powers also sharply limit the court's involvement in immigration regulation (Cox & Rodriguez, 2009). The court has utilized plenary powers since the nineteenth century Chinese Exclusion Act cases to say that the political branches of government have full or complete and therefore unchallengeable power over matters pertaining to the nation's national borders and the nation's self-defense (Saito, 2003, 2007).

The story of plenary powers over immigration begins with the Chinese Exclusion Act cases, which determined that Congress has the power to decide who can come to America, how long they can stay, and when they must leave (Cleveland, 2002; Saito, 2003).[19] Indeed, much of the court's reasoning in these nineteenth century immigration cases is based in legislative supremacy and Congress' plenary powers, as well as Congress' power of delegation. According to the court, the courts have little to say about the use of federal powers in this instance, and the alien receives only the process that is allowed by the political branches. Gradually, in the twentieth century, Congress' plenary powers over immigration would blur into plenary executive power.

Chinese Exclusion Act Cases

During the mid-nineteenth century, the United States was eager to recruit Chinese laborers. The 1868 Burlingame Treaty stated the "inherent and inalienable right of man to change his home and allegiance, and . . . the mutual advantage of free migration (Burlingame Treaty, 1868; Aleinikoff, 1998). With the completion of the transcontinental railroad in 1869 and the economic depression of 1873, Congress looked to curtail immigration, and in 1882 enacted legislation suspending the immigration of new Chinese laborers for ten years (Chinese Exclusion Act, 1882). In 1884 Congress required all Chinese residents who wanted to leave the country temporarily to obtain certificates for re-entry (Aleinikoff, 1998).

In the meantime, Chae Chan Ping, who had resided in the US for 12 years, decided to visit his family in China and obtained one of these certificates (Konvitz, 1953). A few days before he was scheduled to return to the US, another new law went into effect banning the entry of all Chinese workers, including those who held certificates. Ping was excluded, and he subsequently challenged the 1888 Act as a violation of the Burlingame Treaty and his Fifth Amendment due process rights (Konvitz, 1953).

The Supreme Court responded that the courts could not interfere with Congress' power to regulate immigration, which originated from the government's prerogatives over national security, territorial sovereignty, and self-preservation. As a result, the court said, if Congress "considers the presence of foreigners of a different race in this country, who will not assimilate with us, to be dangerous to its peace and security . . . its determination is conclusive upon the judiciary" (*Chae Chan Ping v. United States*).[20]

In 1892, the court upheld the decision of a lone immigration officer to deny entry to Nishimura Ekiu without a hearing, on the basis that she was likely to become a public charge. According to the court, "It is an accepted maxim of international law that every sovereign nation has the power, as inherent in sovereignty, and essential to self-preservation, to forbid the entrance of foreigners within its dominions, or to admit them only in such cases and upon such conditions, as it may see fit to prescribe" (*Nishimura Ekiu v. United States*).[21] It is on such grounds that immigration officers continue to expeditiously remove immigrants at U.S. borders. As the *Ekiu* court said, "as to foreigners, the decisions of executive or administrative officers, acting with powers expressly conferred by Congress are due process of law."

In 1892 Congress also extended its ban on Chinese workers to include Chinese laborers already residing in the US who had not obtained a certificate of residency. Since eligibility for a certificate of residency included the testimony of a "credible white witness," large numbers of Chinese residents, Fong Yue Ting, among them, lost the right to remain in the country. Fong Yue Ting challenged Congress' authority, and the Supreme Court subsequently rejected his claim along with the claims of two other Chinese laborers to remain in the country, thus extending plenary powers over exclusion to now include the deportation of long-term permanent residents.[22] Thus, the federal government would have its precedent for subsequent efforts following 9/11 in NSEERS and other programs to force the registration of long-time residents from specific countries in the Middle East. Equal protection found no traction against government efforts to act with impunity when removing immigrants.[23] Further, the court refused to characterize deportation as punishment that would trigger higher constitutional scrutiny,[24] which provides precedent for efforts to criminalize immigrants, as discussed in Chapter 3.

Plenary Powers during WWII and the Cold War

The most historically compelling component of plenary powers resides in the President's foreign relations powers, which, according to *Curtiss-Wright Export Corp.*, expand plenary powers to the executive branch.[25] According to Justice Sutherland, the foreign affairs powers existed prior to and independent of the Constitution, as an essential sovereign power. According to the court in *Curtiss-Wright Export*:

> [T]he investment of the federal government with the powers of external sovereignty did not depend upon the affirmative grants of the Constitution. The powers to declare and wage war, to conclude peace, to make treaties, if they had never been mentioned in the Constitution, would have vested in the federal government as necessary concomitants of nationality.

Citing the *Chinese Exclusion* cases, *Curtiss-Wright* reiterated that the source of the federal government's foreign affairs powers lies in the fact of independence (sovereignty) itself, rather than in the constitution. It asserted that federal authority over foreign relations operated independently of the Constitution and was inherent in the United States' existence as a sovereign, independent, nation. It also asserted that the power to expel undesirable aliens is one of the powers relating to international affairs. Although not articulated in the constitution, the court suggests this power is "inherently inseparable from the conception of nationality."

Thus, as Alexander Aleinikoff says, "Under the reasoning of Curtiss-Wright, we need no longer scrutinize the Constitution to find the immigration powers. We need simply conclude that the power to regulate the flow of aliens over our borders is inherent in the concept of sovereignty" (Aleinikoff & Martin, 1985, p. 14). *Curtiss-Wright* reinforced the President's plenary powers over foreign affairs and by analogy over immigration control. Foreign affairs power is "the very delicate, plenary and exclusive power of the President as sole organ of the federal government in the field of international relations—a power that does not require as a basis for its exercise an act of Congress" (Curtiss-Wright, 1936). *Curtiss-Wright* blurs the difference between Congressional and Presidential plenary powers over immigration, and also blurs the line between immigration control and national security enforcement. In other words, with this case, the executive branch assumed plenary powers over immigration.

During and following WWII, the executive branch relied on *Curtiss-Wright* as a basis for rounding up and detaining thousands of German, Italian, and Japanese aliens, which was a precursor to the internment of 110,000 persons of Japanese ancestry (non-citizens and citizens). During the Cold War, enemy aliens became identified with the "communist menace." The court invoked plenary powers when it denied immigrants the right to know the charges filed against them, habeas corpus, and basic due process rights to a hearing. In 1950, for example, the court excluded Ellen Knauff, a non-citizen war bride from Germany, after a year of being confined to Ellis Island. Knauff was called a subversive and barred entry on the basis of undisclosed information, which the government contended suggested she had communist affiliations.[26] Knauff argued that her exclusion without a hearing compromised her right to due process (Cole, 1991). The court responded that "whatever the procedure authorized by Congress is, it is due process as far as an alien denied entry is concerned" (Konvitz, 1953).

In ex. rel *Mezei*,[27] the court extended *Knauff* to deny the due process claims of a long-standing U.S. resident seeking re-entry. Mr. Mezei had lived in the United States for 25 years, and left the country to visit his ailing mother in Romania. Saying his 25 years in the US amounted to "a life of unrelieved insignificance," the court confined Mezei at Ellis Island for two years and then denied his re-entry on the grounds that Mezei posed a threat to national security ostensibly because of the time he had just spent behind the Iron Curtain. In this instance, the court repeated its infamous quote from *Knauff* to give credence to applying its deferential standard of review to the Attorney General. Given the huge discretion over immigration that statute delegates to the Attorney General, the *Mezei* case further blurred the line between the Congress and executive for plenary powers purposes.

Justice Frankfurter summed up the court's approach in his concurrence in *Harisiades v. Shaughnessy* (1952),[28] "(W)hether immigration laws have been crude and cruel, whether they may have reflected xenophobia in general or anti-Semitism or anti-Catholicism, the responsibility belongs to Congress." In *Harisiades*, the court approved the removal of three former Communist party members who were rendered deportable under a recently enacted statute. According to immigration scholar David Martin (1983), the court had "come close to saying that even though the Fifth Amendment due process protection applies to all 'persons' we simply do not regard excludable aliens as falling within that category."[29]

Even with the liberalization of immigration law during the 1960s, the court continued to permit harsh treatment of aliens. In 1972 plenary powers were extended to preempt U.S. citizens' claims that their first amendment rights had been violated by the government's refusal to grant a visa to an avowed Marxist who had been invited to speak in the United States. In the late 1970s, in *Fiallo v. Bell*,[30] the court again deferred to the plenary powers of the government to regulate immigration. Then, in 1985, the 11th Circuit held in *Jean v. Nelson* that non-citizens who have not been admitted "have no constitutional rights with regard to their applications, and must be content to accept whatever statutory rights and privileges they are granted by Congress."[31]

When the Cold War ended in 1990, the plenary powers doctrine lost some of its rationale. Suddenly, it seemed, a new day had awakened where human rights rather than sovereignty seemed to be the guiding thread in determining how states must treat individuals within their territory. In fact human rights law shatters the sovereign exception to the rule of law because it extends beyond sovereign boundaries and limits the powers of the sovereign to strip human dignity (Butler, 2004).

Indeed by 2001, it appeared the court might be dialing back its deference to the plenary powers doctrine. The court held in *Zadvydas v. Davis*[32] that Congressional plenary power "is subject to important constitutional limitations," which qualify the government's ability to detain indefinitely permanent residents who are to be deported but who do not have countries willing to accept them. To some, this decision signaled the beginning of the end for plenary powers. Gone were the Cold War days of uniting the three branches of government against a common enemy, or so it seemed.

Regrettably, however, the court continued to interpret the government's own commitments under international human rights law through the lens of sovereignty. According to Saito (1999), Zadvydas "does not signal a fundamental change in the plenary powers doctrine because (it) cites *Mezei* and the *Chinese Exclusion* Case with approval and relies more on ambiguity in the statute than on the Constitution to support its conclusion."

In the meantime, Saito (2003; 2007) suggests that the sovereign's plenary powers over immigration actually grew more severe during this time, and refers to a series of Acts by Congress during the mid-1990s that seemed to reinforce the conclusions made by the 11th Circuit in *Jean v. Nelson* that non-citizens must be content to abide the privileges conferred upon them by acts of Congress.[33] In this instance, Congress further diminished the rights of immigrants.

In 1996 Congress drew its sovereign sword to permit the use of secret evidence without final charges in deportations, and in the Illegal Immigration Reform and Immigrant Responsibility Act (IIRIRA) called for expedited removals and mandatory detention of asylum seekers, mandated the detention and deportation of non-citizens with even very old minor criminal convictions (misdemeanors), restricted access to counsel, and restricted judicial review of immigration matters. Saito suggests the doctrine of plenary powers was behind these restrictive policies.

The executive detention provisions of the 1996 IIRIRA built upon the *Fong Yue*, *Mezei*, and *Knauff* precedents for plenary power, and codified the executive's authority to detain without charge or trial for an indefinite period of time. Once again, immigration was the catalyst for expanding executive powers in the absence of judicial review. As one scholar put it, "just like executive detention powers in general, so has the more specific power to preventively detain suspected terrorists normally been targeted at groups viewed as alien" (Koulish, 2007).

The increase in executive powers over immigration coincided nicely with deliberate legislative attempts to lessen court involvement. Court stripping, a featured part of the IIRIRA, has been an important weapon in the state's arsenal of prerogatives since 9/11. The IIRIRA eliminated judicial review of non-final orders or rulings primarily involving aliens in removal proceedings, and retroactively rendered permanent residents deportable based on prior criminal convictions. It also contained provisions expediting the removal of prospective asylum seekers without affording them the opportunity for judicial review. According to the IIRIRA, only final removal orders directed at aliens were reviewable. Further, Section 1252(a)(s)(B)(ii), entitled "Judicial Review of Orders of Removal," provided that:

> Notwithstanding any provision of law, no court shall have jurisdiction to review . . . (ii) any other decision or action of the Attorney General the authority for which is specified under this subchapter to be in the discretion of the Attorney general, other than the granting of relief under section 1158(a) of this title.

Once again Congress effectively asserted plenary powers for the Attorney General in immigration removal or deportation matters, in effect codifying some of history's most egregious immigration decisions resting on plenary powers.

In addition to the IIRIRA, in 1996 the AEDPA pared down the government's commitment to due process by eliminating judicial review for criminal aliens. According to the AEDPA, "Notwithstanding any other provision of law, no court shall have jurisdiction to review any final order of removal against any alien who is removable by reason of having committed a criminal offense . . ."[34]

In 1997, the Supreme Court reviewed IIRIRA provisions. In *Reno v. AADC*,[35] the INS attempted to deport eight non-citizens on account of their affiliation with the Popular Front for the Liberation of Palestine (PFLP), which the government described as a terrorist organization. Speaking for the court, Justice Scalia upheld Sec. 1252(g), which prohibited the courts from reviewing decisions by the Attorney General to "commence proceedings, adjudicate cases, or execute removal orders against aliens under this Act." Further, the court noted that:

> [t]he Executive should not have to disclose its "real" reasons for deeming nationals of a particular country a special threat—or indeed for simply wishing to antagonize a particular foreign country by focusing on that

country's nationals—and even if it did disclose them a court would be ill equipped to determine their authenticity and utterly unable to assess their adequacy.[36]

While the plenary powers doctrine was not explicit in Reno, the doctrine underlies the court's reasoning. According to the court, "Congress has the power to determine the terms and conditions of a non-citizens presence in the United States and has vested in the Attorney General the power to enforce such provisions; therefore it is not for the Court to second guess the other branches' actions in the typical deportation case . . ."

Following 9/11, plenary powers became the rationale for preemptive action against social groups present in the US. In one fell swoop, the Bush administration skirted decades of advances in state action, international and constitutional law, and created the basis for preventative detention in the PENTTBOM Investigation and detention of "unlawful combatants"; for intelligence gathering in the NSEERS, SEVIS and US-VISIT; and for enhanced border enforcement. The Bush doctrine provided a rationale for the war on terror at home, and it extended unchecked executive powers, based on the foundation, once again restored to prominence, of sovereignty, plenary powers, and the government's role in foreign affairs. This foundation in law would allow securitization strategies to preempt potential threats and, as President Bush said, "take the battle to the enemy, disrupt his plans and confront the worst threats before they emerge" (Mann, 2004, p. 327).

Following 9/11, the Patriot Act invoked plenary powers to give the Attorney General broad authority to detain immigrants who endangered national security. Title IV of the Patriot Act introduced several amendments tightening the INA ("Uniting and Strengthening America by Providing Appropriate Tools Required to Intercept and Obstruct Terrorism") (USA Patriot Act, 2001). Section 412 of the Act authorizes the Attorney General to certify and detain non-citizens if he has "reasonable grounds to believe" that they are engaging, or have engaged, in a terrorist activity or otherwise endanger national security. The Act allows for detention for a period of seven days, after which the Attorney General must commence deportation proceedings, bring criminal charges, or release the detainees.

Even more severe provisions originating in the executive branch make use of exceptional powers over internment. Department of Justice regulations issued on September 20, 2001, extend the detention powers of immigration authorities, and illustrate the dangers associated with privatizing screening and detention. The regulations allow immigration authorities to detain non-citizens suspected of being in violation of an immigration law without charge for up to 48 hours, and for an "additional reasonable period of time" in the event of an "emergency or other extraordinary circumstance." The regulations fail to define the terms, "reasonable period of time," "emergency" or "extraordinary circumstance." "No link with alleged terrorism need be made." As Daniel Moeckli adeptly summarizes:

> The immigration authorities may even indefinitely detain individuals who are not charged with any crime or immigration law violation and against whom no deportation proceedings have been initiated. The detainees do not have to be informed of the reasons for their detention and are not guaranteed a right to contest it.
>
> (2006)[37]

As out of step as plenary powers have been in terms of constitutional or human rights norms, there remain several forms of redress that are available to the immigrant who finds themself victimized by federal officials. The expansiveness of post-9/11 plenary powers does not suggest that the courts might not limit plenary executive powers from time to time. Indeed, The court did just that in its 2006 *Hamdan v. Rumsfeld*[38] decision about Guantanamo military commissions, and in *Hamdi v. Rumsfeld* (2004),[39] the habeas corpus case that reversed the dismissal of a habeas petition brought on behalf of Yasir Hamdi, a U.S. citizen detained indefinitely as an "illegal enemy combatant."

The important point here, however, is that the underlying structure of sovereignty and plenary powers has already carved out extreme powers for the government over immigrants. The fact that such powers are on occasion restrained is important but not crucial to the argument. Sovereignty remains the dominant narrative, and officials embrace their plenary powers when staring down immigrants during factory raids, in border detention camps, and in immigration courts. The sovereignty narrative also serves as the rationale for the abundant discretion that guides immigration decision-making. The power of sovereignty remains fully intact in the immigration control context.

Chapter 3

Criminalizing Immigration

The sovereign has plenary powers with which to engage in wide-scale militarization at the border and inside the country. Sovereigns and "petty-sovereigns" also possess powers of criminal arrest and prosecution, thus criminalizing immigrants and the immigration process. They also have the capacity to engage in surveillance almost at whim. The result is that the State has legal and extra-legal techniques at its disposal in its war on immigrants.

In this chapter I shall examine how the sovereign makes use of the criminal process and constructs the narrative of immigrant criminality. The basis for criminalizing immigrants is "risk management", a neoliberal discipline of control. Risk management provides justification for the sovereign "deciding on the exception," which means making decisions outside the rule of law, and explains much of the criminalization phenomenon.

Criminalization

Criminalization is a tactic in the war on immigrants. It is a form of social control that uses law and legal culture to ostracize and control segments of the population through a myriad of techniques including surveillance, biometrics, extending the reach of the criminal law, and using civil laws to help criminalize people. Such criminalization, for example, includes taking what the law suggests is an administrative offense and turning it into an aggravated felony, a result of recent legislation, regulations, and sovereign decisions. As a result of criminalization, executive powers grow and the rights of the accused shrink. For example, the rights that adhere to the individual in the criminal process no longer hold sway in a civil hearing. Now state agencies can focus on the individual's guilt by association, and can shift the burden of proof from the state to the accused. Thus, by bringing what amounts to criminal charges against immigrants in a civil process, the balance of power that exists between the state and individual in any criminal process becomes even more lopsided in the state's favor. Immigrants don't really stand a chance.

Several scholars have recently documented the criminalization of civil immigration law. Michael Welch (2003) examines the ironies of criminalization,

Mathew Coleman (2007) focuses on the geopolitics of this phenomenon, and Juliet Stumpf (2006) is concerned with the prospect of criminal law swallowing up immigration law. I'm particularly interested in how the criminalization of immigration control demonstrates a culture of risk and adds to the sovereign's tool chest of unaccountable powers against immigrants. In recent years, the list of crimes for which immigrants may be excluded has grown quite extensive.

The key to criminalization has to do with Congress and the DHS creating new crimes out of activities, which until recently had been treated as civil immigration offenses. It also has to do with taking a new approach to offenses that are in the books as both civil and criminal offenses, and treating them as a criminal matter. For example, although an immigrant who enters or attempts to enter the country may be prosecuted under civil or criminal law, until recently such a transgression was treated as a civil matter, and the perpetrator punished under civil provisions or not at all. During the 1970s and 1980s, immigrants caught entering the country would receive voluntary departure or voluntary return (neither of which are perceived as punishment). It was rare for an undocumented entry to face deportation (civil but tantamount to punishment). Although the situation changed somewhat by the late 1980s, particularly following the refugee crisis at the South Texas border with Mexico, such immigrants still usually faced only the civil penalty of deportation.

Criminalization also has to do with applying existing laws in new ways, which now penalize immigrants. The examples here involve identity theft laws being applied to immigrant workers, and charging undocumented entries with conspiracy to commit alien smuggling. Next, criminalization attaches mandatory punishments such as detention and deportation to what used to be civil offenses. Examples include the recently expanded category of "aggravated felonies," as well as reentry following a removal order. Along the way, the criminalization of immigration deepens the image of immigrant as wrongdoer, which in turn expands the range of punishments against this population that an already fearful public seem ready to tolerate. It also shifts attention away from legal norms that ought to guide discretion and towards the subjective and power-laden norms of the sovereign. Although the criminalization of immigration did not start with 9/11, the tragedy injected steroids into the beast, bulked it up with one initiative after another, and helped justify the immigration control industry that came to the fore during the Bush years.

Criminalization Background

Congress first signaled its desire to ramp up its crime-control approach to immigration in 1988. In that year, Congress enacted the Omnibus Anti-Drug Abuse Act of 1988, which created the category of "aggravated felony" that results in deportation. The idea was to deport drug kingpins under murder, firearms, and weapons trafficking charges, not undocumented workers (Coleman, 2007). In 1990 and 1994, Congress expanded the category of aggravated felony, the result of which was a "grab bag of convictions" that included kingpins as well as prostitutes and undocumented re-entries. The category lacked coherence and subjected violent and petty nonviolent offenders to the same broad brush (Coonan, 1998; Kurzban, 2008). By1996, Congress intended to codify a zero tolerance enforcement strategy against immigrants. It enacted the AEDPA, and the 1996 (IIRIRA) Immigration Act, which expanded the category of "aggravated felonies" to include almost all felonies, and to trigger mandatory detention and mandatory removal from the country.[1] There was to be no leniency and no exceptions.

These acts also changed what was meant by a criminal conviction. Potential aggravated felony convictions now counted as warranting deportation. An immigrant could be removed for having committed an aggravated felony without having been convicted of the crime. Also, any sentence of a year or more now counted as evidence of an aggravated felony. Finally, Congress also made the new categories retroactive, so that a 1995 conviction that was not an aggravated felony at the time of the trial could now be an aggravated felony, with mandatory removal as punishment.

The relative ease with which an immigrant could now be rounded up, arrested and branded an aggravated felon was facilitated by post-9/11 efforts to connect crime to terrorism. Coming as it did on the heels of the 1995 Oklahoma City terrorist bombing, for example, the truncated legislative debate for IIRIA made broad-based connections between terrorists and non-citizens convicted of crimes. It didn't matter that Timothy McVeigh, who inspired the legislation, was born and bred in the United States.[2] Representatives Bill McCullom (R-Fl) and Lamar Smith (R-Tx) for example, had no trouble finding connections unsupported by available evidence. McCollum said that:

> Criminal alien provisions in (AEDPA) are also important to the terrorist issue, because oftentimes we find that terrorists or would-be terrorists are criminal aliens and we are not deporting them in a proper fashion. The sooner we get them out of the country, the better procedures we have for that, the less likely we are to have that element in this country, either creating the actual acts of terrorism or directing them in some manner. We need to kick these people out of the country.
>
> (HRW, 2007)

After 9/11 the new DHS began devising parts of its immigration control system. The actors that benefited from these programs were private industry, DHS political appointees and bureaucrats who gained turf and other resources, and elected politicians who made political hay over the fear of terrorism and thus acquired notoriety as well as short-term political gain.

Step I: Criminalizing without Criminal Law Safeguards: Expedited Removal

Expedited removal is a truncated version of the civil immigration process for the purpose of punishing unwanted immigrants with removal without review. It is an important initial step in the crime control assembly line created by the Clinton Immigration Acts and given steroids under Bush. Now it filters out several thousand immigrants, many already inside the United States, in an expedited manner.

It is a procedure that allows a DHS official to order the summary removal of a non-citizen without a hearing or review by an immigration judge or the Board of Immigration Appeals (BIA). The immigration officer has the authority to rule that a person is inadmissible and issue a removal order. The officer can wield this authority upon determining that the person lacks valid entry documents or is attempting entry though fraud or misrepresentation.[3] The removal order carries a five-year bar on return to the United States.

The unprecedented part of the expedited review provision is that the CBP officer's authority is not subject to review. The officer's authority is sovereign. Previously, such decisions were subject to review by an immigration judge and the BIA. Now an officer having a bad day can send a person back to torture or death, and never be second guessed.

The second part of the expedited removal process deals with the situation that arises when the person under interrogation claims to be a refugee (to have been persecuted or to have a well-founded fear of persecution). Persons claiming that they fear to return to their home country or that they intend to apply for political asylum are referred to a second interview, referred to as a "credible fear" interview with an asylum officer. The most unfortunate effects of expedited removal are in evidence at this point in the process. As documented in two sets of studies, first by Hastings Law School and then by the non-profit organization Human Rights First,[4] this second phase, like the first, is secretive and not open to the public. Further, persons having undergone the process note the jarring effects of being asked questions about rape and torture by an armed and uniformed federal law enforcement officer, rather than by someone in judicial robes who is specially trained. According to Human Rights First, "The proceedings are conducted so swiftly that mistakes are inevitable . . . Furthermore, secondary inspection—the stage of the process during which erroneous decisions are most likely to be made—is conducted behind closed doors, with virtually no meaningful scrutiny by independent observers" (2000, p. 1). HRF found that "in 1997 through fiscal year 1999, 99% of all persons subjected to expedited removal were turned away from the United States on the spot at secondary inspection, without any further review to determine whether they had a credible fear of persecution and might be entitled to asylum or had a claim of lawful immigration status" (HRF Executive Summary, October 2000).

Among the thousands of persons turned away at this preliminary stage in the process were U.S. citizens and political refugees. U.S. citizens like Sharon McKnight, who was deported to Jamaica on June 11, 2000:

> After INS inspectors at the airport wrongly questioned the authenticity of her U.S. passport and dismissed as fake the birth certificate presented by her waiting relatives as proof of her birth on Long Island. Ms. McKnight who is 35 years old but has the mental capacity of a young child, was held overnight in shackles and handcuffs, at JFK International Airport, before being sent back to Kingston, Jamaica, where there was no one to meet her. During her time at the airport Ms. McKnight was given nothing to eat and was not allowed to return to the United States after the INS acknowledged its mistake, but she continues to have nightmares and has now filed suit against officials because of the mistreatment she suffered.
> (HRF, October 2000).

Although the expedited removal provision initially was limited to "arriving aliens," who had not yet made it inside the United States, in 2004, the Bush DHS expanded expedited removal to include non-citizens "within" the United States—an unprecedented move which stripped the removal process of any remaining vestige of due process. "For the first time, a non-citizen who has made a land entry into the United States can be removed without the procedural safeguards of a removal hearing, including the right to counsel, right to cross-examine the government's witnesses and examine the government's evidence, and significantly, the right to an impartial adjudicator" (Kenney, August 13, 2004).

Step II: The Fugitive Operations Program

After DHS was created in 2003, one of its first initiatives was the National Fugitive Operations Program (NFOP). The NFOP was a unit within ICE, and since 2003, according to a recent study by Cardozo Law School and the Migration Policy Institute, "no immigration enforcement program has experienced a more dramatic increase in funding, nor expanded its staffing and operations more rapidly, than [NFOP]"[5] (MPI, 2009). According to the ICE website, its mission was to "identify, locate, arrest, or otherwise reduce the fugitive alien population in the United States." The term "fugitive alien" included "an alien who has failed to depart the United States pursuant to a final order of removal, deportation, or exclusion; or has failed to report to a detention and removal officer after receiving notice to do so" (www.ice.gov/ pi/dro/nfop.htm). ICE does not do this work alone. NFOP dispatches Fugitive Operations Teams (FOTs) across the country (MPI, 2009). It also relies on the assistance of "all federal, state, and local law enforcement agencies," through local Joint Fugitive Task Forces.

The "Joint Fugitive Task Forces" are comprised of city, state, and federal officers, which the "Dan Saban for Maricopa County Sheriff" website describes in the following way: "We have a class act of professional law enforcement leaders coming together, checking their egos at the door and doing whatever they can legally do to protect and serve us" (Friday, October 12, 2007). Such a description helps one rest easy when thinking that the FOT has access to fusion center technology, which collects nearly all information gathered by all these different law enforcement units and stores it within interoperable databases. But you cannot help but get nervous when another observer suggests the reality is closer to using this information and power to go "Dog the Bounty Hunter" on the immigrant community (http://flprogressive. blogspot.com/2007/02/fearing-knock-on-door.html).

Indeed, results from the MPI/Cardozo Law School study invoke the image of "Dog the Bounty Hunter" rather than cool and collected professionals. FOTs pursued the lowest hanging fruit, undocumented immigrant entries who had no criminal record. Of the more than 96,000 undocumented immigrants arrested under FTOP between 2003 and 2008, 40% faced no removal order; 27% had criminal convictions, and 9% of those arrested were fugitives from deportation orders who were considered criminals or were considered dangerous (Hsu, 2009). Although FOTs were supposed to arrest fugitive "illegal immigrants with prior convictions," they instead caught people without deportation orders, and did so under the klieg lights of middle of the night neighborhood raids and middle of the day factory raids.

The Cardozo/MPI study discovered that ICE had changed the rules, and the program increasingly went after easier targets. Federal immigration officials had repeatedly told Congress that of "among more than half a million immigrants with outstanding deportation orders, they would concentrate on rounding up the most threatening—criminals and terrorism suspects. Instead . . . they went after easier targets" (Bernstein, February 3, 2009).

Operation Streamline

NFOP was quickly followed by other crime control initiatives. In 2005, Operation Streamline, another DHS initiative, started in Del Rio, Texas and quickly grew to include other regions. It is a one-size-fits-all crime control strategy that focuses on arresting, prosecuting and removing "illegal aliens" (CBP.gov, December 16, 2005). It expanded to the Lower Rio Grande Valley and Laredo Texas, and parts of Arizona. It was designed to criminalize undocumented immigration by charging undocumented entries with a nuisance misdemeanor under 8 USC 1325: "Entry of alien at improper time or place; etc.," rather than with the civil offense of undocumented entry, which had been routine practice for more than a generation.

Operation Streamline forces immigration agents to hand off the immigrant to the federal Marshall's office, where the case goes to a federal magistrate's court, rather than to an immigration judge. Upon a guilty verdict, the immigrant is sentenced to a month behind bars before being handed back over to immigration and removed from the country. The immigrant is detained while the case is pending.

Prior to Operation Streamline, most apprehended undocumented immigrants were subjected to civil process and penalties, or faced no penalty at all. Only 1% were subjected to federal prosecution for the misdemeanor of illegal entry (8USC 1325). Federal prosecutors used their discretion to direct the scarce resources reserved for federal prosecutions towards more substantial criminal activity. According to a DOJ EOUSA memo from Natalie A-Voris, Associate Counsel prior to Operation Streamline:

> ... the Department does not have a specific policy regarding the prosecution of illegal aliens. Instead, the United States Attorneys are charged with establishing such policies based on the particular circumstances and enforcement priorities in their respective districts. . . . As a general rule, SDCA (southern district California) does not prosecute purely economic migrants. Nor are . . . prosecutions based on the "number of times an alien is apprehended." . . . prosecution policies are based on the premise that illegal aliens with the most serious criminal histories should be our first priority for prosecution. As such SDCA has directed its resources to bringing felony (as opposed to misdemeanor) charges against illegal aliens with substantial histories so that SDCA can seek longer prison sentences against those who present the greatest threat to public safety.

Although the rationale for these post-9/11 crime control programs and initiatives was that anti-terrorism was the new priority for federal prosecutors,[6] U.S. attorneys prosecuted almost no immigrants for terrorism-related crimes, but they did prosecute an enormous number of "immigrants with criminal records" rather than pursuing more serious offenders. According to the *New York Times*:

> Federal prosecutions of immigration crimes nearly doubled in the last fiscal year, reaching more than 70,000 immigration cases in the 2008 fiscal year, according to federal data compiled by the Syracuse University research group.
>
> (Moore, 2009)

In FY 2008, in Houston Texas alone, ICE removed a record number of 8,226 "illegal immigrants" with criminal records (Carroll, 2009). Southern California also recorded a new high in federal prosecutions (Gordon, 2008). According to the *NY Times*, "On heavy days, single courtrooms along the border process illegal immigrants on an industrial scale" (Moore, 2009).

Rather than deal with serious cases, the assembly line processes "immigrants with criminal records," a category that is replete with such petty offenses as shoplifting, selling counterfeit DVDs, or being caught smoking pot.[7] Untold numbers of immigrants who live law-abiding lives now have to live in fear of that "pot bust" ten years ago, or some other nuisance crime they committed years ago. Consider the example Parker gave when she testified before the House Committee on Foreign Affairs Subcommittee on the Western Hemisphere:

> Joe Desire, originally from Haiti, signed up for the U.S. military in 1970. At that time, no-one asked Joe if he was an immigrant. A lawful permanent resident, or green card holder, Joe served his adopted country for four years. Now a 52-year old veteran with four U.S. citizen sons, two of whom are in the military themselves, Joe faces mandatory deportation because he was convicted of possession and sale of small amounts of crack cocaine in the mid-90s, for which he spent 16 months in prison.
>
> (Congressional Hearing, 2007)

Although Congress quickly extended its list of crimes for which deportation is mandatory, the real danger to immigrant families rests with the political pressure on prosecutors to bring charges against immigrants, the increased allocation of resources to enforcement efforts, and the cooperation of local law enforcement (see Chapter 6), that results in the DHS detaining and removing increasing numbers of immigrants each year (Vargas, 2005). Based on the 2000 census, the HRW estimates "that approximately 1.6 million spouses and children living in the United States were separated from their parent, husband, or wife because of these deportations" (HRW). As a result of the fear generated by such policies, immigrants learn to hold themselves to a higher standard than citizens, because any arrest, or even a traffic stop, could result in an immigrant's forced removal and separation from their family. According to Parker, "while it may be fair, for example, to deport an immigrant who commits murder within six months of his arrival in the U.S., it may be grossly unfair to deport a parent of young children who has legally lived in the U.S. for 30 years and who was convicted of passing a forged check" (Parker, 2007).

It is important to note, however, that research shows immigrants are less likely than citizens to commit crimes.[8] Thus the intended effect of the 1996 law on immigrants was not so much deterrence as to instill fear, plain and simple. Such prosecutions against immigrants also have a pedagogic effect, which teaches immigrants about the bias and overtly political nature of criminal justice in the United States. Along the way, the integrity of the country's criminal justice institutions is compromised. The resulting horror stories become the stuff of legend in the immigrant's home country, destroying America's reputation for justice one harsh deportation at a time.

According to Solomon Moore:

The emphasis, many federal judges and prosecutors say, has siphoned resources from other crimes, eroded morale among federal lawyers and overloaded the federal court system. Many of those other crimes, including gun trafficking, organized crime and the increasingly violent drug trade, are now routinely referred to state and county officials, who say they often lack the finances or authority to prosecute them effectively.

(Moore, 2009)

Immigration attorney and blogger David Bennion says that "DHS relies on the press to transmit its numbers on 'criminal aliens captured' without digging too deeply into the distinctions between, for instance, armed robbery and possession of prescription drugs in someone else's name. That means it's in DHS' interests to go after low-hanging fruit to pump up the numbers of criminal aliens" (Bennion, 2009). Alison Parker, Human Rights Watch deputy director, concurs with Bennion: "The perception among the American public and even among lawmakers is that the people who are deported are maniacal, homicidal, and rapist criminals . . . In many instances, they are green card holders. They're the family down the street" (Brulliard, 2008).

In addition to pumping up numbers, DHS is also responsible for manufacturing a culture of fear against immigrants. While official anti-immigrant rhetoric presupposes the presence of dangerous criminal aliens in the country, this examination of the number of "criminal aliens captured," presents a different story about DHS in hot pursuit of non-criminals while sowing seeds of fear and confusion in immigrant communities.

The Postville Raid

Perhaps one of the most egregious examples of the Bush era criminalization of immigration came on May 12, 2008, in Postville, Iowa, when ICE raided the Agriprocessors Inc. Meatpacking Company. Three hundred and eighty nine workers were arrested under suspicion of being undocumented immigrants (Hing, 2008). Most of the targets were from Mexico and Guatemala, and a few from Eastern Europe. ICE officials justified the raid by saying it was the result of a long investigation into an identity theft ring that was supposedly being run from inside the plant. It has long been common practice for undocumented immigrants to make use of false social security numbers to gain employment. It is also relevant that the employers and not employees organized the fraud ring.

In all, 302 workers were charged with aggravated identity theft and/or using false social security numbers. The subsequent prosecutions produced evidence suggesting that the "identity theft ring" originated with the employers, not the workers. These claims hid a more salient purpose behind the raid, which was that the United Food and Commercial Workers Union (UFCW) was in the midst of an organizing campaign. Further, the mass raid and subsequent arrests, trials, and sentences ruined the union's organizing efforts in this plant and intimidated workers throughout the meatpacking industry. In all, 297 men and women pled guilty in an expedited and highly unusual criminal hearing, and were sentenced to prison and subsequent deportation (Hing, 2008).

If there was an investigation before the raid, it used fast-food techniques to criminalize immigrants and process them as efficiently as Agriprocessors had processed meat. And when it comes to making sausage, the Constitution, which calls for individualized processing on the merits, never plays a role. How could it? The strategy prepackaged guilty verdicts. DHS distributed a "manual" to defense attorneys for the Postville immigrant workers. According to Lucas Guttentag, American Civil Liberties Union (ACLU) Immigrant Rights Project Director, "this document provides further evidence of the government's disturbing pressure cooker tactics for mass guilty pleas that assumed guilt instead of protecting the constitutional presumption of innocence. Along with the workers, fairness and due process were the victims of the Postville prosecutions" (ACLU, 31 July 2008).

The manual instructed workers to waive their rights and to plead guilty to the charges against them.[9] Its instructions were to expedite the process and rush workers through the system without a criminal trial or immigration proceedings. According to UNLV Law Professor Raquel Aldana:

> This unprecedented criminalization of undocumented workers also has not been accompanied by a comparable infusion of constitutional guarantees in the handling of these cases. ICE conducted the investigation leading to the Postville raid with easy access to immigration databases and employee documents. ICE then executed the raid with easily-procured administrative, not criminal, warrants.
>
> Thus, the protection of stricter Fourth Amendment search and seizure, Fifth Amendment due process, and Sixth Amendment right to counsel constitutional guarantees available to most criminal defendants were unavailable to these workers. Nearly all waived any rights they might have had under extreme prosecutorial pressure. The uncharacteristic speed and efficiency of the Postville raid left workers without adequate opportunity to consult with defense counsel, and none or few had access to immigration lawyers to learn about the immigration consequences of their pleas.
>
> (Aldana, 2008)

Consider the following statement issued by the Society for American Immigration Law Teachers:

> This unprecedented shift to criminalize workers for the use or possession of false work documents has not been accompanied by a comparable infusion of constitutional guarantees in the handling of these cases. ICE conducted the investigation leading to the Postville raid with easy-access

to immigration databases and employee documents, by relying on informants, and then executed the raid with easily-procured administrative, not criminal, warrants. Thus, the protection of stricter Fourth Amendment search and seizure, Fifth Amendment due process, and Sixth Amendment right to counsel constitutional guarantees that apply to criminal investigations and arrests in judicial proceedings were unavailable to these workers. Moreover, the suppression remedy for illegally seized evidence or coerced confessions is quite limited in immigration proceedings. Overwhelmingly, most workers pled guilty in their criminal cases, and thus, relinquished any possibility of raising a Fourth Amendment challenge in court. These workers waived their Fourth Amendment and other due process guarantees under extreme prosecutorial pressure and with little opportunity for adequate legal representation.

(Hing, 2008)

The decision to criminalize the Agriprocessor workplace raid was a deliberate part of the larger immigration control strategy that demands 1) strategic use of state power over immigrants; 2) consolidating state power; 3) delegating state power to private companies; and 4) diminishing the rights immigrants enjoy as persons under the constitution.

Mandatory Detention

One of the important components of criminalization is mandatory detention, followed by mandatory removal. The Postville Raid was unprecedented in its scope also because hundreds of immigrant workers were detained for several months on criminal charges of using false documents, before being removed from the country. In addition, they were dispersed to detention facilities around the country, further separating them from friends, family and attorneys. Mandatory detention signifies a major shift in policy, from "catch and release" policies that were prevalent during the previous decade, to "catch and remove." The one-size-fits-all policy mandates prison for immigrants charged with "inadmissibility" under INA 212(a)(2) or "deportability" under INA 237(a)(2) while in removal proceedings. Mandatory detention also covers immigrants in expedited removal proceedings under INA 235.

Once again, the Clinton Immigration Acts were the forerunners of current mandatory detention policies. AEDPA requires mandatory detention of non-citizens convicted on a broad array of offenses, including minor drug offenses. IIRIRA expanded the list (ACLU, 18 August 1999). Under mandatory detention, the government can hold an immigrant convicted of an aggravated felony for an indefinite period of time, without bond. Immigrants can be held even if they pose no risk to others and no risk of flight. Mandatory detention removes several stages from the master calendar hearing that deals with posting bond and changing venue, and thus the assembly line processing of immigrants occurs more expeditiously. It is also worth noting that immigrant bond hearings have been subjected to a great deal of criticism (Koulish, 1992), but under this new provision, rather than applying bond determinations in a fairer and more equitable manner, the process of most bond determinations is eliminated.

In addition to a draconian policy of mandatory detention, the actual detention conditions for immigrants are inhumane. Consider the following mandatory detention case documented by a recent Amnesty Report, *Jailed Without Justice: Immigration Detention in the USA*:

Mr. B, a 57-year-old lawful permanent resident of the United States for more than forty years with U.S. citizen children and grandchildren, spent four years in mandatory detention while fighting deportation. In August 2003, he pled guilty to two misdemeanors and received probation. As part of his probation, he was required to check in with a probation officer, and he did so regularly. Before Thanksgiving in 2003 his probation officer asked him to come in and when he did so, ICE officers arrested Mr. B based on the misdemeanor convictions and sought to deport him, claiming that his convictions constituted aggravated felonies under immigration law. "I was in complete shock and kept asking my probation officer why I was being taken away. I had never heard of ICE." Mr. B told Amnesty International. His wife returned home from work that day to a voicemail that said she should pick her husband's car up. She told Amnesty International "My husband didn't call me for two or three days. I didn't know what was happening. No one would tell me." Although an immigration judge ruled that his convictions were not aggravated felonies, he remained in detention while his case went through several government appeals. In November 2007, the federal court of appeals found that Mr. B was not an aggravated felon and ordered his immediate release. Although he was no longer subject to deportation, ICE refused to release Mr. B unless he paid bond. Mr. B told Amnesty International "My tears came down my eyes because I learned that I would not be released unless I paid $10,000. I didn't know why." Mr. B's wife raised this money from family and friends; after his release, however, ICE did not return the bond money for over five months. When Mr. B finally received it, his family had to use the money to pay bills. He is still trying to pay back his friends and family, and his daughter has moved back into the home to help him and his wife financially.

(Amnesty International, January 2009)

Mr. B is not alone in his complaints about immigrant detention. He is one of over 400,000 people who are arrested by immigration authorities each year, including some U.S. citizens, four times the number in 2001—with taxpayers paying the $1.72 billion tab (Little, 2009). There are over 28,000 immigrants detained on any given day, and in 2006 alone, DHS arrested over 1.6 million immigrants (see Lutheran Immigration and Refugee Services, 2007; OIG, DHS, April 2006; ACLU, www.aclu.org/immigrants/detention/11771leg 19990818.htm). More than 300,000 people (including children) are detained by immigration authorities each year (Amnesty International, 2009). These people include permanent residents, undocumented immigrants, asylum seekers, survivors of torture and human trafficking. Immigration detention capacity has tripled from less than 10,000 in 1996 to more than 30,000 in 2008 (Amnesty International, 2009).

As detention numbers have increased more than three-fold since the 1990s, U.S. immigration authorities have contracted with about 350 state and county criminal jails to house immigrants pending removal proceedings (Amnesty International, 2009). About 67% of detainees are held in these facilities, and about 50% of these are private detention facilities. Thus it is also important to recognize this policy assures the private detention industry of a constant revenue stream, as discussed in the next chapter.

In its recent report, *Jailed without Justice,* Amnesty International reported that tens of thousands of immigrants languish in detention each year, in horrible conditions and without any judicial review to determine the legality of their detention. Although ICE reported that the average detention stay is 37 days (in 2007), AI has reported an average length of detention of ten months, with some asylum seekers spending over three years in detention before hearing whether or not they are eligible to remain in the United States.

Moreover, the poor conditions have resulted in extreme hardship, including death. Once immigrants are locked away, it seems even their most basic needs are ignored. In a highly acclaimed investigative series, the *Washington Post* in 2008 revealed a system of medical neglect in immigrant detention resulting in the needless death of dozens of immigrants. According to the *Post*:

> The medical neglect they endure is part of the hidden human cost of increasingly strict policies in the post-Sept. 11 United States and a lack of preparation for the impact of those policies. The detainees have less access to lawyers than convicted murderers in maximum-security prisons and some have fewer comforts than al-Qaeda terrorism suspects held at Guantanamo Bay, Cuba.
>
> (Priest & Goldstein, May 11, 2008)

In March 2009, Human Rights Watch and the Florida Immigrant Advocacy Center (FIAC) revealed results from two studies about medical care and immigrant detention. The shared conclusion was that "The medical care system in U.S. immigration detention is dangerously inadequate" (Human Rights Watch, March 2009). Consider the case of Hiu Lui Ng, who:

> . . . suffered cruel and negligent medical care while in (ICE) lock-ups. He died last year from cancer that went undiagnosed for four months

despite his repeated complaints of excruciating pain. . . . In one videotaped incident, Ng was forcibly dragged by detention officers while he cried and screamed in pain. Detention officials denied him medication, medical care and a wheelchair when he was too weak to walk. They cursed at him and accused him of faking his illness.

(Little, March 2009)

The HRW Report focusing on women in detention found that "women in detention described violations such as shackling pregnant detainees or failing to follow up on signs of breast and cervical cancer, as well as affronts to their dignity" (2009). The FIAC Report, "Dying for Decent Care," identified problems resulting in:

. . . poor, sometimes appalling response to health problems. These include: a lack of independent oversight to ensure the quality and effectiveness of detainee medical care; delayed and denied care; shortages of qualified staff; improper care of mentally ill patients and physically disabled patients; problems with medication; difficulty gaining access to medical records; a lack of competent, professional interpreters; cruel and abusive behavior by some clinic and detention staff; unsanitary and overcrowded facilities; and the transfer or segregation of detainees in retaliation for medical complaints.

(Human Rights Watch, March 2009)

In the days of the welfare state, not so long ago, such treatment of human beings would have garnered headlines and immediate redress. The more hardened neoliberal regime, however, provides a different narrative, to humanity's deep chagrin, that suggests that so long as the goal of risk management is still being met, such considerations are of little concern. Immigration detention is the fastest growing prison population in a country that has the world's highest incarceration rate. And within ICE prisons is a culture of cruelty and indifference to human suffering (Little, 2009).

Federal Prosecutions and Carol Lam

In the immigration context, actors have made no bones about the political nature of prosecuting immigrants for crimes and criminalizing the civil offense of entering the country without papers. In this section I focus on the case of U.S. attorneys getting fired for not prosecuting enough immigrants, and the larger issue of coercing federal prosecutions. The issue has to do with the DOJ's outright politicization of federal law, by ordering U.S. attorneys to engage in blanket prosecutions regardless of the merits of an individual case against immigrants. It also has to do with Congress extending the category of aggravated felonies and placing this category within the mission of Operation

Streamline, which destroys the autonomy and integrity of federal prosecutors around the country.

This story begins in 2006 with Carol Lam, U.S. attorney, who was fired by the DOJ ostensibly because she didn't prosecute enough "illegal immigrants." At least that was the official version. Only later was it revealed that she was let go for leading a corruption investigation that involved Randy Duke Cunningham and other high-ranking Republican officials (Moore). Were it not for the Bush administration's wholesale firing of seven U.S. attorneys on December 7, 2006, Carol Lam's dismissal on the grounds that she failed to prosecute immigrants would likely never have raised a stir.

By firing several highly respected U.S. attorneys without explanation, however, the DOJ placed in jeopardy the integrity of the entire federal legal system. So much for the autonomy and integrity of the federal prosecutor's office which, since the Judicial Act of 1789, had been expected to uphold the rule of law. The Judicial Act of 1789, which successfully doled out justice for over two centuries, finally met its match in a Bush administration that cared not one whit for the rule of law. The Bush administration destroyed the integrity and autonomy of federal prosecutors and invited the second-guessing of decisions made by all 93 federal prosecutors around the country. According to Lam, "This . . . creates a chilling effect on the entire U.S. Attorney community." To say the least, it also has a chilling effect on the immigrant community.

The underreported story here is that the State's immigrant control strategizing also undermined the autonomy of the U.S. Attorney's Office. Federal prosecutors were ordered to sacrifice the rule of law for expediency, and spread a very wide net with which to apprehend, brand, detain, and remove undocumented immigrants. Federal prosecutors were ordered to criminalize immigration law and immigrants regardless of the individual merits. Once apprehended and led through a criminal process instead of the "normal" civil process, immigrants were branded as criminals, and prevented from entering or re-entering the country, even if they were already legal permanent residents and had longstanding community and family ties. Such branding as a criminal excluded them from the body politic and prevents them from ever naturalizing.

Lam's "mistake" was clinging to a sense of professionalism that didn't really exist inside the Bush DOJ. It wasn't political or philosophical differences that separated her from the DOJ. She was a conservative Bush appointee who was sympathetic to the President's mission and agenda. However, she also took seriously the mandate that her office had discretion to make decisions informed by judgment and experience, rather than by DHS demands for political expediency under the guise of Operation Streamline, a DHS initiative announced in 2005.

There is nothing unique about immigration's reliance on discretion. All administrative law regimes rely on discretion to fill in the gaps of statutes with their own professional expertise. As Louis Jaffee has written, "the availability of discretion is the necessary condition, psychologically if not logically, of a system of administrative power which purports to be legitimate, or legally valid" (1965, p. 320; Kanstroom, 2006/2007, p. 165).

But immigration is unusual in the amount of discretion it uses and in its reliance upon the sovereign's hand. Daniel Kanstroom suggests that "indeed, much of modern immigration law could fairly be described as a fabric of discretion." Discretionary components of immigration decision-making include:

> choices of whom to prosecute; adjudication of claims for "discretionary" relief; whether bond should be granted; whether a motion to reopen proceedings has established a prima facie case; whether new evidence is material, was not available, and could not have been presented at a former hearing; various "policy-based" decisions; factual determinations; interpretations of statutory terms; and more.
>
> (Kanstroom, 2006/2007, p. 231)

The real problem here is that discretion is exercised in the absence of guiding legal norms. Instead the evidence shows a lack of professional judgment, and paucity of judicial supervision. Unlike other administrative law fields, discretion is the norm in immigration law, which all too often extends the narrative of lawlessness. Whereas in other administrative regimes discretion is the exception, here the exception becomes the rule, as the rules of law are ignored.

Conclusion

Since its origins, a combination of factors has been responsible for pushing immigration law into the remote back eddies of the legal process. In this chapter I have shown how the criminalization of immigration law promotes the marginalization of the immigration legal process. Immigration is one of few fields of law that refer to sovereignty rather than to the constitution for its guiding norms. It is one of few fields of law to promote the plenary powers of the executive branch over discrete individuals. Like other fields of administrative law, immigration law relies on a great deal of discretion. But unlike other fields of administrative law, immigration precludes many Administrative Procedures Act (APA) restrictions and is saturated with discretion throughout the process. Further, in recent years Congress has given sovereign powers to immigration judges and border patrol and ICE officials. For these reasons, the field of immigration differs from other bodies of law in the powers agents exert over its subjects and in its flexibility in being able to shift purpose with the shifting winds of governing ideologies and partisan leaders.

Although immigration law is not altogether outside court review, and is susceptible to scrutiny by Congressional committee, the GAO and Office of the Inspector General, it comes closer to Agamben's "state of exception" than just about any other body of law in the US. It is here, in this most political of legal fields, where lessons exist about how the State might well treat all of its people when in crisis. If nothing else, we get to see where society stands when the juridical order stands on the law's threshold (Agamben, 2005, p. 4).

Chapter 4

Neoliberalism, Risk, and Immigration Control

A grand irony of neoliberal democracy is that the minimal state, its hallmark, gains legitimacy by becoming an almost pervasive presence in people's lives. Its omnipresence is due in part to the overregulation of people it categorizes as a risk, and in part due to surveillance, which the State facilitates and which private firms manage and control. Another irony is that although market ideology suggests the market is society's most efficient regulator, the market draws immigrants into the country and is much less effective at excluding them once they have arrived. Even in economic downturns, the post-industrial economy demands cheap labor. Neoliberalism has no shortage of boxes it paints itself into. The argument for a self-regulating market, therefore, deregulates migrant flows (removing walls and border patrols), and goes so far as to deregulate the border—open borders. The ebbs and flows of unrestricted migration, however, rub up against the neoliberal demands of consumer capitalism, which, in order to police threats to the consumer market, oppresses and excludes the same immigrants the market actively pulls into the country through the push–pull dynamic of migration flow.

Neoliberalism gives itself the challenge of policing the market without hindering the flow of cheap labor. It responds to the challenge with surveillance. Surveillance functions as a tool that advances two parts of the neoliberal agenda: criminalization and consumption capitalism. To advance its agenda it does not rely very much on the old fashioned "statist" top-down approach. Rather, state power is now decentralized and delegated to state and local governments, as well as outsourced to private firms. Rather than diminishing state power, these technologies extend its reach over suspected undocumented immigrants. The tentacles of state power do not reach so much into the immigrants' soul or psyche, as had been the intent of past approaches to social control. Rather, the neoliberal uses surveillance technologies to assess and manage the risk associated with immigration and immigrants. Risk management is the neoliberal social control ideology that connects the sovereignist and free marketer. Risk management provides the justification for the decisions the sovereign makes after he decides on the exception. Bush's punitive immigrant control policies, directed mostly against immigrants of color and manifested in workplace and neighborhood raids, mandatory detention and removal policies, etc., illustrates the everyday operation of sovereignty justified by risk management. In such instances, Majia Nadesan suggests, "the decision for exclusion finds justification in the logics of risk management and public safety (2008, p. 35).

Risk Management

In recent years, the risk management industry has had to address the fear of immigration generated in the aftermath of 9/11. Risk management technologies consist of surveillance, biometrics, RFIDs and databases, all of which are designed to create, control, and contain fear. "By means of this process of fear cultivation, the surveillance systems become 'necessary' interventions, worth any cost, inconvenience, or more profound alteration of educational environments" (Monahan, 2006).

During the heyday of the welfare state era (the New Deal through the 1970s), the government assumed responsibility for its citizens, a phenomenon many people still take for granted and some critics suggest is paternalistic. Neoliberalism, which is constructed around the idea of market efficiency and choice, shifts responsibility from the government to the individual, thus relieving the state of a good many social and political responsibilities.

When dealing with people who do not accept its societal norms, the welfare state deploys strategies of social control that Michel Foucault referred to as normalization. Normalization occurs within disciplining institutions, such as the prison, and endeavors to rehabilitate criminals through case histories and diagnostics, and on a wider scale by aggregating data to target dysfunctions in society in order to normalize the entire population back into the mainstream of normalized society (Nadesan, 2008, p. 34). When rehabilitation fails, punitive measures are deployed.

Even though neoliberalism shifts responsibility to individuals, it does not trust them; quite the opposite. It subordinates the individual's subjectivity to its own ideological interests, which means it decides when and how to trust citizens through the method of risk management. By assessing risk, the neoliberal regime justifies its a priori decision to trust and rely upon those who happen to be active purveyors of consumer capitalism.

Under neoliberalism, risk management, rather than normalization, becomes the preferred method of social control. Risk management calls for surveillance. Neoliberal authorities "couple surveillance with 'targeted government' to identify and manage risk" (Nadesan, 2008, p. 34; see also Valverde & Mopas, 2004). Thus individuals who fail to take responsibility (for abiding by neoliberal norms) are subject to various forms of guidance and discipline by experts because they ostensibly threaten the values associated with property and consumer capitalism. According to Majia Nadesan:

> In a sense, neoliberal government presupposes an impossibility—the rational, self-governing neoliberal agents who always act (or learn to act)

responsibly in accord with neoliberal value orientations—and the ruptures that point to the impossibility of the neoliberal fantasy result in ever more invasive efforts to property produce, manage, and discipline neoliberal subjects.

(2009, p. 34)

Nadesan highlights another important irony in neoliberal governance. The rhetorical adherence to minimizing government and accentuating responsibility instead produces postmodern policies in which "expert knowledge, employed by private and governmental agents, is extended and refined to better represent and act upon recalcitrant and/or risky populations who belie the neoliberal fantasy" (2009, p. 34). Such a regime, Dean says, "attempts to govern as much through domination—a word that covers a myriad of conditions—as it does through freedom" (as cited in Nadeson, 2008, p. 34).

In other words, the only part of the state that has been minimized under neoliberalism is the part that deals with social welfare programs. In the meantime concern for the poor, sick and elderly morphs into strategies to discipline and contain them.

Surveillance

Briefly, the neoliberal process of domination over immigrants functions through surveillance and databases. As newcomers to society arrive, they are categorized in multiple ways. In terms of law, they may be categorized as fitting into some undocumented, temporary, or permanent status. Typically, as their status gets closer to becoming permanent, the newcomer becomes eligible for greater entitlements and benefits. Such entitlements and benefits adhere to identities that have been submitted to some national database. This identity is referred to as an individual's "virtual identity," which becomes the newcomer's key to gain entry into the benefits and entitlements that a society reserves for its own members. The virtual identity is a representation that has been captured, retained in a national registry database, and is subsequently capable of being modified and massaged.

The process of coming under surveillance consists of a basic tradeoff: anonymity for freedom (goods, benefits, legal status and even citizenship). David Lyon notes that "to gain privileges or entitlements, (passports, driver's licenses, credit cards, and mortgages, among other things) the ID holder must present a card that refers to a database record, and each time a transaction is made the virtual identity is modified" (Lyon, 2007, p. 125). Once in the system, you come under surveillance, a phenomenon that allows Jeff Bezos at Amazon books to list books of interest whenever you log on. According to Nikolas Rose:

Problems of the individualization of the citizen have formed in a whole variety of sites and practices—of consumption, of finance, of police, of health, of insurance—to which securitization of identity can appear as a solution. Does this person have sufficient funds to make this purchase; is this citizen entitled to enter this national territory? . . . is this person a good insurance risk? The image of control by totalizing surveillance is misleading. Control is better understood as operating through conditional access to circuits of consumption and civility: constant scrutiny of the right of individuals to access certain kinds of flows of consumption goods . . .

(Rose, 1999, pp. 183–208)

The same surveillance logic also explains how law enforcement tracks the whereabouts of immigrants in places like Maricopa County, Arizona, where Sheriff Joe Arpaio and his posse conduct raids in their neighborhoods and places of employment. Arpaio's "governing through crime," as Jonathan Simon refers to this side of the surveillance phenomenon, treats ostensibly non-punitive social relationships (employer–employee) with punitive crime control techniques (Miller, 2007).

Arpaio and Amazon share the same ideology, make use of the same technology, and have access to the same virtual identities. These virtual identities are accessible to both circuits of securitization and of consumption. The circuits of securitization that are of concern to Arpaio are the reverse side of the circuits of consumption that interest Amazon. So each time immigrants gain access to "circuits of consumption," it provides opportunities for Sheriff Arpaio and his posse, and others to gain access to them and subject them to punitive forms of criminalization (Rose, 1999).

Such is the neoliberal form of governance that has gained currency during the Bush era. Citizenship is reduced to consumerism and government responsibilities shift from social welfare to crime control. The era was launched when, after 9/11, the President told Americans to go shopping as a sign of patriotism. Although Barack Obama's election and the economic crisis he followed into office suggest the demise of neoliberal governance, the effects of the immigration regime that Bush established likely will be long-lasting. Bush's cronies were inspired by the 1973 Chilean coup and used it as a model for their own attempt to wreak free market havoc on border control policy. As several memos released after Bush left office show, he came a lot closer to achieving a Pinochet-like model for the United States than many people imagined. Naomi Klein's *Shock Doctrine* adeptly documents how the thunderous events around 9/11 enabled the Bush administration to orchestrate a neoliberal coup against immigrants without encountering much criticism in the press. By the time the country and courts regained their senses around Election Day 2006, the State had already reconfigured itself along the lines of the neoliberal agenda that Milton Friedman envisioned for Chile and that Richard Nixon conceded could never be implemented in America. It's not the first time that Nixon was wrong.

Background to Bush Neoliberalism

The origins of the neoliberal part of the Bush era immigration control regime can be found in the writings of Milton Friedman (Harvey, 2005; Klein, 2007). Friedman was the architect of the neoliberal revolution. Back in 1947, Friedman and Friedrich Hayek formed the Mont Pelerin Society, which boasted the mission of promoting neoliberal values (Harvey, 2005; Klein, 2007). During this post-WWII period, neoliberal thinking was relegated to the back rooms of conservative salons and parlors (Klein, 2007). John Maynard Keynes' analysis provided the philosophical foundation for much of the New Deal and subsequent development of the welfare state.[1] The idea behind the welfare state was support for full employment and the establishment of a social safety net. Friedman critiqued state intervention as an inefficient impediment on the market (Klein, 2007).

Friedman's ideas remained on the periphery of the political agenda until 1973, when neoliberal ideas were first put into action in Chile following the U.S.-backed coup against the democratically-elected socialist Allende government. After the coup, Augusto Pinochet turned to a business elite in Chile that had been trained at the University of Chicago. Starting in 1975, this elite dismantled the existing Keynesian and developmentalist compromises between management and labor, the State and the market, trade and development. In its place, the Chicago boys transformed the Chilean government into a neoliberal regime, which privatized all state assets except copper, and opened the country to foreign investment (Harvey 2005; Klein, 2007).

The Chilean counterrevolution was a reaction against the welfare state, that is, against the Keynesian economics in which the State moderates market forces and makes them less brutal through unemployment insurance, welfare, and so forth (Riesco, 2003). The problem for elites is that Keynesianism eats into their profit margins. Thus Wall Street, a major sponsor of the University of Chicago set out to dismantle New Deal Keynesianism, wherever it lay.

Friedman believed in a radical vision of society in which profit and the market drove every aspect of life. Friedman called for abolishing all trade protections, deregulating all prices, and eviscerating government services. Thus Friedman's agenda is the minimal state. The only acceptable role is for the state to enforce contracts and protect borders. Everything else, and by this he means education, the post office, national parks and so forth, should be left to the "free market," ostensibly because these things can be bought and sold for profit. For obvious reasons such ideas have proven unpopular and unattainable through elections. How to go about this? Friedman, in 1982, called for economic shock treatment: "only a crisis, actual or perceived produces real change. When that crisis occurs, the actions that are taken depend on the ideas that are lying around. That I believe, is our basic function, to develop alternatives to existing policies, to keep them alive and available until the politically impossible becomes politically inevitable" (Klein, 2007).

Friedman thought he had an acolyte in Richard Nixon, and was quite chagrined to see Nixon go on to impose wage and price controls on the U.S. economy.[2] Friedman's real acolyte was Donald Rumsfeld who later taught Friedman's basic principles to George Bush. Nixon indeed was sympathetic to Friedman, but realized he could not get re-elected in 1972 if he implemented Friedman's neoliberal agenda during his first term. Nixon convinced Friedman that Friedman's brand of neoliberalism could never garner the public approval needed to be politically viable in a democracy. Although Nixon wouldn't jeopardize his own political viability, he had no problem unleashing the forces of Friedmanism upon Latin America. With Nixon's tacit support, Chile was turned into a laboratory for Friedman and his Chicago boys. The lesson learned is that although neoliberalism was anathema to democracy, it could indeed function in a dictatorship (Klein, 2007).

For many policy makers and academics, the 1970s were also the beginning of the end of New Deal liberalism and the beginning of post-New Deal neoliberalism. The country experienced social and economic changes that ripened the political economy for a shift to the neoliberal paradigm during the 1980s. The Reagan Presidency epitomized this shift in paradigm from the welfare state, social safety nets and unionism to competitiveness in the new global economy.

In the decades that followed, culminating in Bush's post-9/11 America, the industrial sectors of society started giving way to post-industrial service and technology sectors, which increasingly replaced America's manufacturing base. The liberalization of markets opened the U.S. economy to global markets and offshore production, which in turn led to deindustrialization. This shift in paradigm also led to the economy's growing reliance upon cheap, exploitable and flexible labor, the sort that immigrant workers have represented for more than a century (Brenner & Theodore, 2003).

Immigration and Free Trade: Guest Worker Provisions

In many ways, temporary immigrant labor is a quintessential neoliberal phenomenon. Common sense suggests that immigrant labor is desired for its productive capacity and disdained for its reproductive capacity, which ostensibly places demands on the state for social benefits. Such is the neoliberal way: unregulated markets, flexibility, informality, and individualized worker relationships with employers. The neoliberal does not want to bear the costs associated with providing social benefits. Thus immigrant labor embodies the desired characteristics: unregulated markets, flexibility, informality, and individualized worker relationships with employers. It is anti-union and functions largely outside legal regulation. Above all, perhaps, undocumented immigration has inspired the immigration control industry, which is discussed in detail in Chapter 4.

Historically, migrant flows into the country have been met with existing state of the art social control mechanisms—from Haymarket to Operation Wetback, urban red squads to RFIDs and mandatory detention— intended not so much to expel as to register and subordinate immigrants into pliable and movable cogs in the workplace and docile neighbors. During the 1950s, immigration control served as a backdrop for efforts to rid the country of suspected disloyal and unwanted Latinos. During the 1960s, as a result of the Immigration Act of 1965, persons coming across the border faced hemispheric restrictions, and thus, for the first time, attention was focused on counting Latino immigrants crossing the border. Such recordkeeping and categorization slowly turned the public's attention to unauthorized entries. During the 1970s, Jimmy Carter began militarizing the border, forcing undocumented immigrants for the first time to contend with more aggressive border control strategies, and traverse Vietnam-era sensors and traps to get into the country (LeMay, 1987; Daniels, 2004).

During the 1980s, border-crossers had ideological labels from El Salvador and Nicaragua attached to them. During this time, the credo "the enemies of our enemies were our friends," really came into play, as Nicaraguan refugees easily passed through the obstacle course to settle in Miami, Los Angeles, DC and elsewhere, while Salvadorans were forced to undergo a much more strenuous vetting process, and were far more liable to be denied of relief from deportation, detention, deportation and for many, death at the hands of the government and death squads (Koulish, 1992; Gibney & Hanson, 2005). During the 1990s, immigrant workers were part of the NAFTA debate, where the idea of open borders was accepted for trade but not for people, who faced increasing legal restrictions and physical barriers against entry into the country.

Temporary Workers

Temporary guest workers, both undocumented or temporarily documented and unskilled are the quintessential neoliberal phenomenon, and have been since guest worker programs were first institutionalized to compensate for labor shortages during WWI. In 1917, the Department of Labor initiated the country's first temporary guest worker program for agricultural workers from Mexico (Calavita, 1992). In part due to labor shortages caused by the war, and in part caused by the country's first qualitative immigration restrictions (in 1917), the government brought in over 70,000 guest workers from 1917–1921.

In 1942, the U.S. government negotiated the "Mexican Labor Program," referred to as the Bracero agreement. The Bracero Agreement was designed to alleviate labor shortages by allowing Mexicans to work in the United States on a temporary basis (Calavita, 1992; Koulish, 1996). In 1951, Congress passed Public Law 78, which gave the Bracero program a permanent statutory basis for the next 13 years. This extension was enacted in response to political pressure from growers. It was also a response to growing fears of labor shortages during the Korean War. Until its demise, the Bracero program allowed about 200,000 unskilled Mexican laborers annually to enter the country as guest-workers, mostly doing agricultural work. During the program's 22-year tenure, about 4.8 million Braceros contracted for work inside the United States (Koulish, 2008). As Kitty Calavita put it:

> The Bracero program became synonymous with substandard wages and living conditions. Although guarantees regarding wages, duration of employment, housing, health insurance, and other specifics were written into bracero contracts, these protections were poorly enforced and routinely circumvented . . .
>
> Also well-documented was the downward pressure on local farm workers' wages. Although bracero contracts required employers to pay "prevailing wages" and growers had to demonstrate that a shortage of labor existed before being certified to contract braceros, study after study found that in regions where braceros were concentrated, workers' bargaining power declined and wages fell.
>
> (Calavita, 1992)

Following the end of the Korean War, the U.S. economy fell into recession, which along with intensifying fears of communism instigated by Senator Joseph McCarthy (R-Wi), increased political pressure to "do something" about illegal immigrants in 1953–1954. The government's response was perhaps the first systematic effort to militarize the borders and immigration control. In 1954, the INS launched "Operation Wetback," which organized a mass round-up of suspected undocumented immigrants. In all, the INS apprehended over 1 million undocumented immigrants (Calavita, 1992).

But even recession and McCarthyism couldn't end the growers' addiction to cheap Mexican labor (Durand & Massey, 2006). During "Operation Wetback," Congress more than doubled the number of bracero visas (Durand & Massey, 2006, p. 37). In addition, in 1952 Congress established the H-2 visa program, which allowed employers to hire temporary immigrant laborers for agricultural and nonagricultural positions in case of certified labor shortages. While the H-2 program overlapped with the Bracero agreement and continues to the present, it is very restrictive: guest workers may only enter the US to fill jobs for which no American workers can be found (Calavita, 1992). According to Nicholas Laham, "since there are very few jobs where no American workers can be found, only a limited number of guest workers have been allowed to enter the United States under the H-2 program" (p. 63).

In many ways the H-2 Program continues the exploitation of workers begun under the Bracero program. The program is employer specific, which makes the migrant worker exceedingly dependent upon the employer, and susceptible to exploitation and abuse. Furthermore, the meager number of visas issued annually does almost nothing to mitigate problems associated with undocumented labor. Because the number of guest worker visas typically does not come close to satisfying either the demand for or the supply of cheap labor, the H-2 program serves as an advertisement for potential laborers and thus, like a magnet, induces them to cross the border. Rather than helping to lessen undocumented immigration, the H-2 visa program historically has attracted cheap labor over the border. At the same time, a pool of immigrant workers is created as a result of these programs in response to market demands, a pool that is subject to gross exploitation by unscrupulous employers and scapegoated by the State.

The importance of temporary immigrant labor is even greater as a result of the global economy. In addition to having established an apparatus capable of managing millions of temporary workers, the World Trade Organization (WTO) General Agreement on Trade in Services (GATS) did the administration's bidding in the international arena by paving the road for international agreements regarding temporary workers. Such guest worker proposals helped frame immigration within a neoliberal trade context, opening another door to privatized control over immigration, and providing an abundance of potential business for the border industrial complex.

Perhaps the most salient international provision relating to guest workers was Mode 4 of the GATS, which helped reduce migrant workers to the status of commodities. The GATS agreement categorizes international service industries in four modes, depending on the location of the provider and the consumer at the time the service is rendered. Mode 4 applies specifically to the "temporary movement of natural persons (workers as opposed to corporate entities) across borders to provide services." The key stipulation of Mode 4 required migrant workers to be employed by firms with a commercial presence where the service is provided, or be under contract for the provision of a service. This stipulation mandates visas that are employer or contract-bound; workers must be employed to retain legal status. The alternative is detention and deportation, which leads to the criminalization of a great many people.

Once he was elected President, Bush was quite receptive to these global neoliberal currents. By 2001, Bush, who had been a neoliberal border state governor, had come into office with a special affinity for Vincente Fox, Mexico's first non-PRI President and fellow neoliberal aficionado. They hoped to develop an alliance that would serve their shared belief in free trade. In February 2001, Bush announced the creation of "an orderly framework for migration that ensures humane treatment (and) legal security, and dignifies labor conditions" (Gibney & Hansen, 2005). In August 2001, Bush and Fox reached a preliminary agreement that allowed guest workers to apply for legal residency status after a certain period of time in the United States. Fox called for the agreement to be finalized by the end of 2001. On September 10, 2001, *Business Week* reported that the United States was about to undergo a sea change in immigration policy. President Bush, along with Mexican President Vincente Fox, was preparing to propose changes in immigration policy that would consider "regularization" of status for unauthorized Mexicans, and facilitate the entrance of Mexican temporary workers into the United States. Even after 9/11 guest workers remained on the Bush agenda. In September 2005, for example, Bush announced that "a complex process" would have to be completed before guest worker programs could be implemented.

Criminalizing Day Labor

One of the recent currents of immigrant labor has to do with day laborers, a neoliberal (deregulated) version of the bracero (Valenzuela, 2006). The day laborer phenomenon avoids legal regulation as well as most circuits of consumption. It also coincides with the build-up of anti-immigrant militarization since the mid-1990s. According to Abel Valenzuela, author of the first systematic study of day laborers in the United States:

> The reasons behind the growth of day laborers . . . involve the complex interaction between forces of labor supply and demand, patterns of industrial change, and increased migration flows to the United States. On the demand side . . . there has been a push for greater market flexibility in all sectors of the U.S. economy . . . On the supply side . . . workers are increasingly turning to day-labor hiring sites, and other contingent work like temp. agencies and labor brokers, following the deterioration of job opportunities . . . plant closings, mass layoffs . . . in old industrial centers . . .
>
> (Valenzuela, 2006, p. 6)

Valenzuela's studies depict the situation of day laborers on street corners and Home Depot parking lots, among other places, seeking temporary employment in such diverse places as urban Baltimore, suburban Long Island, and small town Hazelton, Pennsylvania (Valenzuela, 2006). In all about 120,000 day laborers are out looking for work every day. About three-fourths are undocumented. About half work for homeowners, while 43% work for contractors. As Valenzuela has found, day laborers represent new immigrant flows "outside traditional ports of entry cities like New York, Los Angeles, and Chicago." "New migratory circuits have developed in the South and parts of the east and Midwest, especially in small cities and towns with abundant . . . low wage opportunities" (Valenzuela, 2006, p. 6). As PBS' POV producers noted in their documentary about day labor in Farmingville Long Island, "it is a migration that globalization is carrying beyond border areas and major cities and into small cities and towns across America" (www.pbs.org/pov/pov2004/farmingville/about.html, accessed March 6, 2009). Immigration scholar Aiwha Ong suggests that the lesson here is that "under neoliberal restructuring, weaker social groups such as poor economic migrants—are essentially given over to deregulation by supranational entities which relegate many to unregulated work with little security and few rights" (2006).

Hence the disciplinary pressure on day laborers is much more than the pressure that GATT, bracero or H-2 regulations applied to temporary immigrants. With law, even with such weak regulations as those issued under bracero and H-2 rules, comes constraints on government power. When dealing with day laborers, employer sanctions are lifted. A loophole in the 1986 employer sanctions law means sanctions kick in only when immigrants are being hired for three days or more. Ostensibly, the day laborer is the only party to the day labor relationship that is subjected to discipline and punishment. The employer can act with virtual impunity.

Such is the neoliberal ideal situation: a deregulated market that polices the worker. Many of the same suburbanites who benefit from the cheap day labor also object to seeing these workers on their downtown street corners seeking work. For day laborers, the same socio-economic forces that draw them to their suburban destinations also remove their legal protections and add police intimidation and harassment to their troubles.

This double bind plays out almost every day in cities and towns across America. Just consider how, in early 2007 in south-east Baltimore, an ICE unit that was supposed to be pursuing "high risk" criminal aliens walked into a local 7/11 store where day laborers were known to gather daily to solicit work, and arrested all Latinos on the premises. A *Washington Post* report revealed that arresting the day laborers provided a convenient way for this ICE unit to meet its arrest quota of 1,000 aliens, since this one stop yielded 24 Latino men (Aizenman, February 19, 2009).

In Baltimore as well as in Riverside, California, in violation of federal rules law enforcement agents are given quotas, which threaten officers with less desirable schedules if they do not make enough arrests. As a result they conduct raids on neighborhoods that are known day-labor locales, and make arrests of day laborers. The agents were required to make 150 arrests in January 2009, and so they conducted raids and identification checks at the San Bernardino Greyhound bus station (Olsen, February 2, 2009). On October 21, 2008, in the Jackson Heights section of Queens, NY, local police sprang out of police vans and arrested over a dozen day laborers, charging them with "obstruction of traffic"(Arce & Auken, October 29, 2008). One day laborer who was arrested that day richly describes what transpired:

> We gather here every day before dawn and hope to find work for the day. Most of us come from Mexico and Central America, but there are also workers from Ecuador and Colombia. . . . The police arrived in two vans. There were three policemen in uniform in each van . . . There were 12 of us, and the police ask for IDs. Some of us, like myself, had IDs, but they arrested us anyway. We were handcuffed and taken to the stationhouse in

Queens. The police took our pictures and fingerprints, and then we were put in jail cells. Later on were taken in handcuffs to the Queens courthouse and were put in jail cells again before being taken before a judge. The charge was "obstruction of traffic." We were let go after 7 p.m. on the condition that we stay out of trouble for six months. I want to say that we are here to work and support our families because our countries are very poor. Work has slowed down. I do construction or house cleaning work.

(www.wsws.org/articles/2008/oct2008/
immi-o29.shtml)

The workers were not turned over to ICE, nor were they placed in mandatory deportation or forcibly removed from the country. "Obstruction of traffic" ordinances are one of myriads of local nuisance ordinances that local police use to pursue, manage and control unwanted day laborers.

Farmingville police also arrested several day laborers for criminal trespass (Trumbull, April 2006). In 2007, the town council of Cave Creek, Arizona enacted an ordinance that prevented Hector Lopez, a longtime resident, from uttering the words, "I need work," on Cave Creek sidewalks. With this nuisance ordinance, the Cave Creek council, at the urging of Sheriff Joe Arpaio, the local Maricopa county sheriff, was able to put another anti-immigrant tool in Arpaio's nativist arsenal. In fact, this and other enforcement tools enabled Arpaio's sheriffs and local police to harass Cave Creek's entire Latino population when it made use of the town's public streets and sidewalks.

By 2006 and 2007, almost any mention around law enforcement of day laborers and guest workers was accompanied by workplace raids. Given the estimated 12 million undocumented immigrants in the country, these raids are quite disruptive, but even more important is the fear they inspire among immigrants.

When Michel Foucault focused on disciplining societies, he emphasized the normalizing power that worked through such institutions as factories, prisons, and armies. The story of day laborers moves Foucault's narrative outside brick and mortar institutions to open-air markets, public streets, sidewalks, and parking lots. Local suburban communities are often where local homeowners, contractors, and even officials interested in the economic revitalization of their communities solicit the new immigrants to come work. At the same time, however, day laborers are increasingly perceived as "evidence of illegal immigration out of control" (Kettles, 2009). This double bind awaited day laborers as they arrived in Farmingville Long Island during the late 1990s, when about 1,500 immigrants wound up in this community (pop. 15,000) seeking employment in landscaping, construction, and restaurant businesses. According to local contractors, restaurateurs, and homeowners, the local economy would have come to a standstill were it not for the "Mexican's willingness to do hard, low paying, and sometimes dangerous labor" (Kettles, 2009). But that didn't stop local residents from beating and stabbing the immigrants in the basement of a temporary work site. Nor did it prevent the local Farmingville city council from drumming up nuisance ordinances to harass the newcomers. Nor should it have, if Foucault's discussion of decentralized power is to be believed.

Although Farmingville seems to have repeated the well-worn theme of immigration being about supply and demand and push and pull dynamics, differences lie in new immigrant destinations and hyped-up official and unofficial responses to the sudden presence of new immigrants. While the logic of exclusion would criminalize day labor, criminalization is a disciplinary power that constructs a version of reality from the neoliberal agenda to maintain a population of docile and compliant laborers. The disciplining power of federal law enforcement (ICE) is obvious. Uniforms, guns, badges, and arrest equal power. A bit trickier is making sense of how the normalizing judgment of zero-tolerance policing coincides with neoliberalism.

The nut of this argument has to do with policing human mobility. Mobility is an essential feature of both neoliberalism and immigration. Migration is a major feature "of the flexible capitalism that now dominates the world of production, exchange and consumption" (Lyon, 2007, p. 120). As Lyon suggests, "the information economy is an important aspect of this globalizing world, but so is mobile labor, which means that employment records also migrate." It follows that keeping track of mobile labor has created a huge demand for database firms to compete for government business. Further, the government response to 9/11 created incredible demand for information about immigrants and all people entering and leaving the country. The idea was to prevent the next terrorist from crossing the border. And thus was born the post-9/11 surveillance component of the immigration regime, which enabled the State to move pro-actively against perceived threats against homeland security.

Even if such immigrants were not offered up to the deportation machine, an arrest for violating the nuisance ordinance would have created a record that did not previously exist. With such records in hand, local police authorities have the ability to add the immigrants' personal information into inter and intra-national anti-immigrant databases. Under neoliberal logic, data collection is even more important than detention or deportation. It is also more important than the division between immigrant and citizen, and helps redefine the boundary between skilled and unskilled. The new dividing line divides people who are registered from the unregistered.

The harassment scenarios discussed above reinforce and are reinforced by the surveillance components of the immigration control industry. The surveillance industry plays out in the field of immigration in several ways. First, passport entries represent the surveillance archetype. Not only did the first national registries follow the creation of the passport system, but passports and a new version for internal travel—Real ID— now include society's most advanced identifying features—biometrics—which allow the State to sort out and monitor who belongs and where they go. Second, the country's 12–14 million undocumented immigrants represent the only group in society that is not surveilled, which presents a huge opportunity for the state and surveillance industry.

In addition to tracking immigrants as prospective threats to national security, information systems were also deployed to track migrants as potential threats to the post-9/11 marketplace. The neoliberal agenda blurs the distinction between markets and society. The market is comprised of cogs and commodities; society is comprised of human beings. By commodifying parts of society, neoliberalism ignores the social needs of immigrants as human beings. As a result, immigrants in the global market are both necessary cogs and perceived threats. The tension created by the agenda also blurs the distinction between neoliberal and sovereignist approaches to immigration control. No longer subjects, they have been stripped bare of their dignity and humanity; they also become easy victims of sovereign impunity. In this way, I argue, sovereignty partners up with neoliberalism to strip the immigrant of constitutional rights and other human trappings of dignity that might impede the commodification process. With constitutional rights, immigrants might be expected to demand that the government assume some responsibility for the social welfare of immigrants and their families. But since immigrants are no longer described as "persons" under the Constitution they have no standing to demand social welfare from the government. Thus neoliberalism's market metaphors advance the theory that the executive can treat immigrants with impunity. It further removes the expectation that immigrants deserve due process and other checks on sovereign power.

Private Enterprise and Neoliberalism

Capitalism creates huge incentives for employees to treat immigrants as commodities, ensuring a plentiful and well-disciplined labor supply for industry. This occurs by ensuring that arrests are high, detention centers are full and that the revolving door of entries and removals keeps spinning. It is also important to keep a significant number of immigrant workers running free, as long as they are "virtually imprisoned" with counterintelligence technologies. Following 9/11, the military-industrial complex saw an opportunity to reap profits by engaging in immigration control and quickly mobilized its lobbyists to create policy around its new spy technologies. Such companies as ManTech, Accenture, VeriChip, Anteon and others quickly convinced the new DHS and sympathetic members of Congress that they had devised the most effective and efficient spy tools that could help protect the homeland while keeping a watchful eye on the "alien other." For example, during the immigration reform debate in 2005, VeriChip Chairman Scott Silverman offered to privatize the management of millions of guest workers (Koulish, 2008). The VeriChip "RFID" is a subcutaneous identification tag that would be injected into the flesh of guest workers as they register for the program at Ellis Island centers (Koulish, 2008). In sum, the neoliberal state allies with private companies in a decentralized manner for the purpose of extending its own social control tentacles. It morphs sovereignty and neoliberalism into a new securitization beast.

Guest worker policies also provide the security-industrial complex with additional opportunities at the border. Inspired by the shock of 9/11, the federal government created the DHS and moved immigration services and enforcement within it. Perhaps more than any other department in the federal government, DHS, immediately contracted out many of its responsibilities and operations to private contractors. This scenario has been well-documented with regards to the Iraq War. It is also the case with border enforcement. With CCA, Blackwater, Lockheed Martin and others as gatekeepers, guest workers, like other entries, would come face to face with law and order activities twice removed from public scrutiny. The lack of accountability here is cause for alarm even if corporate cultures were steeped in values favorable to immigrant rights. Regrettably, that is not the case.

The looming presence of "virtual" technologies, mercenaries and military contractors as front-line defenders of American sovereignty is cause for alarm well beyond the potential consequences of individual human rights violations. It suggests this country's "deciders" are less interested in physical border fences that would harm trade and impede the flow of cheap labor, than in securing a system of "virtual fences" that would facilitate wholesale control over migrants in the name of profit.

The Least Dangerous Branch as Neoliberal Enabler

Although the executive branch under Nixon basically punted on neoliberalizing the economy during the 1970s, the courts during this time established an infrastructure that would soon help pave the way for neoliberalism. The court's support for neoliberalism is most evident in the steps it took towards redefining the "state action doctrine," intended to reduce state intervention in the market. According to *Burdeau v. McDowell* "(the fourth amendment) . . . was intended as a restraint upon the activities of sovereign authority, and was not intended to be a limitation upon other than governmental agencies." Since Burdeau, the court has never held that private searches implicate a fourth amendment interest, unless the private actor is regarded as having acted as an "instrument" or agent of the state.

Next, private contractors were not considered state actors for purposes of Bivens or 42 USC 1983 "under color of law" liability. According to the court, there is no basis for filing a federal civil rights lawsuit under 42 USC 1983 against an individual who is not a "state actor." For example, according to the court in *National Collegiate Athletic Association v. Tarkanian*, the only proper defendants in a Section 1983 claim represent the state in some capacity, whether they act in accordance with their authority or misuse it. *Tarkanian* raises serious questions about accountability and liability issues related to the conditions of confinement within private facilities. The Office of the Inspector General reported in 2003 on serious infractions against private immigrant detention facilities, including routine abuse of basic prisoner rights, denial of attorney access, mental and physical abuse, denial of health and medical treatment, prison overcrowding, and a lack of showers and toilets. Inmates in public facilities have channels for redressing grievances though the Office of the Inspector General (OIG) and litigation, but similarly aggrieved counterparts in private facilities lack of such redress. As a result, immigrants have a hard time seeking redress from companies that employ individuals who might abuse them.

By using private contractors, the executive branch can further limit Congressional oversight of immigration policy. Although the Congress enacts the budget for ICE, the executive hires the contractors and Congress' access to these contracts is limited. Further, private companies need not divulge information to Congress or the public, and they are less rule-bound than public entities and make decisions behind closed doors. Finally, they are not subject to the notice and comment provisions of the APA.

Private contractors also are exempt from civil service rules and the constraints associated with having a unionized workforce. Thus the private security industry, for example, can pay its employees less than what it would pay unionized workers, and put them on jail blocks or the street with neither firearms training nor rigorous background checks. The lack of professionalism, high turnover rates and ad hoc decision-making that results can place immigrant populations at a great risk.

Consider a field of law in which officials may gather and use secret evidence, expedite immigrant removals, where there is no review of final orders of removal, where mandatory and indefinite detention exists, along with secretive changes of venue, exorbitant bonds, restricted access to counsel and restricted judicial review. As I have discussed, the unfettered exercise of sovereignty in these instances showcase a system that is anathema to the democratic process. Due process safeguards, for example, which prohibit prosecutions based on "outrageous investigative techniques, applies only to the government." Thus, any procedures attached to the private processing of potential guest workers in "Ellis Island Centers," for example, or to the street questioning by private contractors of a Hispanic resident walking into a Circle K grocery store to buy milk or cigarettes without a wallet, would not necessarily be prohibited from using "outrageous investigative techniques."

Under this regime, according to Mark Dow, "The buck stops nowhere. While the INS (now ICE) pretends to be open to scrutiny, . . . corporate offices . . . make no secret of their antipathy to oversight, at least not in materials directed to shareholders" (2004, p. 90). Indeed, the transfer of liability (from government to private entity) provides an incentive for government to outsource in the first place. This phenomenon also provides an incredible opportunity for radical privatization, taking advantage of plenary executive powers to facilitate outsourcing beyond the review authority of the courts or Congress.

Detention: Ending Catch and Release

As a result, the Customs and Border Protection's Expedited Removal Program has contracted with KBR to oversee the expansion of the federal government's capacity to detain immigrants. This $385 million KBR contract would set up temporary processing, detention and deportation facilities. Indeed, the KBR deal is part of an extraordinary mad rush to build new private detention sites. Private prison companies are competing for an immigrant "super jail" facility (2,800 beds) in Laredo, Texas, and in December 2005 Corrections Corporation of America (CCA) announced a contract with ICE to hold up to 600 immigrant detainees in Tyler, Texas.[3]

Privatizing immigrant detention is nothing new (Dow, 2004; Fernandes, 2007; Barry, 2009). During the early 1980s, the federal government began experimenting with incarcerating people for profit, using immigrant detention as its guinea pig. According to some, the private prison industry was born in 1980 during a fundraiser in Nashville, Tennessee for then Presidential candidate Ronald Reagan. The Chairman of the Tennessee Republican party and the Corrections Commissioner of Virginia and his counterpart in Tennessee together set up what became known as the CCA. In 1984 CCA, the private-incarceration leader, cut its first deal with the federal government to operate INS detention centers in Houston and Laredo, Texas. When asked how to sell his product— prisoners—Tom Beasley, a CCA co-founder said, "You just sell it like you were selling cars, or real estate, or hamburgers." Indeed CCA was backed financially by the Massey Burch Investment Group, which funded Kentucky Fried Chicken. Since then, private incarceration has become a boom industry as well as a lightning rod for human rights abuse litigation (Dow, 2004).

What is new is the expansion of privatization after 9/11 and its use in establishing a social control apparatus ostensibly for non-citizens but which is applicable to citizens as well. According to Deepa Fernandes, "in the aftermath of 9/11, the private prison industry has once again experienced a boom as national security has been involved to sweep up and jail an unprecedented number of immigrants. Immigrants are currently the fastest growing segment of the prison population in the U.S. today" (2007).[4] Clearly, a close nexus exists between immigrant detention policies and the new boom market in private detention. In the months following February 2006, when President Bush proposed increasing spending on immigrant detention, CCA shares climbed 27%. Of 9/11, the chairman of the Cornell Companies (one of the top four private prison companies) said:

> It can only be good, with the focus on people that are illegal and also of Middle Eastern descent . . . there are over 900,000 undocumented individuals of Middle Eastern descent. That's half our entire prison population . . . The federal business is the best business for us . . . and the events of September 11 (are) increasing that level of business.
>
> (Bacon, 2005)

As a result, the private prison industry is increasingly in a position to direct immigration detention policy. The question remains whether private immigrant detention is a good thing. Private detention facilities are one-stop shops for immigrant processing. The DHS contracts are to train and supply security guards and screeners, and to build, manage and maintain detention facilities. Security guards and screeners make decisions related to political asylum and other forms of relief from deportation and arrest, and hold quite a lot of power over the conditions of confinement within the detention facility. Guards have control over access to phones, lawyers, visitors, food, restrooms, and medical care. Given the logic of private prisons, for example, which is to keep their beds full and immigrants locked up, privatization threatens the legal integrity of immigrant processing, which until recently has been premised upon the idea that non-citizens should not be incarcerated.

When private companies have control over the custodial functions of government, they assume quasi-judicial responsibilities that affect the legal status and well-being of immigrant detainees, raising important questions. According to Ira Robins:

> To what extent for example, should a private corporation use force—perhaps serious or deadly force—against a prisoner? It is difficult enough to control violence in the present public-correctional system. It will be much more difficult to assure that violence is administered only to the extent required by circumstances when the state relinquishes direct responsibility. Another important concern whether a private employee should be entitled to make recommendations to parole boards, or to bring charges against a prisoner for an institutional violation, possibly resulting in the forfeiture of good crime credits towards release. By dispersing accountability, the possibility for vindictiveness increases. An employee who is now in charge of reviewing disciplinary cases at a privately run INS facility in Houston told a *New York Times* reporter last year: "I am the Supreme Court."
>
> (Bacon, 2005)

Private guards wear badges, uniforms, carry guns, and drive cars with sirens; they make arrests and as far as the individual is concerned, represent the coercive force of the state. They wield as much power as any state actor but are not held nearly as accountable to the rule of law.

Another problem with privatizing detention is the secretiveness of the process. Screeners and guards make decisions with virtually no oversight. Interviews and hearings are closed to the public and family. Further, non-citizens are secretly shuffled from one detention facility to another, without notice to family or counsel. This shell game has been documented and has non-citizens ending up in facilities long distances away from legal counsel and family.

Even more extreme are contingency plans that could detain and deport large numbers of immigrants "at the command of the president." The plan contains echoes of Japanese internment camps during WWII, as well as contingency internment plans for Middle-Eastern non-citizens established during the 1980s. On October 17, 2006, President Bush signed into law the John Warner Defense Authorization Act. It allows the President to declare a "public emergency" and station troops anywhere in America and take control of state-based National Guard units without the consent of the governor or local authorities in order to "suppress public disorder." In a manner reminiscent of the government raids preceding Japanese internment during WWII and other notorious raids against immigrant communities during times of national insecurity, the Warner Act would facilitate militarized police round-ups and detention of protesters, so called "illegal aliens," "potential terrorists", and other "undesirables" for detention in facilities already contracted for and under construction by Halliburton (Koulish, 2008). In January 2006, the DHS awarded a $385 million contingency contract to KBR to establish temporary Detention and Removal Operation (DRO) facilities. There is nothing secret about such legislation and regulations. They are part of a larger effort to enhance executive powers and diminish judicial review of immigration matters. Under cover of a trumped-up "immigration emergency" and the frenzied militarization of the southern border, detention camps are being constructed right under our noses, camps designed for anyone who resists the foreign and domestic agenda of the Bush administration. With rare exception, they remain in place under Obama.

Chapter 5

Privatization of Immigration Control

Introduction

Few would have imagined, prior to the Bush years and 9/11, that government efforts to protect the homeland and its borders would be doled out to the highest bidder. Even Milton Friedman, the father of modern American neoliberalism, suggested that immigration was off limits to free market profiteers and should be reserved for government. But Secretary of Defense Donald Rumsfeld, a Friedman acolyte, had other ideas. Even though he said he felt smarter when Friedman was in the room, Rumsfeld eagerly and quickly leapt out of his mentor's shadow on September 10, 2001 to declare war on his own bureaucracy, the Pentagon and its big government bureaucratic ways (Klein, 2007).[1] Rumsfeld declared privatization and outsourcing were the solution to this problem (Roberts, 2008). The next day—9/11— Rumsfeld and the rest of the Bush administration saw the tragedy as the free market opportunity of their professional lifetimes and they ran with it. With the American people and Washington insiders in a daze following the tragedy, Rumsfeld and his fellow neoconservatives quickly privatized the war in Iraq, and, after first opposing the creation of a DHS, Rumsfeld's cronies designed the new Department along a similar neoliberal track. DHS would be the perfect hydra, ripe for outsourcing with no central headquarters but with 22 agencies. Unlike Friedman, the Bush administration tried to privatize many new projects and activities intended to secure the homeland, linking its efforts to the war on terror. Within DHS, the administration privatized everything in sight, especially immigration, the unwanted stepchild of every previous bureaucratic home (Klinenberg & Frank, December 15, 2005).

One of the unintended consequences of outsourcing immigration control is that biometric technology snafus have replaced bureaucratic ineptitude and deprivations of basic rights for immigrants as the government's most pressing concern (GAO, 2003). Biometric technology offers an ostensibly foolproof method to safely secure the homeland by tracking and identifying people as they cross the border, while leaving no marks on the immigrant body. It also invites abuse. With biometrics, exclusion, marginalization, and detention can be achieved virtually (as opposed to physically). Immigrants can be "virtually detained" in their neighborhoods and workplaces, forced underground with powerful disincentives to have their voices heard and become active members of their work or home communities.

In *Lockdown America: Police and Prisons in the Age of Crisis*, Christian Parenti examines immigration enforcement in the context of race and class polarization in Reagan's America (1999, p. 159). Parenti refers to the Reagan INS' strategy for "Interior Integrated Enforcement." Parenti's argument makes the bold but accurate comparison between low intensity conflict (LIC) strategies and the fear of increasing pockets of poor and disenfranchised populations in urban centers around the country. Following Parenti, I'd point out the increasing reliance of counterintelligence, LIC forces on technology. Parenti explains how high-tech computers and law enforcement intelligence systems are "mechanisms for tracking, controlling, and intimidating whole populations" (Parenti, 1999, p. 149). He suggests that "the effects of power [are] constant, even while its application is intermittent" (p. 149). In other words, Parenti continues, "immigrants will fear the law more intensely in that INS/police intelligence systems are automatic, infallible, and instantaneous. The electronic dragnet will force internalization of the INS gaze," forcing migrants even further underground (p. 149).

Following Agamben, I imagine undocumented immigrants as twenty-first century homo sacers, stripped of political rights, yet participating anyway. This points to what is contested terrain for undocumented immigrants in this country. Although the polity is off limits, other avenues such as the market and local communities become sites for immigrants to thrive in and create social change. For generations, the State along with the activities of right-wing nativists have oppressed undocumented immigrants. At each turn, however, there has also been an often overlooked story of immigrant resistance. Take, for example, the May 1, 2006, "Day Without Immigrants" General Strike and nationwide protest that revealed a potential threat to the immigration control narrative (Hamilton, 2006). Millions of undocumented immigrants who exist beneath the glaring regulatory gaze of the State became a social and political force.[2] To a government that had been fooled by a handful of terrorists who in the days before 9/11 had broken through the country's sovereign defenses, the sight of more than 1 million mostly undocumented immigrants parading in the streets of its major cities must have been horrifying.

This is the link people perceive between undocumented immigrants and terrorists. It is the fear of not knowing who the hell these people are. The dominant narrative would have us believe that homo sacer can organize terroristic acts just as easily as he lives a law abiding and productive existence. Since homo sacer in the guise of the undocumented immigrant has already eluded legal rules, the idea is for law to give way to sovereignty, in order for the sovereign to impose its unchecked powers upon this potential threat.

In this chapter, I examine the privatized parts to this sovereign regime, which presumes that by outsourcing sovereign powers to private corporations, the government can do a better job subjecting this population to social control. This regime is intended to marginalize and exclude immigrants from social and political participation, in order to keep them isolated, fearful and thus docile in their role as surplus labor.

The problem for the immigrant control system is that by pushing undocumented immigrants further into the shadows, the immigrant control system tags almost everyone other than undocumented immigrants. In a strange sense, they remain "free" by having escaped the gaze of privatized technologies. What do I mean by this? Many immigrant control technologies cropped up after 9/11. These technologies allow the State and private corporations to engage in surveillance and counterintelligence operations. The "double bind," for immigrant controllers is that undocumented immigrants escape the "gaze," precisely because of the fact that they have no papers. "Having papers" puts you in the Border Crossing Information System (BCIS) database system that subjects you to high-tech social control. The labyrinth of RFID technologies, smart cards and interoperable databases can now track almost everyone in society—regardless of their immigration status—except the undocumented people the system has spent billions of dollars to monitor, track and survey.

This is a challenge that neoliberalism outsources, in order to effectively strip the traveler/foreigner naked, and make her body/soul transparent to the gaze of the State. Recently the State has upped the stakes for foreigners and citizens alike, perhaps hoping to smoke the undocumented immigrant out of his/her ethnic enclave. Did you know that CBP agents can now take your laptop or other digital devices as you enter the country, copy and image the data and then data-mine it, all without having any suspicion that you did anything wrong?

In April 2008, in *U.S. v. Arnold*,[3] the ninth Circuit Court of Appeals ruled that the Fourth Amendment does not require government agents to have reasonable suspicion before searching laptops or other digital devices at the border, including international airports. The decision gives CBP sovereign powers over all the information you accumulate in your computer, and you have nothing to say about it, no redress. The significance of this decision is difficult to overstate if you accept that computers are like the human mind, "because of its ability to record ideas, e-mail, Internet chats and web-surfing" (*U.S. v. Arnold*). According to an amicus brief that EFF entered for Arnold, "the executive branch of our government seeks blanket authority to read to read, seize, and store all of the information retrievable from the laptop computers and other electronic devices carried by travelers who cross our national borders" (EFF Amici for *U.S. v. Arnold*).[4] The decision allows your data to end up in the same BCIS database that has put people wrongly on watch lists, do not admit lists and so forth, and that can prevent you from boarding an airplane, or even from getting a job. Furthermore the contents of someone's computer may hold information about people that have never even left the country. Thus their identifying information, like yours, could end up on the same watch lists. Like homo sacer, and regardless of immigration status, your rights and dignity are stripped bare.

The homo sacer is the mirror image of the sovereign. Immigration technologies are tools for effectively banning homo sacer from society, but not from the country. Through the immigration technologies created as part of the NSEERS, US-VISIT, Real ID, and virtual fence programs, the State and private contractors gain access to confidential and personal information and make it available to a wide range of other people. The wide net observes all of us coming and going from work, entering and leaving the country, and at almost every transactional activity in between, in hopes of catching undocumented immigrants as they surface at some official site of interaction with the real world.

A privatized and decentralized system of control promises a more efficient and effective means of surveilling all of us. In this respect, the federal government not only gets a force multiplier in terms of enforcement capability, but also in terms of plausible deniability for abusive and racist raids done in its name. Think of the Postville meatpacking plant, or the ongoing neighborhood raids committed in the name of homeland security. Concerns about privacy, redress, accountability, and due process long ago gave way to sovereign concerns, but now even these concerns pale before the billions of dollars thrown into a Kafkaesque procurement process that still struggles with making sure immigrants, not birds or raindrops, trigger high-tech border sensors.

Fortunately, few people would have also imagined that the high-priced failures of the Bush administration would have played out so publicly as to open a space for the new administration to reexamine some fundamental components of immigration control. The hegemony of sovereign controls over immigration has come into question. Further, neoliberalism has come so near to utter exhaustion and collapse that the new Presidential administration of Barack Obama and the new 111th Congress have an opportunity to dramatically shift the direction of immigration control politics. Whether they actually will exploit the opportunity remains to be seen.

Introducing the Immigration Control Industry[5]

Securing cheap labor and subjecting it to social control has been a sine qua non of immigration policy since the nineteenth century. The difference now is that guest worker proposals and other forms of visa relaxation help frame immigration within a neoliberal trade context, which opens the door to privatized control. To be sure, the Clinton administration supported border walls and fences in San Diego and El Paso, coinciding with the 1994 enactment of NAFTA, which liberalized trade between the US, Mexico, and Canada (Dunn, 2009).[6] Still, when compared to what would follow, border control efforts during the Clinton years were piecemeal and had not yet cohered around neoliberal logic.

Although George W. Bush paraded down Pennsylvania Avenue on January 20, 2001 with a neoliberal agenda in his pocket, about half the country (actually slightly more than half) had voted against the Bush agenda. According to Naomi Klein in *Shock Doctrine*, the 9/11 tragedy was a catalyst in Bush efforts to institutionalize the neoliberal logic. Such institutionalization would have no qualms exploiting human tragedy to augment state power and increase America's competitiveness in the changing global economy (2007). It mattered little that such increased state power would occur on the backs on immigrants. If anything, the political silence of immigrants made it easier to unleash the forces of neoliberalism precisely because it was thought their voices were not heard.

Consider what followed in short order after the planes hit the towers. On September 10, 2001, President Bush was pursuing dramatically different immigration tactics along neoliberal lines.[7] The signs of these tactics were apparent early in 2001. In early February, 2001, Secretary of State Colin Powell commented, "Our common border is no longer a line that divides us, but a region that unites our nations, reflecting our common aspirations, values, and culture" (February 4, 2001).[8] A week later Bush met Mexican President Vincente Fox at Fox's San Cristobal, Guanajuanta ranch to discuss immigration and trade. Fox, the pro-business PAN candidate for President, had been elected on a free trade and open borders agenda, and had forged a solid working relationship with Bush while the latter was Governor of Texas. Together the two men were committed to an alliance premised upon a cross-border neoliberal logic.

On September 11, 2001, two airplanes crashing into the Twin Towers and a third plane hitting the Pentagon ushered in a sea change. Almost immediately, a climate of war replaced the permissive immigration climate of early 2001. The differences between pre- and post-9/11 approaches to immigration appear dramatic. Whereas Bush and Fox had endeavored to welcome immigrants and embrace a bilateral approach to resolving immigration problems, an avalanche of post-9/11 policies showed the administration turning its back on the international community and invoking the nationalist exclusionary powers of sovereignty to remove and socially control non-citizens. I shall argue, however, that guest worker programs and border fences are merely flip sides of the same immigration control coin. All Bush did after 9/11 was flip the coin and pursue the tail side of the same neoliberal strategy.

After 9/11, the Bush administration enacted the Patriot Act, Title IV of which tightened the INA to increase the authority to detain. Title IV, Section 410 authorized the Attorney General to certify and detain non-citizens if "reasonable grounds" existed to believe they were engaging in terrorist activity, or endangering national security." On September 20, 2001, DOJ regulations similarly increased and expanded detention powers. Also, immediately following 9/11, Bush issued the Homeland Security Presidential Directive 2, "Combating terrorism through Immigration Policies," which began the process of bureaucratically intermingling immigration and security.

Next, on March 21, 2002, the Bush administration issued Executive Order 13260, which established an advisory council, as reconstituted by statute in the DHS and called the Homeland Security Advisory Council (HSAC).[9] It is here where sub-governments were formed and private actors gained direct access to the immigration control policy process. An HSAC subcommittee was the Secure Borders and Open Doors Advisory Committee (SBODAC), which focused attention on border control.[10] Its private culture was evident in that notices of meetings were not published in the federal register, nor were the meetings themselves required to be open to the public. Such secrecy allowed HSAC to show little concern for potential conflicts of interest. For example, HSAC directed funds to Sybase Inc., whose president, John Chen, was also co-chair of SBODAC. Sybase also had close financial connections to the Republican Party, and is financially controlled by Marvin Bush, the President's brother, whose company Winston Partners owns more than $3.5 million worth of shares of Sybase. In sum, the infrastructure for surveilling, catching, detaining, and removing aliens had become a financially lucrative cash cow for big business, former administration officials and even members of the President's family (Koulish, 2008).

In 2003, the INS was abolished and its functions were transferred into the new DHS. Never before in the history of the federal immigration bureaucracy has it found a match like it has in the DHS. If one were to pick one public bureaucracy that was ripe to be hollowed out, outsourced, and privatized, one could not have chosen one more suited to the task than the immigration bureaucracy. It is important to recognize that the immigration bureaucracy has always been considered among the federal bureaucracy's most inept and least professional agencies. This is relevant because it shows the agency's susceptibility to being hijacked by private interests.

During the early days of immigrant processing in south Texas, federal immigrant inspectors were patronage appointments of the King Ranch, the largest landholder in the region (Montejano, 1987; Koulish, 1996). In 1902, the Commissioner General for Immigration observed inspectors "who . . . lack in a greater or less degree the qualifications, hysterical or mental, to discharge with efficiency the very exacting duties essential to a successful enforcement of the law" (Koulish, 1996). In 1903, when Congress created the professional position of "Immigration Officer," with civil service status, the immigration officers remained ill trained and poorly-qualified. In 1935, when border patrol officers were classified under civil service provisions, they were categorized at a lower level than the immigration hierarchy believed appropriate. Border patrol salaries were "relatively low" compared to what law enforcement officers received in other federal agencies. As a result, "border inspectors frequently took the civil service examination for other federal agencies that offered more competitive salaries" (Koulish, 1996). It is also important to note that the host bureaucracies for immigration never wanted immigration under their purview. Immigration has passed through many bureaucratic homes throughout its existence—from the Department of State, to Commerce, to Commerce and Labor (1903), to Labor (1913), to Justice (1940), to Homeland Security (2003) (LeMay, 1987; Koulish, 1996).

Each successive transition for immigration agencies followed this pattern: There was little or no debate in Congress, and no support from new bureaucratic home. Sometimes the new placement occurred over the prospective host's objection. The only instance in which this pattern was not followed was in 2003, when the DHS welcomed immigration agencies with open arms. For once, immigration agencies had found a welcoming home. Little did they know that the host bureaucracy wanted them only to outsource their services to military contractors.

In 2003 this hollowed-out shell of an agency was placed in a Department whose priority was to hollow out agencies.[11] Increasingly, decisions would be placed into private hands and follow a market logic. New programs were immediately outsourced. For example, the DHS started a procurement process of outsourcing billions of dollars to defense contractors for the purpose of building the border fence and a virtual border fence, which would include digital databases for the purpose of collecting information about people entering the country and immigrants already residing in the country. The largest chunk of cash was allocated to SBInet, another secretive office in the CPB agency, in charge of overseeing virtual fence contracting, which includes decisions about programs dealing with immigrant workers—such as those arrested in the Iowa Raid. After September 2006, the SBInet office was filled with Boeing employees,[12] who worked in close proximity with SBInet director Greg Giddens to manage, oversee and implement the project. The lines between government and private contractors had become inextricably blurred. Slowly, or rather, swiftly, private contractors began eating up the budgetary pie that Congress was allocating for purposes of immigration control.

How can we explain the susceptibility of immigration control to neoliberalization? I would suggest several reasons, which I shall mention only briefly here.

The most important reason, I believe, is that immigration policy rests upon the foundation of sovereignty and plenary powers, which condenses state powers into the hands of a few pro-business decision-makers inside the executive branch.

Sovereignty is a quasi-legal status that places decision-makers above and outside the law. Since its inception during the 1880s, immigration control policy has rested upon this dangerous sovereign foundation, which has allowed leaders to target and demonize immigrant populations on a whim, or rather, according to prevailing political winds. Immigration is one of very few legal fields governed by the doctrine of sovereignty, rather than the constitution. The key to sovereignty is recognizing that there is no accountability and no reference to the rule of law or constitutional norms. In fact, the sovereign stands outside and above the law. Because of its core in sovereignty, immigration historically has been one of this country's most racist, backward, and hate-filled areas of public policy.

Sovereignty gives plenary powers to the political branches, which allow them to reign over immigrants with near impunity. Immigration control was renowned for its generous use and abuse of discretion before privatization, which now makes it particularly susceptible to profiteering.[13] Freeman and Minow notes that "War profiteering is a serious problem not only because it diverts public monies—the money of citizens—to private hands though overcharging and fraud, but also because it can jeopardize peacemaking and broader confidence in government" (2009, p. 145). Journalist Deepa Fernandes refocuses concern over profiteering to the border, where, she says, "[t]here is big money to be made as the government dramatically increases its reliance on the private sector to help carry out its war on terror. On the home front, the prime targets of this war are immigrants" (Fernandes, 2007; Koulish, 2008).

But for one traumatic moment in American politics, Bush and his cronies would not have been able to make immigration into the neoliberal guinea pig it has become. Following 9/11, the Bush administration, guided by a neoliberal frame and post-9/11 security agenda, moved swiftly to transform immigration into a security issue and place immigrant communities under suspicion. Bush used 9/11 to hasten development of his neoliberal agenda. Keep in mind Bush, Donald Rumsfeld, and Dick Cheney were committed to the idea of hollowing out government services. One of the least-reported ironies of 9/11 is that on 9/11 Secretary of Defense Donald Rumsfeld proposed to transform the Pentagon along neoliberal lines. Similarly, Bush's plans on 9/10 coincided with the WTO agenda to treat migrants like commodities. Like Bush's plan, which he reintroduced in 2006, Mode 4 of the GATS, negotiated in the WTO, would reduce migrant workers to the status of commodities, which possess no human rights, as discussed above.[14]

Although the public is no longer terrified, as it was in the days and months following 9/11, and although the Congress is no longer as reluctant to challenge the President as it was in 2002–2003, the Congress and public remain wary of overt challenges to administration claims of national security in the "war on terror", or however it is now described. Consider the July 2008 vote in Congress on FISA, to see how reluctant even a Democratic-controlled Congress remains to challenge the President on national security grounds.[15] Further, the government has sunk billions of dollars into the border fence, and given such sunk costs, is unlikely to reverse course. The "war on terror" has become a permanent fixture in American politics and culture, and is assimilated into every policy proposal that appears even tangentially related to protecting Americans from terrorists.

Background: NSEERS

After 9/11, the government hastened efforts to track the entry and exit of non-citizens from particular countries. The "National Security Entry-Exit

Registration System (NSEERS) program was introduced in June 2002, requiring non-citizen men age 16 and over from 25 predominantly Muslim countries to register with the government at ports of entry and local immigration offices for fingerprints, photographing and questioning.[16] NSEERS legitimated the use of profiling by national origin, ethnicity and religion as a tool of immigration control. A total of 290,526 people registered, including almost 86,000 men already living within the US on temporary visas from Muslim countries. Any of them found to be out of status were subject to immediate deportation. Of the total, 13,799 were referred to investigation and received notices to appear for deportation proceedings, and 2,870 were detained.[17] The NSEER program netted no terror-related convictions, but instilled a great deal of fear in immigrant communities around the country.[18]

The origin of efforts to track entries and exits actually can be found in Section 110 of the U.S. Illegal Immigration Reform and Immigration Responsibility Act of 1996, which mandated the INS to develop an automated entry–exit control system that would "collect a record of every alien departing the United States and match records of departure with the record of the alien's arrival in the United States" (Illegal Immigration Reform and Immigrant Responsibility Act, Public Law 104–208, 110 Stat. 3009, Sec. 110 (IIRIRA)). Originally, the motivation for this provision was to track visa overstays. After 9/11, the use of security technology was subsumed under the rationale for the war on terror, exemplified by the NSEERS program. Regrettably, as many reports about NSEERS have concluded, "the NSEERS program was unsuccessful as a counterterrorism tool" (p. 6).

According to *NSEERS: The Consequences of America's Efforts to Secure its Borders*, a report conducted by the law school at Penn State:

> . . . many individuals impacted by the NSEERS do not appear to have terrorism charges or criminal histories. Notably, many . . . have meaningful family, business and cultural ties to the United States. Indeed, more than seven years after its implementation, NSEERS continues to impact the Arab-American community. Impacted individuals include those who are married to United States citizens or meaningfully employed . . . This scenario has torn apart Arab-American families . . .
>
> (p. 6)

Rather than being a lone failed experiment, however, NSEERS ushered in the new era of biometric anti-immigrant control technology. At around the same time, the Patriot Act (2001) included entry–exit provisions as did the Enhanced Border Security and Visa Entry Reform Act of 2002 (Pub.L. No. 107–56, 115 Stat. 272 2001). These provisions accounted for the introduction of biometric technology and a combination of facial recognition and electronic fingerprint scanning. Coming as part of the post-9/11 response, the Enhanced Border Security Bill passed Congress with no opposing votes.

US-VISIT and Western Hemisphere Travel Initiative (WHTI)

By January 2004, the NSEER Program had become the archetype for a copycat program called U.S. Visitor and Immigrant Status Indicator Technology (US-VISIT). The US-VISIT program requires all foreigners entering the US on short-term visas to be fingerprinted, photographed and submit biographical information. US-VISIT was deployed at 115 airports and 15 seaports in January 2004, and 50 land ports were phased in by December 2004.[19]

The official purpose of US-VISIT is to "enhance national security", and "ensure the integrity of the immigration system. Data collection begins in consular offices with the collection of finger scans and digital photographs, which are taken again upon arrival in the US for verification purposes. According to the Heritage Foundation, "when completed, it will record visitors through the use of fingerprint scanners and digital photos and will integrate existing databases to push good information across agencies. In this way, it will pick out people who are security risks, while cutting costs . . ." (2004).[20]

Although US-VISIT is supposed to verify the identity of individuals as they enter and leave the country, the program has been plagued by problems with concerns over personal privacy. So far, only the entry procedures have been deployed. Although entry verification procedures have been in place for years, US-VISIT has had many more problems with its procedures for biometric exit procedures. The GAO reports that:

> DHS reports that the proposed air and sea exit solution provides less security and privacy than other alternatives. Adequate security and privacy controls are needed to assure that personally identifiable information is secured against unauthorized access, use, disclosure, or retention. Such controls are especially needed for government agencies, where maintaining public trust is essential. In the case of US-VISIT, one of its stated goals is to protect the security and privacy of U.S. citizens and visitors.
>
> (GAO-09–96, p. 4)

By outsourcing responsibility to ticket agents to assume control over biometric fingerprinting, the GAO concludes, this process failed to account for the risks to managing the individual's personal privacy. Regardless of the concern for privacy in the final regulations, the US-VISIT smart technology design reveals blatant disregard for individual privacy. Weaknesses in the privacy protections for the exit requirements in US-VISIT, and in the inter-operability design, risk spreading the personal information of individual travelers well beyond the US-VISIT database.

Under the Bush Doctrine approach to immigration control, the government endeavors to spread intelligence-gathering tentacles across the United States into state and local police offices, as well as abroad. Data is stored in government databases in agencies throughout the federal, state and local governments. According to US-VISIT Director Robert Mocny, "by enhancing the interoperability of DHS's and the FBI's biometric systems, we are able to give federal, state and local decision-makers information that helps them better protect our communities and our nation" (http://media-newswire.com/release_1079956.html). As of May 2005, about 25 million individuals have submitted data; 590 of whom have been denied admission for crimes and immigration violations. According to DHA, there is no evidence that US-VISIT has caught a wanted terrorist (EPIC Report, http://epic.org/privacy/us-visit/).

The US-VISIT program has also experimented with using RFID (radio frequency identification), imprinted on miniscule microchips (half the size of a grain of sand). The RFID tag can be read silently and invisibly by radio waves from up to 150 feet or so, even through clothing. It can also link to medical records, and serve as a payment device when associated with a credit card. RFIDs provide additional capacity for tracking non-citizens already in this country. They are being embedded in I-94 entry documents, passports, and border crossing cards, which non-citizens are urged to carry with them at all times. The future use of RFIDs as an immigration control mechanism was not lost on former Secretary of Homeland Security Tom Ridge who became head of Savi Technologies, an RFID design and manufacturing company.

It is important to note that RFIDs and other forms of technology-based monitoring systems are easily transferable from US-VISIT to other immigration programs, for example, proposed guest worker programs, WHTI and passport programs. The RFID watchdog group, "Spychips.com", reported on May 18, 2006 that the Board Chairman of VeriChip, Scott Silverman,

> bandied about the idea of chipping foreigners on national television Tuesday, emboldened by the Bush administration call to know "who is in our country and why they are here." He told Fox & Friends that the VeriChip could be used to register guest workers, verify their identities as they cross the border, and "be used for enforcement purposes at the employer level." He added, "We have talked to many people in Washington about using it. . . ."
>
> (www.rinf.com/columnists/news/
> rfid-implants-for-guest-workers)

In February 2007, however, the GAO told Congress that RFID failed to "meet a key goal of US-VISIT—ensuring that visitors who enter the country are the same ones who leave" (2007).[21]

Although RFID failed with US-VISIT, it is flourishing with the Western Hemisphere Travel Initiative (WHTI), Enhanced Drivers' Licenses (EDLs) in Washington state and New York, and passports (House Committee Homeland Security Hearings, http://epic.org/privacy/us-visit/chertoff_020907.pdf). The WHTI requires all persons traveling by air outside the United States to present a passport or other valid travel documents to enter or re-enter the United States (http://travel.state.gov/travel/cbpmc/cbpmc_2223.html). WHTI is the result of the Intelligence Reform and Terrorism Prevention Act of 2004 (IRTPA), which requires all travelers to present a passport or other documentation that allows DHS to quickly and reliably identify a traveler.

As of November 2008, RFID readers were scheduled for 39 ports of entry, which is about 95% of all land border crossings. Beginning summer 2009, U.S. citizens and Canadians entering the United States at sea or land ports will be required to carry a passport, passport card or WHTI-compliant document such as an EDL. RFIDs will be embedded in WHTI compliant documents. The RFID technology will allow CBP agents to read a person's information before they even get to the customs and border crossing office to present their papers. DHS awarded the $64 million Enterprise Gateway for Leading Edge Technology (EAGLE) contract to Unisys[22] to process secure WHTI RFID-enabled documents (passport cards, EDLs, Trusted Traveler cards and border crossing cards) (www.unisys.com/about__unisys/news_a_events/01288853.htm).

By integrating RFID technology into WHTI passport cards and EDLs, DHS officers, and anyone else with access to an RFID reader gain the ability to invade personal privacy by never having to show grounds for suspicion before stopping an individual and asking a personal question. Although border agents do not need to have reasonable suspicion of wrongdoing to ask such questions at the port of entry, they do need reasonable suspicion of individual wrong-doing before approaching an individual and asking questions or demanding papers. Once an agent can read the contents of immigration, and/or identity papers, without reasonable suspicion of wrongdoing, then everyone becomes suspect and the system's Orwellian qualities overwhelm any rhetorical concern for individual privacy.

Although DHS has failed to safeguard personal privacy, it has no qualms about pursuing aggressive interoperability strategies among US-VISIT, WHTI and SBI (GAO February, 2008). The intent behind such interoperability ostensibly is to help cut down on delays caused by having to handle and assess the huge number of documents that can be presented to CBP at the border. A one-size-fits-all identity card is certainly a solution to the abundance of possible identity documents—over 80,000—that according to the 9/11 Commission an individual might present at a border gate to CBP. RFIDs are defended on the grounds that they enhance system efficiency and save time at the border crossing station, shaving off about 6–8 seconds per person and 14 seconds per vehicle. At the Bridge of America at the U.S.–Mexico border, for example, RFID technology would reduce the delay to cross the bridge by about two hours (www.rfidnews.org/2008/11/21/episode-24-passport-card-update). RFID's overly broad potential, however, threatens to expose the personal information of millions of foreigners and citizens to government offices and corporate giants.

In theory, interoperability is facilitated by post-9/11 databases that combine data from criminal and terrorist investigations at the federal, state, and local level, and that are accessible in the private sector. Efforts at interoperability culminated in 2008, as the *Washington Post* reported, in a network called the BCIS: "The federal government has been using its system of border checkpoints to greatly expand a database on travelers entering the country by collecting information on all U.S. citizens crossing by land, compiling data that will be stored for 15 years and may be used in criminal and intelligence investigations," wrote Ellen Nakashima. Not only is it described as "part of a broader effort to guard against terrorist threats," it also "reflects the growing number of government systems containing personal information on Americans that can be shared for a broad range of law enforcement and intelligence purposes, some of which are exempt from some Privacy Act protections" (Nakashima, August 20, 2008).

The plan is to enter US-VISIT and WHTI data into the Border Crossing Information System and then to link it with the Non-Federal Entity Data System, which will store data from Real ID and other border security programs. I take this to suggest that all data taken from individuals who cross the border or its functional equivalents could end up in US-VISIT and BCIS databases. Considering the ninth Circuit opinion in the Arnold case, the dangers to civil liberties are palpable. The ninth Circuit ruled that CBP can take, copy, image, and disseminate data taken from the laptop computer of anybody who crosses the border or enters the country at an international airport. Not only does this decision jeopardize all the thoughts (translated into web surfing, emails, and so on) of the person crossing the border, it also places at risk all the data of anybody this person has been in communication with.

The interoperability of US-VISIT enhances the danger by disseminating personal data to federal, state and local databases as well as to private companies. The US-VISIT program links to other DHS and DOS databases.[23] These databases can then be made available to foreign governments, corporations, and state and local law enforcement officials. In other words, the BCIS is the database for a national ID. Since the personal information for almost everyone who enters, exits and drives in the US will be entered into this database, it remains to be seen how this is not a national ID system, unless you are an undocumented immigrant. It also invites abuse. As a result, people living in the US will fall into one of two categories: 1) subjected to monitoring, tracking and surveillance, which means you are not undocumented but are nonetheless suspect because your data is in the database; 2) not subjected to such monitoring because you are undocumented, which makes you a suspect. Everyone becomes suspect in this preemptive counterintelligence network, and virtually everyone's data can end up in the same database. The fear of the alien other subjects everyone to being scrutinized by this Orwellian police state operation.

The interoperability of databases is facilitated by post-9/11 business alliances that comprise important parts of the immigration control policy making and administration team. The cost of the US-VISIT program is projected at over $10 billion. Accenture Ltd. was awarded the US-VISIT prime contract on May 28, 2004, and has entered into subcontracts with Raytheon, a runner-up on the virtual fence contract, SRA Intl., and the Titan Corporation. Together this corporate team calls itself the "Smart Border Alliance." Accenture is an offshore company headquartered in Bermuda, which allows it to avoid paying U.S. corporate income tax. Republican strategist and Bush donor and John McCain campaign advisor Charles Black lobbied on Accenture's behalf to gain the US-VISIT contract. The contract gave Accenture so much discretion with which to shape the program and avoid waste and abuse that the nonpartisan group Taxpayers for Common Sense likened it to a "blank check."

Further, the Anteon Corp. (now owned by General Dynamics), which led an alliance that lost the US-VISIT contract, was instead awarded the contract to provide secure identification and border-control card technology for the Homeland Security Department's Bureau of Citizenship and Immigration Services, with optical card scanners and technology to read almost 20 million border crossing cards and permanent residency cards. In August 2004, Anteon received a $74 million surveillance-training contract for the DHS' Bureau of Customs and Border Protection. According to Anteon president and CEO Joseph Kampf, "our focus on position in the marketplace with the DOD, intelligence community and DHS has really paid off." Indeed, over 90% of Aneteon's business comes from government contracts in these three areas, with border crossing identification a growth area. According to Kampf:

> We think border crossing security will continue to grow over the next two years, perhaps becoming one of the fastest paced markets in the federal government . . . The whole concept of validating who people are as they travel and cross land, sea and air will, I think, would be an explosive marketplace. It will be one in which we have a significant footprint.
>
> (http://alexconstantine.blogspot.com/2007_07_
> 01_archive.html; Koulish, 2008)

SBInet

During Bush's second term as President, starting in 2006, Boeing was given an extraordinary amount of control over immigration control policy in the United States. Its clout came from being SBInet's primary contractor. SBInet is the brand name given to Bush's virtual war against aliens and terrorists at the U.S.–Mexico border. SBInet, initiated in 2006, is a virtual border fence composed of cameras, radars and other sensors strung on towers and linked to operation centers (Lipowics, 2008). It boasts an integrated system of personnel, infrastructure, technology, and rapid response to secure the northern and southern land borders of the United States. The SBInet mission, as far as one exists, is to map SBI technologies of control onto specific plans and projects, including construction of the physical and virtual border fences.

SBInet is part of the Secure Border Initiative (SBI), which is the overarching DHS program to organize border protection, interior enforcement of immigration and customs laws, and guest worker programs. With such a broad mission, SBI assumes control over a great deal of the immigration control machinery. The SBI Program Management Office (PMO) exists within CBP. According to CPB Commissioner W. Ralph Basham, SBI encompasses all of CBP's border security efforts and has already changed the way CBP employees do their job:

> Secure Border Initiative is instrumental to CBP achieving its mission . . . SBI directly impacts CBP's priority mission to prevent terrorists and their weapons from entering the U.S. while not stifling the flow of legitimate trade and travel . . . Through SBInet, CBP will be more effective at detecting, identifying and interdicting illegal cross border activities.
>
> (http://governmentdocs.org/docs/upl204/foi255/ doc2041/2041.pdf)

Gregory Giddens, Executive Director of SBInet, and presumably his successor as well, also served as director of the Secure Border Coordination Council, which unites all relevant agency heads under the SBI banner, and reports directly to the DHS deputy secretary. In reality, therefore, the SBI director (Greg Giddens, 2006–2008, Jack Borkowski, 2008) reports directly to the (deputy) secretary of DHS, not the CPB commissioner. Thus, the SBI director is a top immigration control bureaucrat, without the burden of having to administer a real bureaucracy.

At a projected cost of $8 billion, SBInet quickly became known as one of this country's most ridiculous wastes of taxpayer revenue ever diverted to Boeing and its boondoggle partners. It quickly overshadowed legislative efforts at comprehensive immigration control as the most ridiculed part of U.S. immigration policy.

In the Bush administration, the shadow DHS staff in SBI could outsource advice from Boeing and Capgemini, a consulting subsidiary of CACI. According to the Capgemini website:

> Capgemini provided technical and strategic assistance, including the rollout of initiatives detailing an efficiency and detention capacity model to demonstrate the impact of alternative initiatives on the required detention space. Capgemini also used its Accelerated Solutions Environment to establish detailed implementation plans for each reengineering recommendation.
>
> (www.us.capgemini.com/)

Decisions that involve billions of dollars and affect millions of people are thus made by a small, select, group of people—SBInet employees—married to the private sector—Boeing SBInet employees, who is not democratically accountable, and who encouraged decision-makers to blur the distinction between the public interest and the corporate bottom line.

From the looks of Project 28 (see pp. 92–4), it is difficult to say whether CBP leads Boeing or Boeing leads CBP. As important as SBI Director Jack Borkowski is to border control, the reality is that he works alongside Boeing SBInet program director Jack Chenevey. The GAO reported in February 2008 that SBInet had been designed and was operating with little input from CBP (GAO, February 27 2008, p. 5). The SBI office is replete with public officials and private sector "professionals" who function interchangeably; although they may not work in the same office, they attend the same meetings, provide nearly the same Congressional testimony, and interchangeably attend to the same SBI/DHS mission. In sum, military contractors are perhaps the driving force behind immigration control policy at the border. Decisions are not made about the border without these folks being in the room.

Indeed, the rationale is simply that the market is better equipped—in terms of efficacy and cost savings—to make decisions about border security than government agencies. And by marketplace, I refer to behemoth military contractors, not free enterprise. As the recent history of these programs suggest, this rationale is dead wrong.

Boeing's Virtual Fence

In May 2006, the federal government solicited bids from military contractors Boeing, Lockheed Martin, Raytheon, Ericsson, and Northrop Grumman for a multibillion-dollar contract to build a "virtual fence" of unmanned aerial vehicles, ground surveillance satellites, motion-detection video equipment, and databases to store information on the identity of millions of non-citizens along the border. On September 20, 2006, Boeing, a major aerospace, defense, and aircraft contracting firm, was awarded a three-year, $2.5 billion contract with the DHS to create a virtual fence along the U.S.–Mexico border.[24]

According to the Boeing website, its mission is to "gain operational control of the border." Described by an SBInet subcontractor as a combination of law enforcement and surveillance systems, the new SBInet project promised to include up to 1,800 radar towers along the border, along with motion detectors; a radar system that can transmit images to border agents; and cameras that can spot people from 14 kilometers away. In addition, the plans call for the development of infrastructure and logistical support to be able to "remove all removable aliens." Finally, Boeing plans to use unmanned aerial vehicles that could be launched from the backs of border patrol trucks.

Some of Boeing's workload was delegated to subcontractors, including Booz Allen Hamilton Inc., Centech Group, DRS Technologies, Kollsman, Unisys

Global Public Sector, a division of L-3 Communications Holdings Inc., Perot Systems, U.S.IS, and others. According to Unisys Vice President of Homeland Security, Brian Seagrave, Unisys was placed in charge of the SBInet systems engineering, infrastructure, and configuring and installing several key software packages, including the "common operating picture" (COP) which Seagrave describes as SBInet's brain. Unisys' experience in this field includes police department systems and a range of surveillance and detection contracts.

Part of the problem with the privatization of immigration control is that the system allows subcontractors to be in charge of oversight of the process. In February 2007, for example, Congressman Henry Waxman, chair of the House Committee on Oversight and Government Reform, pointed out the conflict of interest inherent in hiring Booz Allen Hamilton Inc., a Boeing sub-contractor, to oversee SBInet. Booz Allen has had a relationship with Boeing since 1970, and since 1993 has assisted Boeing in maintaining its market share in the airplane industry. According to Waxman, his committee received a list of 50 contractor personnel involved in contract oversight and management, including personnel from Booz Allen (Lipowicz, February 8, 2007).

The next problem concerns the DHS procurement process, which has an unanticipated impact on policy, and highlights the surreptitious nature of outsourcing. The policy regime shifts from being government-centered to market-centered. By outsourcing government responsibilities to Boeing, the defense contractor can then embed its specific military contractor stamp upon what had been a public policy.

The rationale behind wholesale outsourcing once again is that the market is better equipped than the government to handle a project as complicated as SBInet. By market is meant Boeing, which then subcontracts to partner companies to help manage and oversee the project, including the process of distributing and overseeing the contracts themselves.

In this privatized world the focus is on troubles with the procurement process rather than with excessive government power or due process for immigrants. The humanity of immigrants at this point has been so diminished that immigrants are perceived as no different than birds and wild coyotes when it comes to considering SBInet's effectiveness.

To see how Boeing achieves sovereign status over aspects of border control, I point to the procurement process. The SBInet contract with Boeing highlights deleterious effects of the neoliberal philosophy.[25] Congressman John Yarmouth (D-Ky) correctly described the LSI procurement approach within privatization doctrine: "there is a methodology in the world, and it seems to be adopted as doctrine, irrefutable doctrine, in many Government circles: the private sector is always more efficient and effective than the Government sector. And I think what we have seen in this particular situation is evidence to the contrary"[26] (Waxman Hearings, 2007, p. 22).

According to Eugene Gholz, a defense industry expert, "(Such) contracts are huge and technologically complex. They strive to create what Defense calls 'interoperability'—the ability to share data seamlessly across disparate platforms manufactured by different contractors" (see pp. 87–88). Thus the Boeing contract, a lead system integrator (LSI) contract, bundles the individual parts and delegates it and a huge amount of discretion to the LSI. The only way this remains accountable is if the CBP closely monitors the LSI's discretionary decisions.[27] That did not occur in this case.

As disparate as some components of SBInet might seem—border fence, interior controls, arrest and detention, guest worker—decisions are made under the umbrella owned and controlled by Boeing and its subsidiaries.

> The contract structure means few people have the total picture of the finished product the government is buying at a cost that could reach $30 billion . . . with approval from DHS officials, the company will design every part of the border program from communications equipment to how agents process apprehended immigrants—the department has issued three task orders for work with one more set to come out soon.
>
> (Phillips, 2007)

The LSI assumes control over nearly everything related to the project, including the incredibly important function of framing complex policy matters for public consumption. Nothing gets by Boeing to CBP unless it is first vetted by the LSI, which claims a "right of first refusal" (for itself or its subsidiaries) regarding its own contracts. "The . . . contract asks Boeing to design the project itself, with the work performed incrementally through a series of individually negotiated task orders. It is responsible for 'doling out . . . work to sub-contractors, often including themselves'" (*Aviatorweek*, August 20, 2007).

Thus another problem with outsourcing is that much of the government information about SBInet is little more than Boeing propaganda, cloaked as public policy.

The popularity of the LSI approach among neoliberal administrators can be explained as an outgrowth of disaster capitalism. In ordinary times, the public would never stand for such usurpation of power by the likes of Boeing as seen in this DHS process. But by the time the public is again responsive, the system of systems would already be well underway, away from public scrutiny, with billions of dollars of sunk costs already in the virtual fence. As a result, there is really no redress for any aggrieved persons to object to Boeing's authority, as evidenced by the train of events subsequent to the April 1, 2008 statement that Boeing's prototype Project 28 had failed.

Project 28

Problems with the LSI procurement approach are highlighted in the case of Project 28, which is the pilot 28-mile stretch of virtual fence, consisting of a wireless network; nine 98-foot-high towers;[28] the P28 Common Operating Picture (COP);[29] enhanced communications; and upgraded agent vehicles along the Arizona–Mexico border. The idea behind Project 28 and the rest of the virtual fence is that when an immigrant crosses the virtual fence, they are instantly detected by cameras and sensors on the tower, whose images are then relayed—via real time electronic images—to a (sub)contracted communications center. The contractor employee takes manual command of the camera, and zooms in to identify the number of individuals and their means of transportation. The employee then "classifies the threat" and transmits the data, including coordinates, to border patrol agents who receive it via laptop computers in their vehicles (Richey, July 9, 2007).

The problems that plagued Project 28 and the entire virtual fence project had to do with huge cost overruns, delays, and Boeing misleading SBI about the purpose of Project 28. It was supposed to provide a real world and real time template for the virtual fence; Boeing later suggested it was nothing but an experiment.[30] Although Boeing was able to manufacture the discrete components for the virtual fence, it couldn't assemble the parts into a functioning virtual fence. Boeing couldn't relay the images and data from the cameras and sensors to the communications center and then back again into the field for border patrol and state and local officers to apprehend the undocumented immigrant. Although anywhere else along the 2,017-mile stretch of border, trained border patrol officers could identify, evaluate and then act upon the perceived threat, along this 28-mile stretch of border, the act of identification, evaluation and apprehension were separated into three distinct units (a camera, a Boeing employee, and a border patrol agent), that couldn't communicate because of a high tech snafu. According to the GAO, the COP software was not suited to process and distribute "the type of information being collected by the cameras, radars, and sensors . . . it was taking too long for radar information to display in command centers and newly deployed radars were being activated by rain or other environmental factors, making the system unusable" (GAO-08–508-T, 2008, p. 9).

Boeing submitted three corrective action plans through the second half of 2007, and by February 22, 2008, the DHS, under pressure from Boeing, approved Boeing's work product, noting that Boeing had met its contractual requirements, even though the system still failed to function. The border patrol and SBI signed off on Boeing's progress even though they acknowledged that completion of Project 28 would be delayed until 2009.

At about the same time, it was also announced that Boeing would continue with two new border fence segments—Tuscon-1 and Ajo-1—which, according to plan, would cover 60 miles of the U.S. southern border near Yuma, Arizona, and would be deployed in 2009. After the failed Project 28 test, Boeing also announced that it expected to be given the contract to begin laying down a virtual fence along the Canadian border (Rotstein, May 10, 2008). There is nothing like failure to merit obtaining additional government contracts.

All the while, Rep. Chris Carney and Rep. Bennie Thompson (chair, House Homeland Security Committee) scheduled several Congressional hearings, with increasingly critical themes. Boeing and SBInet directors took issue, but

Rep Carney responded by saying the system "works about 30% of the time," as he conveyed the following personal anecdote, as reported in the *Times-Tribune*. "Carney said he saw an incident where two illegal immigrants crossed in front of a project camera. Carney said that a technician tried to electronically reposition the camera to track them, but the picture was out of focus, the camera moved too slowly, and the illegal immigrants got away" (Krawczeniuk, February 20, 2008). Carney has since concluded that Boeing did not bring its "A-team" to the SBInet project and asks, "my question was how far down the alphabet was that team? (McCarter, May 14, 2008).

By the end of 2008, CBP announced it would postpone plans for the SBI virtual fence, and concentrate instead on completing the pedestrian fence. According to CBP deputy commissioner Jay Ahern, the highest priority is to build a system of physical fences and barriers that will keep people and vehicles from illegally crossing the U.S.–Mexico border (Cole, September 10, 2008). Boeing gets to keep the X million plus dollars in contracts it sunk into the project, which is quite a raise since its first $20 million dollar work order in September 2006 (Cole, September 10, 2008).

Homeland Security Information Network (HSIN)

Finally, the Homeland Security Information Network (HSIN) was designed, by contract, by ManTech International. It is worth noting that Congressman Richard Renzi (R-AR), one of House's most vocal advocates for increased funding for the DHS is the son of ManTech Executive Vice-President Eugene Renzi. ManTech was charged with developing an information-sharing system, which is called the U.S. public and private partnership (Shorrock, 2008), which links public sector agencies and the private sector to "significantly strengthen the flow of real-time threat information to state, local, and private sector partners, and provides a platform for communities through the classified SECRET level to state offices." For example, data can to be shared with as many as 600 federal, state and local agencies, including police departments, fire and emergency responders, governors' offices, and agencies within DHS. In all, HSIN has 40,000 users, 90% of whom are from the private sector, and any of whom may add information that subsequently remains there for five years. As Fernandes suggested, HSIN "catches immigrants in the name of protecting against foreign terrorist threats" (2006). And once their names are on the list, they remain on the list regardless of the reason for putting them there. In short, catching aliens is a lucrative business made all the more so by exploiting already blurred distinctions between immigration and national security.

Regrettably, few people in America are aware of Accenture, Anteon, and Man-tech, let alone the power they wield to develop and implement immigration control policy. Given the power such companies hold over individual immigrants, one would think that immigration authorities would care to see that only well-trained professionals had access to HSIN and could input data, which is not the case. One of the perks of privatizing is that the masters of this virtual domain are less accountable for mistakes and outright abuse. They would also be less likely to have the training required to avoid such undesirable outcomes. Few are well trained; fewer are accountable to the constitution and some are not liable for the misuse of coercive force.

Real ID

While Boeing's power over the virtual fence grew despite its repeated failures, L-1 Solutions[31] has been consolidating control over the biotechnology identification market and Real ID, which establishes a de facto national ID card under the auspices of being an anti-terrorist, anti "illegal alien" measure. Real ID standardizes state driver's license design and the minimum data elements to be collected and stored about each licensee. It isolates undocumented residents by rendering them ineligible for a driver's license.[32] Real ID is an anti-immigrant law by omission and exclusion. Their exclusion actually provides incentives for undocumented immigrants to retreat further into the shadows of the law, making most of them more difficult to reach and monitor, as long as they stay off planes and don't get stopped by the police. Real ID strips undocumented immigrants of their basic rights as persons under the fourteenth amendment. By forcing undocumented immigrants underground, Real ID reinforces their status as one of Agamben's homo sacer, as it increases their reluctance to reach out to law enforcement, the courts or emergency rooms.

When Congress enacted the Real ID Act in 2005, authored by Rep. James Sensenbrenner (R-Wis.), few people noticed, and few of those who did take note really appreciated just how radical a piece of legislation this was. The Act was surreptitiously passed without hearings or debate; it was tucked inside an $81 billion bill for "supporting troops," and "tsunami relief."[33] Back in 2005, few dared to oppose such a measure, and regrettably, few deigned to read it.

According to Sensenbrenner, the Real ID Act would make it more difficult for terrorists and undocumented immigrants to obtain legitimate identification documents and travel freely around the country. In reality, the Real ID Act beefs up the securitization of migrants and nudges domestic policy closer to adopting a national identification card.

Under Real ID, all driver's licenses would have "physical security features," and a "common machine readable zone (mrz)." Personal information for every driver in the country would be stored in a huge database controlled by each state's DMV, but accessible at the federal level.

To become eligible for a Real ID, an applicant would have to present documentation of one of the following statuses:

> a citizen or national of the U.S.; an alien lawfully admitted for permanent or temporary residence in the U.S.; has conditional permanent residence

in the U.S.; has an approved application for asylum or has entered the U.S. in refugee status; has a valid, unexpired non-immigrant visa or non-immigrant status; has a pending application for asylum in the U.S.; has a pending or approved application for temporary protected status in the U.S.; has approved deferred action status or; has a pending application for adjustment of status to lawful permanent resident status in the U.S.

In addition to excluding undocumented immigrants, these provisions also exclude legal immigrants "who may have been victims of abuse and whose abusers destroy, steal or otherwise control their documents, or citizens who happen to be Native Americans, victims of natural disasters, domestic violence victims, homeless, military personnel, or elderly individuals" (EPIC, 2008). Without the proper documentation, and with few exceptions, individuals cannot obtain a Real ID. Nor can they board an airplane, enter a federal building, nuclear power plant, or use an existing ID to claim social security benefits or open a bank account.

Federalization of Real ID

Real ID is a federal policy that coerces partnerships with the States. It is largely unfunded by the federal government, and it promises to increase the workload of already overcrowded and under-resourced DMV offices around the country. According to the existing norms of federalism, the federal government needs a good reason to interfere with a State's issuance of driver's licenses. As the 9/11 Commission concluded, national security presents that federal interest. However, the federal government cannot require the States to participate in Real ID. In *NY v. U.S.*,[34] the Supreme Court ruled that the tenth Amendment prevents the federal government from forcing a state to enact or enforce a federal regulatory program. Thus, States can choose to not comply with Real ID, as 19 states have done. It is also important to note that the Real ID law cannot function without States appropriating moneys and, in many instances, changing their laws and revamping their DMV capabilities. In short, Real ID only works if the States contribute money, resources, and staff.

Once States opt-in to the program, Real ID then conditions the federal government's acceptance of state-issued licenses on the States' meeting certain federal standards (Harper, 2007, p. 3). Thus, although each State license may retain cosmetic differences, they are essentially the same in terms of their data and biometric specs. According to ACLU Congressional testimony, "the National ID System is created by the mandate that all states make their databases of licensee information interoperable and that they engage in unprece-dented data sharing about licensees (http://hsgac.senate.gov/public/_files/testimonySparapani.pdf). The federal government thus uses a State respons-ibility and State machinery to implement a federal program, "blurring the lines of authority and obscuring the workings of government and citizens and taxpayers," which is dangerous on several grounds (Harper, 2007). When it comes to accountability and redress, or honoring existing law, DHS covers its eyes and points to the States. It provides no accountability and argues that accountability and redress will occur within the individual States.

DMV staff decisions would be final. Consider the State DMV employee who has nearly unreviewable powers to verify source documents, including complex immigration documents, birth certificates, social security cards, foreign passports, permanent resident cards, EADs, visas, certificates of citizenship, naturalization documents, and perhaps even more obscure immigration documents.[35] According to EPIC, "It is questionable how well State DMV employees would be able to spot fraudulent documents, especially documents as rarely seen as consular reports of birth abroad [. . .] when it is difficult for counterfeit documents to be spotted by federal employees whose primary job is verification of source documents" (2008, p. 9).

The final regulations avoided the issue of redress and accountability, and as a result, nobody reviews the process, and no right of appeal is given to the applicant for a careless and mistaken decision. It is quite possible that a DMV employee will hand out a "scarlet letter" driver's license just because the name on the applicant's birth certificate didn't include the nickname displayed in the database. Such typos and other errors are quite prevalent, and yet they could prevent an applicant from receiving a Real ID license and transform a law abiding resident into a suspect.[36]

Immigrants who fail the database check, and fail to prove they have lawful status through verifiable documentation, or because they rely on foreign documents other than an official passport (www.realnightmare.org/about/2/), can be issued a second tier, different-colored driver's license, which highlights their second-tier status in society. Such a "scarlet letter" card guarantees a great deal of scrutiny from public or private officials who see it, making the holder a suspicious figure at the retail shop, bank, or for that matter at a routine traffic stop.

The process turns State MVA employees into immigration officers, "forcing them to ask prospective driver's about their immigration status and then assess the validity of documents—a troublesome chore even for well-trained immigration officers" (Koulish, 2008). Not only do MVA employees become de facto immigration officers, but consider the administrative delays and mistakes that are likely to follow as poorly-trained employees grapple with the complexities of immigration law:

> . . . despite the complexity of our immigration laws, which rivals that of our tax code, and the numerous legal categories that allow an individual to obtain legal status in the United States, and the even greater number of documents that verify that status. Training for motor vehicles employees could not possibly cover all of the technicalities of the immigration laws. And immigration databases are notoriously incomplete and error-ridden and might fail to verify the status of people who are in fact legally present.

And many non-citizens who have lawful status, particularly refugees, might be unable to obtain federally-qualified licenses simply because they do not have official passports from their home countries.

(www.realnightmare.org/about/2/)

Privacy is one of those slippery slope issues that many people don't fight for until it is gone. With Real ID, privacy as James Madison imagined it all but disappears. In 1974, Congress enacted the Privacy Act as a response to the abuse of executive powers in the Nixon administration. The Act says in part: "No agency shall disclose any record which is contained in a system of records by any means of communication to any person, or to another agency, except pursuant to a written request by, or with the prior written consent of, the individual to whom the record pertains . . ." (The Privacy Act of 1974, 5 USC 552a). Because Rep. Sensenbrenner failed to include a directive to DHS to abide by the Privacy Act, the final rules suggest that DHS need not comply with this post-Nixon corrective to abuses of power. In response, Senator Joseph Lieberman said that "the concept that federal agencies need explicit Congressional authorization to protect Americans' privacy is just plain wrong. In fact, our government is obligated to ensure that programs and regulations do not unduly jeopardize an individual's right to privacy" (EPIC, 2008, p. 10).

In this example of passing the buck, the federal government diminishes expectations that people have for the individual privacy of persons and property.[37] In the meantime, the final regulations for Real ID hint strongly that DHS would like to see Real ID morph into a national ID card, where it will be used for voter registration and as a border-crossing document. (ACLU Report, 2008, p. 8). As the various identification card programs consolidate under the control of L-1 Solutions, and as the technology becomes interchangeable, Real ID can also be used as a pre-clearance for employment, federal subsidized housing and obtaining government-backed loans (ACLU Report, 2008).

Real ID lays out the infrastructure for a national ID card by standardizing "common machine-readable technology" and assuring the development of a shared information database. According to the Center for Democracy and Technology report "Unlicensed Fraud," a single national database makes personal information vulnerable to fraud, especially given the federal government's poor record at information security and preventing insider fraud. The Privacy Rights Clearinghouse is quite concerned about Real ID's vulnerability to identity theft and fraud. It argues that insider fraud is inevitable because it already occurs in other systems, and Real ID makes no effort to diminish the likelihood of fraud in this new system. By interlinking state databases Real ID provides multiple parties with access to personal data, which the Clearinghouse suggests is a recipe for fraud (ACLU Report, 2008).

Of greatest concern is that the machine-readable technology allows for the transfer of the data on the cards to and among private parties. As the ACLU

Real ID Report says, "Already, many bars and clubs collect their customers' information by swiping driver's licenses handed over to prove legal drinking age" (ACLU, www.realnightmare.org/). Real ID would expand the capacity for such parallel private sector databases, "free from the limited privacy rules in effect for the government" (ACLU Report, 2008). DHS has also failed to demand the 2-D bar codes on these cards be encrypted to minimize dangers of identity theft.

Real ID proponents, and proponents of a national ID card, contend that non-criminals have no reason to fear such loss of privacy because they have nothing to hide. This argument is patently absurd. Many "non-criminals" have very good reason to want to remain anonymous and not have their identity entered into such a national database. For these people, the absence of privacy and the interlinking nature of the database create the potential for real danger. For example, 19 states have confidentiality laws protecting domestic violence survivors. Real ID recognizes the conundrum presented by individuals who need to retain anonymity for safety reasons. According to the final rule of Real ID, "A DMV may apply an alternative address on a driver's license or identification card if the individual's address is entitled to be suppressed under a state or federal law or suppressed by a court order including an administrative order issued by a state or federal court" (http://news.cnet.com/8301-10784_3-9867257-7.html).[38]

The broader concern, however, is that the true name and address as well as "source documents" (birth certificate), are stored in the DMV database, which can be accessed by any DMV agent anywhere in the country, as well as sheriffs, the federal government, and the private contractor. So, although the store clerk may not be able to gain access to an individual's real address, the same is not true for the DMV worker, the local sheriff, and L-1 staffer. In its effects, the Real ID driver's license comes very close to a national ID card. According to the L-1[39] website, "the Real ID Act, in concert with the 9/11 report, recognizes the increasing value of the U.S. driver license and its role as the primary citizen ID in the U.S. today" (www.digimarc.com/govt/realid.asp).

According to DHS regulations, each state would have to keep copies of the applicants' documents and a digital photograph (Wald, December 1, 2008). The digital photo required by Real ID must meet international standards adopted by the ICAO, a UN agency, for compatibility with facial recognition software. Such compatibility with local, state, national and international systems allows an ID to be horse traded around the globe. Further, an individual's "full legal name" and "true address" must be stored in the DMV database, which means that a breach would enable an abuse victim to be identified and located.

Next, the database has multiple access points that increase the likelihood of a breach. In the old system, before Real ID was enacted, DMV databases were discrete and separate. Victims of domestic abuse, for example, who moved to another jurisdiction and applied for a new driver's license with a new address expected that their driver's license could not lead an ex-spouse or other potential abuser to their front door. The Real ID system requires interlinking DMV databases and makes all driver's records and personal documents available to almost anyone at an access point. The multiplier effect is huge in terms of gaining access to an individual's personal information and tracking them anywhere in the country.

L-I Identity Solutions to Real ID

When Real ID was enacted in 2005, two private companies, Viisage Corp. and Digimarc, were the two heavyweight players in the driver's license and identity card business. In June 2006, Viisage was awarded contracts with DMV offices in Pennsylvania, Wisconsin, Maryland, and Arkansas to provide Real ID compatible driver's licenses (*Business Wire*, June 13, 2006). In 2006, Viisage merged with another high-tech identity player, Identix and was renamed L-1 Identity Solutions. In March 2008, it was announced that L-1 Solutions would purchase the ID systems industry-leading Digimark Corporation (Reuters, June 23, 2008). Previously, Digimarc had about 70% of the driver's license market. Quickly, L-1 controlled about 95% of the market, and by 2008, boasted $100 million in federal contracts for identification cards.

L-1 Solutions has consolidated the biometrics industry and gained near monopoly control over government identification programs. According to industry analyst Jeff Kessler, the "consolidation of identification programs should affect nearly all initiatives . . . PassCard, Western Hemisphere Travel Initiative, US-VISIT, TWIC, and Real ID . . ." (www.thesecurityanalyst.com/blog/?p=15, 2008). For example, in March 2008 L-1 picked up the contract for the government smart passport card program. With such contracts and market share, L-1 now has the potential to help the government create a police state under the auspices of securing national and homeland security.

It is safe to say that not only has L-1 become the de facto producer and issuer of the Real ID driver's licenses, it has become a one-stop shopping center for the government's identity card needs. Increasing L-1's clout is the fact that its lobbying voice in Congress and at DHS is both powerful and effective. The L-1 Board of Directors includes George Tenet, Admiral Loy, former head Secretary of the U.S. Department of Transportation, Deputy Under-Secretary of the Transportation Security Administration (TSA) John Lawler, former member of Congress, B.G. Buddy Beck, and former FBI director Louis Freeh.

With monopoly control, absence of privacy restrictions, and leadership positions handed out to former heads of the FBI and CIA, L-1 Identity Solutions raises important conflicts of interest challenges to the new Administration. Back in the 1960s and 1970s, CointelPro spied on and blackmailed citizens and other residents on account of their political affiliation and involvement in social movements. CointelPro efforts to create a police state were hampered by deficiencies in technology and by laws that demanded accountability and oversight and regard for privacy. The Real ID era removes such deficiencies from a system that can potentially help public and private interests keep tabs on all people in the US based on their race, ethnicity, political party, or any other criteria.

E-Verify

Along with Real ID comes E-Verify, another national database that is designed to contain information about all people who are employed in the United States. E-Verify is an outgrowth of the 1986 Immigration Reform and Control Act (IRCA) provision that made it illegal for employers to "knowingly" employ unauthorized workers. IRCA created a paper-based system that required every employee to fill out the I-9 form, an employment eligibility verification form that says the individual is authorized to work in the United States, and is presented along with identification documents. Employers were to keep copies of the documents on-file for three years. Sensing problems with this paper-based system, Congress, when it enacted the IIRIRA in 1996, required INS to create three pilot programs to test electronic methods of verifying employment eligibility. The three test programs were narrowed down to the *Basic Pilot*, later known as *E-Verify*. Basic Pilot was developed in 1997. According to Cesar Cuahtemoc Garcia Hernandez:

> The BPP was designed to provide a check for employers who met the letter of the law but not the spirit of the I-9 form's verification process. No longer would it be enough for an employer to make a good faith determination that the documents they were shown were authentic and accurate. Under the BPP the federal government would make the final call—and it would do so immediately.
>
> (*Z Magazine*, July 2008)

E-Verify is an electronic verification system implemented in all 50 states that tracks the data that is collected when an employee fills out an I-9. The lessons learned provide a warning to those who suggest that databases offer an airtight way to manage risk in society. The most important warning is that the system is highly flawed. Several recent investigations have found that the E-Verify system "is riddled with errors, is exorbitantly expensive, and results in discrimination against foreign-born individuals who are, in fact, authorized to work here" (Hernandez, 2008). A 2008 GAO report on E-Verify found:

> About 7 percent of the queries cannot be immediately confirmed as work authorized by SSA, and about 1 percent cannot be immediately confirmed as work authorized by [U.S. Citizenship and Immigration Services] because employees' information queried through the system does not match information in SSA or DHS databases . . . because employees'

citizenship status or other information, such as name changes, is not up to date in the [Social Security Administration] database, generally because individuals have not notified SSA of information changes that occurred.

(GAO Report, 2008)

Just when a bevy of government and NGO sponsored studies of E-Verify were being released to the public highlighting serious deficiencies, the Congress endeavored to extend E-Verify to create a national, mandatory employment verification system.[40] Although that effort failed, DHS Secretary Chertoff quickly picked up the E-Verify gauntlet and issued regulations extending the use of E-Verify.

Why, you might ask, would the Bush administration extend the program when it was proving itself to be a failure? The answer is that its success had very little to do with the accuracy of the database, and was not diminished by an error-ridden program or one replete with discrimination. Success was defined ideologically. The outcomes that mattered were those that advanced the risk management agenda.

Conclusion

In spite of major failures, the privatization of immigration control has achieved perhaps the greatest success of all. It has enhanced sovereign powers by privatizing them. It has further removed decision-makers from the sometimes messy but absolutely necessary realm of democratic accountability, and it has sunk billions of dollars into a privatized regime and developed a huge infrastructure of interlinking data bases so as to make it very difficult for the new administration to reverse course.

Perhaps it doesn't even matter that none of the many privatized high tech ventures can claim to have succeeded during the past eight years. US-VISIT still cannot figure out how to develop and implement a biometric exit program, which means that it can track who enters the country but has no record of who leaves. But it shares biographic and biometric data information with DHS and other federal agencies that make use of data mining.[41] The Real ID program has encountered resistance from the states, forcing the federal government to repeatedly postpone implementation dates and impose penalties for failure to comply. The virtual fence still cannot integrate its various component parts, leaving undocumented immigrants to enter the country just out of focus of the Project 28 cameras. In the meantime, however, vast databases with millions of names exist, with multiple entry points allowing federal agents, local and state police, foreign governments, and private corporations to identify individuals to place them on "watch lists," exclude them, seek their removal from the country, and so forth. Regrettably the absence of quality control measures means that rampant mistakes leading to abuses of individuals' civil and human rights persist unchecked. And of greatest importance is that this counterintelligence network contains no information on the people it intended to target, undocumented immigrants, and by association, potential terrorists.

Cory Doctorow's recent short story about the privatization of border control captures the fear inspired by these programs. In Doctorow's account, "custom agents grill travelers about their search inquiries, public places are swept by Webcams and officials look for terrorist connections in social networking sites" (LaVallee, 2007). The concern here is that such gigantic data bases invite abuse. Doctorow's nemesis could just as easily be the consortium of information gathering corporations that comprise SBInet. They successfully destroy privacy. It matters little to the government if an innocent person is wrongly accused.

Chapter 6

Race, Class, and the Border Fence Fiasco

> In my forty odd years of studying the U.S.–Mexico border I have never seen anything suggested by either government that is so wrong headed and destructive to our communities and our people as this border wall.
>
> (Tony Zavaleta, Ph.D., Vice President of External Affairs at the University of Texas at Brownsville and Texas Southmost College, quoted on the No Border Wall website)

Sovereignty of the Border Fence

On April 1, 2008, DHS Secretary Michael Chertoff announced that he was relying on a provision of the Real ID Act of 2005 to ignore existing law in his quest to construct a border wall along 700 miles of the U.S.–Mexico border. The Real ID provisions of the 2005 Real ID Act granted Chertoff statutory authority to waive federal law in construction of the fence: "Notwithstanding any other provision of law, the Secretary of Homeland Security shall have the authority to waive all legal requirements such Secretary, in such Secretary's sole discretion, determines necessary to ensure expeditious construction of the barriers and roads under this section" (Real ID). Chertoff's authority also draws upon nearly unreviewable discretion that is granted him by the Secure Borders Act of 2006 and the Consolidated Appropriations Act of 2008. These laws handed Chertoff the power to decide where the fence would be placed and who would be displaced by the fence. The ad hoc and arbitrary decision-making by Congress that gave such power to Chertoff, and Chertoff's subsequent actions highlight a culture of reckless disregard for law, immigration, national security, and for the people who reside at the border. When Georgio Agamben wrote about sovereignty, this is what he was getting at: situations when government leaders rely on the law in order to step outside its grasp.

On April 1, Chertoff stepped into a deconstitutionalized zone where actions are controlled by almost nothing but the voices inside his own head, and perhaps also coming from the White House and Boeing. Of course, Chertoff and his underlings are constrained by DHS culture, but the newness of DHS, and its absence of culture, gives Chertoff leeway to go his own way. In the absence of law and culture, almost nothing controls where and how DHS will construct the U.S.–Mexico border fence.

No political appointee has ever been granted the power Congress has granted to Chertoff and that Chertoff thereafter claimed for himself at the border. Specifically, Chertoff's waiver authority allows DHS to move forward without compliance with numerous procedural and substantive requirements of law.[1] He has used his unprecedented power to "waive in their entirety" 36 laws, including the Endangered Species Act, the Migratory Bird Treaty Act, the National Environmental Policy Act, the Coastal Zone Management Act, the Clean Water Act, the Clean Air Act, the National Historic Preservation Act, the National American Graves Protection and Repatriation Act, American Indian Religious Freedom Act, and the National Environmental Policy Act, as well as others, to override court challenges to the construction of fences and walls. Many of these federal laws enforced human rights as well as civil rights.[2]

There was no national security rationale for placing the fence in one place rather than another. Chertoff's decisions were informed by the larger SBI strategy, which involves the U.S. Army Corps of Engineers (USACE) and Boeing. In fact, according to a recent article in the *Texas Observer*, DHS referred decisions about where the border fence would be placed to the SBI office of then SBI director Greg Giddens:

> Questioned more about where the data came from, the staffer said she would enquire further. The next day she called back. "The border fence is being handled by Greg Giddens at the Secure Border Initiative Office within the U.S. Customs and Border Protection office," she said. Giddens is executive director of the SBI, as it is called, which is in charge of SBInet, a consortium of private contractors led by Boeing Co.
>
> (Bosque, 2008)

It is important to note that the USACE, which has a monopoly of control over the levees upon which parts of the fence were built, is also one of the federal government's most outsourced agencies. In this regard, the USACE is a proxy for private and secretive entities making public decisions that are guided by the desire for making profit rather than concern for national security or the public good.

Since the USACE, CBP, and Boeing SBI divisions helped map out fence locations, it makes sense that decisions were based on expediency and the desire to protect the property rights of wealthy border residents.[3] According to the University of Texas working group that testified before the OAS: "The government has not provided justification for its differential treatment of properties along the border as it has not explained why certain lucrative properties are not to be affected by border wall construction" (www.utexas. edu/law/academics/centers/humanrights/publications/Background_and_ Context.pdf, p. 14).

In fall 2008, the Rapoport Center conducted a study on the border fence and found the construction of a border barrier and the necessary taking of property associated with it would have substantial disproportional impacts on marginalized and underrepresented groups in Cameron County, Texas: ". . . the general placement of the fence along the Mexican border ensures that poor Hispanic immigrant families are those who would mostly likely to be affected by its construction" (Wilson et al., 2008, p. 9).

For example, while Chertoff condemned the modest property of Eloise Tamez (see p. 116), a Spanish Land Grant property, along with over 100 other similarly situated property owners in South Texas, he didn't ask anything of the owners of the River Bend Resort and Country Club, a popular winter retreat, just 6.7 miles down the road heading south-east from Tamez' property (Story, March 11, 2008). Unlike Tamez, River Bend guests will have unfettered access to the River. Had Chertoff followed the existing levee as the map for the fence, the fence would have cut off the resort from the golf course that it owns. As it is, the resort, golf course, country club, and vacation rentals will be unaffected by the fence (Nedderman, Dulitzky & Gilman, 2008).

Chertoff also missed the Grajeno, Texas border property of Ray L. Hunt, (Hunt Consolidated, Inc.) a friend of the Bush family and contributor to the Bush Presidential library. Hunt donated at least $35 million to Southern Methodist University to help fund the Bush Library. Back in 2001, Bush appointed Hunt to the Foreign Intelligence Advisory Board, where Hunt received a security clearance and access to classified intelligence (Nedderman, Dulitzky & Gilman, 2008). Although an 18-foot-high border fence is supposed to cut through the next door property of Daniel Garza, a 74-year-old retiree born and raised in Granjeno, it stops abruptly just short of Hunt's property line (Nedderman, Dulitzky & Gilman, 2008; Story, 2008).

By ignoring the law and protecting wealthy property owners, there is no question that DHS misused its grant of sovereign power from Congress. Such lack of transparency also gives rise to serious questions about how decisions are made regarding the amount of fencing the government has proposed and its precise location. By keeping such matters secret, and then acting in seemingly arbitrary ways, the government made it difficult for people living on the border to plan their lives and livelihoods, or to organize their neighbors to resist the fence.

Although claims to sovereignty explain how Chertoff got away with ignoring domestic law, ostensibly for the purpose of preserving it, the continuing war on terror provides a rationale for how the administration can ignore international commitments to the American Convention on Human Rights and Duties of Man, interpreted in light of the American Convention on Human Rights. International law holds that a sovereign's restriction of rights must be proportionate to the State's ultimate objective. It also suggests that national security objectives do not give States free reign to restrict rights in unreasonable ways (Nedderman, working group, 14). When it comes to protecting border residence from abusive decision-making authority at the border, international law protections follow the path of domestic law. International law prevents the government from: 1) taking property in a manner that is disproportionate to its goal of protecting the border; 2) disparately applying its sovereign powers; 3) degrading the environment; and 4) violating the rights of indigenous communities protected under international human rights law. The Bush administration's dismissal of its international obligations in this instance reinforces the perception that it doesn't really care about them. International law would allow the sovereign to step outside the law, but only insofar as the least invasive option is selected. Similarly, the sovereign could only engage in discrimination against border residents, if it first demonstrated that its objectives could not be satisfied any other way (Nedderman).[4] Chertoff's intentions were to suspend the law for its own sake; to build the fence for its own sake.

The border fence storyline lends further credence to the notion of a lawless Bush administration. According to Arnoldo Garcia, Senior Policy Associate with the National Network for Immigrant and Refugee Rights,

> it is time for Congress to reconsider building a Berlin-type militarized wall along the U.S.–Mexico border. . . . What good does it do to spend hundreds of millions of dollars on a border wall when half the undocumented immigrants enter the United States with non-immigrant visas, not through the U.S.–Mexico border?
>
> (www.nnirr.org/news/index.php?op=
> read&id=130&type=8)

Fence Fiasco

What makes the border fence a fiasco? The fence is intended to prevent terrorism, but all the 9/11 terrorists entered the country via legal means. None gained entry through Mexico. In fact, the only border that has played a role in rumored terrorist plots against the US has been the Canadian border, where no serious plans exist for a wall or fence (U-T Obstructing Human Rights, June 2008). As Representative Phil Gingrey stated regarding the Secure Fence Act in 2006: "If we are really concerned about terrorists, we ought to be much more concerned about our northern border, where there are many more miles of unprotected border without camera sensors, without fencing" (Congressional Record, September 14, 2006, p. H6587).

The border fence also intends to keep out undocumented immigrants, which earlier attempts at fence construction failed to do. Recent studies attempting to find correlations between the border fence and "illegal immigration," however, have failed to find any. The border fence in San Diego, for example, "did not have a discernible impact on the influx of unauthorized aliens coming across the border" (Haddal, Kim, & Garcia, 2009). Even Michael Chertoff has conceded that there have been numerous breaches where fences have been built.[5] Border fence construction since the 1990s shows fences were never intended to deter undocumented entries. Rather, the design of the fence in Operation Blockade and Hold the Line sought to control, manage and direct the migrant flow from Mexico into the US and, like a toothpaste tube, to squeeze in some areas only to increase the flow in other areas. According to the CRS, however, fences that channel immigration into more remote areas do not deter immigration. All they do is to secure migrant deaths (Haddal et al., 2009). The only result of this boondoggle is the likelihood of more migrant deaths and more Boeing (and subcontractor) profits.

Border Fence Attempts

In no small part, the construction of the border fence is part of a larger effort to militarize the U.S.–Mexico border, and thus strategically control the population there. After more than a decade of border militarization with "Operation Gatekeeper" and "Operation Hold the Line," and the deployment of the National Guard, the government finally got serious about building a 700-mile fence along a 2,017-mile border. Actually, I think it is more accurate to say it got serious about creating a fence-building industry and corresponding narrative. I don't think it was ever serious about constructing a 700-mile fence – at least not one that actually keeps people out. Such a fence would have conflicted with the reigning free market ideology that relies on cheap labor. Constructing a 2,000-mile border fence is also impossible in practical and budgetary terms. It is not cost effective. Costs are estimated at 2–4 million dollars per mile of border fencing. The terrain in many border areas is too rugged and in other areas a fence or wall would cause flooding and other disasters. Still, the government enacted the Secure Fence Act, formed the Secure Border Initiative, and outsourced responsibility for building the fence to private contractors. The Secure Fence Act sanctioned public funding to augment yet another corporate boondoggle.

Timothy Dunn, author of *The Militarization of the U.S. Border*, sees militarization not so much in terms of the deployment of armed forces at the border, although that is part of it, but in terms of the use of military rhetoric, tactics and technology (Dunn, 1996). Dunn defines militarization in terms of LIC, a military tactic popularized in such third world settings as Latin America during the early 1980s. LIC is about "maintaining social control over targeted civilian populations through broad range of measures (many not obviously coercive) via the coordinated efforts of police, paramilitary, and military forces" (Dunn, 1996, p. 20).

Although the first immigration officers were spotted on horseback patrolling the border in South Texas as early as 1901, the first official State-sponsored movement against undocumented immigrants came when the border patrol was established in 1924. The border patrol did not face a "real problem" with "illegal immigration" until after the 1965 Immigration Act, when a cap was established for immigration from the Western Hemisphere. For the first time, significant numbers of immigrants from the Western Hemisphere wanted to enter the country but were prevented by the cap from doing so. The result was undocumented immigration. Once such a population of people existed, it was only a matter of time before a narrative was developed to subordinate them.

During the 1970s and 1980s, the militarization of the border made do with leftover Vietnam era technology. In 1977, Jimmy Carter proposed increasing the border patrol's resources. He also proposed the Alien Adjustment and Employment Act of 1977, which laid out "a set of actions to help markedly reduce the increasing flow of undocumented aliens in this country and to regulate the presence of the millions of undocumented aliens already here" (S.2252/HR 9531). It would take Carter's proposal almost a decade to get enacted as the Immigration Reform and Control Act of 1986.

During the Reagan era, LIC was waged throughout much of Central America, the results of which led refugees through Mexico to the U.S. border. The Refugee Crisis at the Texas–Mexico border in 1988–1990 was a direct result of Reagan's LIC policies in El Salvador and Guatemala. During the Reagan years, the INS introduced high tech air support, OH-6 spotter-observation helicopters from the U.S. Army, night-vision and infrared scopes, and low-light television surveillance systems. Soon the border patrol introduced SWAT teams, military-trained and armed BP officers who ride in armored personnel carriers, shoot M-16s, and keep grenade launchers handy.

President George H.W. Bush intensified border militarization. Emphasis on drug enforcement at the border resulted in the purchase and deployment of more helicopters and additional electronic surveillance equipment. Among other things, Bush established the relationship between INS and the military. This complicates the border control situation. While border patrol agents are trained to use minimum force and to protect the constitutional rights of the accused, the military ethic presumes guilt and responds to situations with overwhelming force. According to Anthony Romero, ACLU Executive Director, ". . . federal law enforcement officers are the best equipped and trained to deal with these kinds of civilian law enforcement needs . . . Soldiers are trained to kill the enemy, and they lack the training to conduct proper law enforcement" (Kouri, 2006). The military has helped with such construction projects as Operation Blockade, resulting in the construction of a 7-mile corrugated steel fence between San Diego and Tijuana. The Bush Sr. years can also saw the construction of the first physical barriers (not quite a wall or fence) along the border in the San Diego, California area (Haddal et al., 2009).

The Clinton administration was responsible for constructing the first border walls and fences. In 1993, Sandia National Laboratories, a military think tank, released a "border security" study for INS. The study recommended construction of a triple fence in the San Diego/Tijuana area. During this time, the INS launched Operation Gatekeeper in the San Diego border region, a deterrence strategy that deployed more than 1,000 border patrol agents to the region before 1994 and about 2,200 after 1994.

In 1993, Operation Hold the Line was launched in the El Paso/Juarez border region. Then border patrol sector chief Silvestre Reyes (now member of Congress) shifted border patrol personnel throughout the sector to the boundary line in El Paso. He deployed agents along the Rio Grande River every quarter mile within eyesight of each other. According to the Center for Immigration Studies (CIS), "by mobilizing his sector's resources along the border around the clock, he converted what had been a widely breached river and fence between the busy cities of El Paso and Ciudad Juarez, Mexico, into an effective deterrent" (*Houston Chronicle*, June 1, 1995). In addition to border patrol agents, these operations also introduced post-Vietnam era technologies, including infra-red telescopes, heat sensors, ground sensors, new computer systems to track people, surveillance cameras, and helicopters. They also resulted in the construction of a fence in San Diego that reached the Pacific Ocean.

During this period, a study of human rights conditions along the border revealed that customs and border patrol officials discriminated against people on the basis of skin color and ethnicity, and that border control activities failed to discern differences in immigration status (Koulish, 1994). These findings reinforced the perception that immigration officials are not constrained in their actions by the rule of law. Rather their activities are informed by mandates to control border populations.

In 1996, the IIRIRA included in its provisions a grant of broad authority to the government to construct barriers along the border (see IIRIRA, Pub.L. 104–208, Div. C, Section 102(a)-(c)). The IIRIRA also gave the government the power to take land in the border area when the government deems the land essential to "control and guard the boundaries and borders of the United States" (see id., Section 102(d); 8 U.S. Code 1102(b)). In 1999, Operation Safeguard began at the Arizona border with Sonora, Mexico, along with Operation Rio Grande. Drawing upon the PR successes of the previous programs, they attracted attention to the idea of separating Anglos from Mexicans, while hyping the subtext of Mexicans being a threat to the United States.

From the standpoint of actually deterring undocumented immigrants, the Clinton administration efforts at the border were an abject failure. In 1993, there were about 3 million undocumented immigrants in the United States. The number tripled a decade later. It is estimated that Operations Gatekeeper and Hold the Line resulted in the death of about 3,000 people trying to cross the border along more dangerous and remote routes in Arizona, New Mexico and Texas (Reyes, 2003). According to a 2003 GAO Report, ". . . the border patrol has realized its goal of shifting illegal alien traffic away from urban areas into more remote areas. However, rather than being deterred from attempting illegal entry, many aliens have instead risked injury and death by trying to cross mountains, deserts, and rivers" (GAO, June 16, 2003).

Failure has never discouraged the Bush administration from pushing forward. In recent years, the military role in border security has evolved. The Joint Task Force North, a military unit affiliated with U.S. Northern Command, has lent services to the BP, and state governors in Arizona and Texas have dispatched National Guard Units from their states to the border. In all, as of summer 2006 about 6,000 National Guard Troops were assuming the surveillance and infrastructure duties of the border patrol. According to DHS spokesperson Jarrod Agen, the National Guard is being assimilated into the border protection apparatus and may assume surveillance responsibilities and intelligence gathering for the border patrol. Among other activities, the National Guard may assume surveillance responsibilities and intelligence gathering for the BP. In addition to the National Guard, in 2002 the Department of Defense agreed to deploy its initial 1,600 federal soldiers as deputized border patrol and customs service agents at our borders, bringing state of the art military technology.

Secure Fence Act of 2006

In 2006, Congress passed the Secure Fence Act, which was sponsored by Peter King (R-NY) and passed both chambers with broad bipartisan support (Secure Fence Act of 2006, pp. 109–367). According to its sponsors, it was intended to protect the border from terrorists. According to one border patrol officer, the fence is designed to keep WMDs from getting into the country (www. youtube.com/watch?v=GUMFfV_qbNM&feature=related).

The Secure Fence Act was a bone thrown to Congressional neoconservatives in the aftermath of contentious failed attempts in 2006 at "comprehensive immigration reform." Since few people wanted to risk being labeled soft on terrorism in this election year, support came with the unspoken promise that the issue would just go away for a while. There was little opposition. Once passed, it was quickly amended in December 2007 as part of the Consolidated Appropriations Act FY 2008, which orders DHS to construct at least 700 miles of fence, but leaves it up to DHS to decide where. The 2008 Consolidated Appropriations Act is famous for significantly increasing DHS's discretion over where to construct the fencing.[6]

Since Congress gave ambiguous orders about the length of the fence, such decisions were left to DHS discretion. The Consolidated Appropriations Act requires construction of not less than 700 miles of intermittent fencing, leaving DHS with the discretion to find alternatives to border fencing along 1,300 or so miles of the 2,017 mile-long border from San Ysidro, California to Brownsville, Texas (Congressional Research Service). The 2008 Act also gave DHS given additional flexibility to decide on alternatives to fencing,[7] such as vehicle barriers or virtual fencing, ground sensors, remote video surveillance systems, and truck-mounted mobile surveillance systems to detect illegal border crossings.[8]

Where it decided to build a fence, the DHS decided on the construction of a double reinforced steel and concrete fence between California and Texas. An 18-foot high fence would cut through cities and deserts along the border. It didn't help matters, according to the mayor of Eagle Pass that, "[w]e found out they had no idea of what life is like on the border, and many couldn't find the Rio Grande with a map" (*The Washington Times*, February 21, 2008). The USACE's task was to oversee construction of the border fence. It outsourced to military contractors much of the planning design, construction, management, and oversight of the border fence.[9]

Fence Contracts

Following the dismal failure of outsourcing construction of the San Diego stretch of the fence to the Golden State Fence Company, which hired undocumented labor, this time the USACE awarded the contract to such companies as the Boeing subsidiary Power Contracting Inc, Tempe-based Sundt Construction, known for having built the top secret town of Los Alamos and moving the London Bridge to Arizona, and Kiewit Brothers.

The problem for Kiewit was that it was both a beneficiary and a victim of DHS' sovereign power over this project. In constructing a portion of the fence at Pipe Organ National Park Arizona, for example, Kiewit was not held to account by USACE for environmental regulations that would have prevented the flooding it caused on private property and government buildings in Lukeville, Arizona and Sonoyta, Sonora, Mexico. According to environmentalists at the Center for Biological Diversity, the 7-foot flood waters along 200 feet of the fence were predictable and would have been avoided had USACE and Kiewit followed existing environmental regulations. Regrettably for them, and the people of these two border towns, Secretary Chertoff arrogantly announced he would ignore the environmental regulations (Brady McCombs, *Arizona Daily Star*, August 15, 2008).

UT-Brownsville/Texas Southmost College

Among the areas in Chertoff's path as he lay down the map for constructing the border fence were universities, incorporated municipalities, private property, Indian Reservations, and national park reserves. Rather than deal with the nuances of each taking, Chertoff chose instead to embark on a one-size-fits-all method of eminent domain. The only exceptions to his cookie-cutter design consisted of the private property of wealthy landowners and Republican contributors and supporters.

In October 2007, the University of Texas-Brownsville (UT-B) received a letter from DHS requesting the right of entry onto University property.

The request, according to the UT-B website, which the University refused to sign,

> sought access to survey University land for up to 18 months to store equipment and supplies, take samples and to do any other work they found necessary for the proposed construction of the fence. It also stipulated that the government would not be responsible for any damage done to property during their work preparing to construct the fence.
>
> (http://blue.utb.edu/newsandinfo/
> UpdateBorderFenceIssue.htm)

DHS wanted to cut in half the University of Texas-Brownsville and related Texas Southmost College. UT-Brownsville has a 425-acre campus on a site that was once an Army cavalry base (Fort Brown) at the southernmost point in Texas. All that separates UT-Brownsville from Matamoros, Mexico is the Rio Grande River, the Gateway International Bridge Point of Entry, a U.S. National Historic Landmark at Fort Brown, and parts of the UT-B/Fort Brown 18-hole golf course.

The demand letter threatened to go the route of eminent domain if the University failed to accept its plans. Eminent domain is "the power of the sovereign to take property for public use without the owner's consent upon making just compensation" (Medoff & Sklar, 1999, p. 118). The sovereign may delegate its eminent domain authority to government agencies and private entities (Medoff & Sklar, 1999, p. 118). DHS proposed using its eminent domain authority to erect an 18-foot high, solid border fence—including a 50-yard wide "dead zone" where people are not permitted—right through the middle of campus (Galuszka, September 18, 2008). In a letter to alumni, UT-Brownsville President Juliet V. Garcia responded:

> What is being demanded, under threat of legal action, is unimpeded access by military and civilian agencies to a UT System campus and its state and locally financed buildings for an extended period of time for purposes of determining if land and buildings will be condemned and seized . . . I believe there is sufficient cause for serious concern.
>
> (January 23, 2008)

According to Dr. Antonio Zavaleta, Vice President for External Affairs at UT Brownsville/Texas Southmost College, the federal government's attempt to build a fence in the middle of the University campus misreads the thinking of people living at the border. According to Zavaleta, the fence would destroy a great deal of economic development in the region since NAFTA in 1994, and would violently fracture economic development (however uneven) in the border zone. He also suggests that the Bush administration has hypocritically turned its back on its own core neoliberal belief in free trade.

In a YouTube video, Zavaleta pointed out the parts of his campus that would end up on the Mexican side of the border wall, thus demonstrating the ridiculous nature of the Chertoff proposal. The original plan would have placed the part of the campus that houses the services that facilitate cross-border interactions on the Mexican side of the fence. Included on the south side of the fence was the university's International Technology, Education and Commerce campus (ITECC), which is a mile west of the main campus and is the hub for technology training. The original plans also would have placed several U.S. business and state and federal agencies, including the U.S. Export Assistance Office; the U.S. Small Business Administration Office and the U.S. Export/Import Business Office on the wrong side of the wall. According to Zavaleta, the federal government believed the issue simply did not warrant much consideration.

To allow students, professionals, workers, clients, and customs to get in and out of this zone, and students to classes, the border wall would have to allow for an enormous gate that would allow a thousand entries and exits during the course of a day. The gate would also have to be staffed by border agents or private contractors who would check the entry and exit papers of students crossing campus to get to class. "Students would have had to bring passports and go through border checkpoints just to attend some classes" (Galuszka). Of such a gate, President Garcia also wrote, "having an opening in an 18 foot high fence for the purpose of channeling illegal entrants alongside our golf teams and adjacent to the baseball park, the new soccer field and the REK Center would greatly endanger our students" (www.insidehighered.com/news/2008/01/23/fence).

Consider also that students from Mexico (about 400 of them) would spend much of their day showing ID documents to government authorities, first at the International Bridge and then at this gate. Under the original plan, students or anyone else from the US who would like to travel to Mexico or Central America would have to somehow get to the Mexican side of the fence in order to get a visa to go to Mexico or beyond. Nor, as Garcia says, is the fence conducive to the university's mission,

> which is in part to convene the cultures of its community, foster an appreciation of the unique heritage of the Lower Rio Grande Valley, encourage the development and application of bilingual abilities in its students and provide academic leadership to be intellectual, cultural, social, and economic life of the bi-national urban region it serves.
>
> (*Inside Higher Ed*, January 23, 2008)

It is worth noting that many of UT-B's 17,000-plus student body are of Mexican ancestry, and about 400 are Mexican citizens. In defending his decision to divide the university campus with a border wall, Chertoff suggested the campus had become a haven for undocumented immigrants. Chertoff's claim is unsubstantiated by border patrol apprehension records. Bob Lucio, head golf coach at UTB, added his own observation, saying there was no urgency regarding undocumented border crossings. "They were back in the 1980s when you had a lot of refugees from conflicts in Central America, but not now" (Galuszka, 2008).

Two events helped resolve this particular controversy. Barack Obama came to town. Following Obama, the U.S. House of Representatives came to Brownsville to hold hearings on the border fence. In March 2008, at a speech given at UTB, then candidate Barack Obama called plans to build the border fence through the campus of UT-B "foolish" and "an example of not consulting with local and state officials who understand these communities and who can best figure out how to solve the problem" (OhMyGov!.com). In April 2008, the House Natural Resources Committee, Subcommittee on National Parks Forests and Public Lands, led by Rep Raul Grijalva came to Brownsville to hold a hearing on the border fence. Rep. Tom Tancredo headlined the hearing by suggesting the border fence should be placed to the north of Brownsville, causing an uproar that hurt Chertoff's cause. According to the Harlingen, Texas, *Valley Morning Star*:

> Boos and hisses emanated from the audience for a Congressional field hearing when Republican U.S. Rep. Tom Tancredo of Colorado dismissed residents' concerns that the effort to build 670 miles of fencing along the U.S.–Mexico border by year's end would damage the environment and destroy a centuries-old bond between residents on both sides of the Rio Grande. Late in the five-hour hearing, Tancredo returned to a comment made earlier by panelist Betty Perez, a rancher and local activist. Perez said, "It really isn't a border to most of us who live down here." Tancredo dismissed Perez's remarks as a "multiculturalist attitude toward borders." As jeers rose, Tancredo added, "I suggest that you build this fence around the northern part of your city."
>
> (*Valley Morning Star*, April 28, 2008)

These events at the border attracted a good deal of press attention and came at about the same time the federal government withdrew its condemnation lawsuit against UT-B, following a compromise reached after extensive negotiations in the court of District Court Judge Andrew Hanen, whose court has played host to dozens of border fence condemnation trials. The settlement allowed surveyors for the federal government onto University land in exchange for several minor concessions. In return, in July 2008, the University agreed to improve its own security fence along its southern perimeter in exchange for altering the plan for the fence to transect the University campus. Shortly thereafter, DHS' original border fence plan was revised to place the fence to the south of ITECC, but it would still meander to the north of the Fort Brown Memorial Golf Course and remnants of historic Fort Texas. The fence would also force UT-B to move its baseball field, which is located adjacent to the levee and would intrude on the Education and Business Complex located just off campus.

On August 1, 2008, after a long hearing in Hanen's court, a court order was issued in which it was announced that the border fence would not intrude upon UT-B. Instead, UT-B would upgrade its fence, with sensors and cameras (and flowers), and purchase land that that was located between UT-B and the point of entry at the U.S. Gateway Bridge (Sieff, October 2, 2008).

Land Grants and Sovereign Eminent Domain Power in South Texas

Landowners of modest means who also happen to live at the border's edge have been targeted by DHS. Some of these property owners are original land grant families that received tracts of land from Spain more than 200 years ago. The U.S. government assumed conservator status for the land grants as part of the Treaty of Guadalupe Hidalgo in 1846 that ended the Mexican–American War and transferred territory north of the Rio Grande and south of the Nueces River from Mexico to the United States. The government's taking of land grant property for the Border erases Native American and Hispanic ties with their pre-American legacy.

Consider Eloise Tamez' property in El Calaboz, which is located ten miles west of the UT-Brownsville campus, in Cameron County along the Rio Grande River.

Tamez' family inherited the property pursuant to the San Pedro de Carricitos Land Grant, of the Nuevo Santander region of South Texas, established by Spain in 1743. Prior to the Spanish empire, her land was shared by indigenous ancestors in the Chiricahua and Lipan Nde' (Apache) tribes. In those days, the area was referred to as "Ta ma ho lipam" (the place where the Lipan pray). Tamez' ancestor, Pedro Villareal, who was interred in a cemetery on the land, received 12,730 acres of land from the Spanish Viceroy in 1784.

Tamez' family established ranching and farming operations on the land, per the terms of the land grant, and have since continued working this land for more than 265 years (*Tamez v. Chertoff*, complaint for Injunctive and Declaratory Relief). Tamez described her property in a recent interview on Democracy Now:

> This three acres that I have here is the remnant of the San Pedro de Carricitos Land Grant that was awarded to my family back in 1767. And I remember my father and my grandfather used to farm this part of this area, plus what's over on the other side of the levee, as well as

lands that my grandmother had that went all the way up to the river's edge. So there is no dollar value for this land in comparison to those memories of how hard it was for my father and my grandfather to carve a life for us.

(www.democracynow.org/2008/2/27/
holes_in_the_wall_texas_border)

After the Secure Fence Act charged Chertoff with the task of building the border fence, he invoked eminent domain powers to seize land in the wall's path. He then employed the Declaration of Taking Act (DTA), an expedited condemnation process that denies property owners access to due process and a full trial. In August, 2007, Chertoff announced that property owners in South Texas would be served with waivers requesting unimpeded access to their land (Story, March 11, 2008).

In 2007, DHS served Eloise Tamez with a "Right of Way for Survey and Site Assessment," "Certificate of Acceptance," and sued her under the DTA for "immediate access to land and the ability to take down structures, bore holes, destroy plantings and crops, and take other measures as contractors of the (DHS) may consider necessary . . ." Contrary to existing law, Chertoff pursued DTA expedited condemnation proceedings, as opposed to normal condemnation proceedings, which the law allowed. In an unusual challenge to Chertoff's eminent domain authority, Tamez and seven other landowners charged Chertoff with abusing his eminent domain authority. Tamez' lawyer Peter Schey argued that Chertoff failed to follow due process and violated the federal law that prohibits the expedited condemnation process (Story, 2008). As a result, Tamez filed suit against Chertoff.

The complaint in *Tamez et al. v. Chertoff* alleged that Chertoff misinformed Tamez about her rights by incorrectly threatening to use expedited condemnation proceedings against her and other property owners.[10] Chertoff also failed to comply with the Consolidated Appropriations Act requirement that directed Chertoff to first consult with Tamez and to clearly define the interest he had in the property, and failed to attempt to fix a price with Tamez, which the law also requires (Complaint, pp. 2–3).[11] The law requires "consultation with private property owners and cities and other stake-holders to minimize the impact on the environment, culture, commerce, and quality of life for the communities and residents located near the sites at which border fencing may be constructed" (Complaint, p. 3).

In March 2008, Judge Hanen granted Tamez and other South Texas border landowners a partial victory. Judge Hanen ordered DHS to enter into negotiations with the property owners before moving to condemn their property. According to Judge Hanen, "Dr. Tamez correctly asserts that negotiations are a prerequisite to the exercise of the power of eminent domain" under federal law. The court further concluded that Secretary Chertoff had presented "insufficient evidence . . . as to whether there has been bona fide efforts to negotiate with Dr. Tamez (Garcia, March 7, 2008). At the same time, however, Hanen ruled that DHS could move to condemn the land if the parties were unable to negotiate a fixed price, using DTA.[12] In December 2008, Hanen ruled that juries will decide the value of the properties in question, which is what the property owners had requested and contradicts the request of federal prosecutors to rely on appointed land commissions (Sherman, December 18, 2008).

The taking of the land grant property and defacing it with a fence is an example of cultural imperialism. Similar actions of cultural violence have occurred throughout the border area during this long project. For example, actions in South Texas are quite similar to CBP behavior in Arizona when border patrol occupied the Tohono O'odham's sacred Baboquivari Mountain in 2004 while O'odham leaders were at the United Nations in New York pressing for protection of the sacred site (Norrell, March 22, 2004). Such arrogance expresses the context within which Chertoff's decisions were made. Individuals and local communities mattered not one whit to the larger goals of hegemony.

Eagle Pass/Piedras Negras

> They're going to put up some fence, and it's going to be in Eagle Pass just to make an example of the mouthy mayor of Eagle Pass. –
> (Mayor Chad Foster, as quoted in the *Houston Chronicle*)

In addition to planning the bisection of a university campus, and forcibly removing land grant families, DHS also ordered the town of Eagle Pass (pop. 25,000), Texas, to temporarily turn over 233 acres of land so it could survey the land before building the fence. The new fence at Eagle Pass would bypass an industrial park, and instead cut off a city park, new residential subdivision and the municipal water intake from the rest of the city. Eagle Pass mayor Chad Foster wondered, "I puzzled a while over why the fence would bypass the industrial park and go through the city park." According to the Rapaport center Working group, "he was reportedly utterly unsuccessful finding 'any logical answers from Homeland Security as to why certain areas (in Eagle Pass) have been targeted for fencing over other areas'" (Nedderman, p. 13). The border fence in Eagle Pass shows the federal government's insistence in having its way with a local government without any consultation.

At issue here is the DHS decision to ignore the same law that granted it sovereign powers. More precisely, it chose to reject the consultation proposal made to assist DHS with the requirement of the Consolidated Appropriations Act of FY 2008 (Section 564 of Public Law 110–161). The provision, which was written into the Appropriations Omnibus Act by Sen. Kay Bailey Hutchinson, R-Tx, and Rep. Ciro Rodriguez, D-San Antonio, requires DHS to consult with local governments and communities located near the sites where the border fence will be constructed.[13] The law also says that no funds will be released for Border Security Fencing, Infrastructure and Technology until DHS has complied with the provision (www.offthekuff.com/mt/archives/ 011017.html).

According to Eagle Pass Mayor Chad Foster "They came in here from Washington like storm troopers, dictating what we were going to do and how we were going to do it," said Mr. Foster in describing Homeland Security efforts to explain its fence project. "They steamrolled us. We tried telling them that in building a fence on this border, one size does not fit all" (*Washington Times*, February 21, 2008). The government warned Eagle Pass it would use its powers of eminent domain to secure access to the property. Eminent domain allows the government to take land so long as it is accompanied by just compensation for the property. The more complicated issue has to do with federalism and the taking of locally controlled land, which already exists for the public good.

On January 14, 2008, U.S. District Judge Alia Moses Ludlum in Texas Western District Court ordered the city of Eagle Pass to surrender 233 acres of city-owned land. But the city of Eagle Pass never knew they were being sued, and thus had no opportunity to be present at the hearing. According to Monica Westberg-Stewart, committee chairperson of the Texas Border Coalition, "Informing the city after the judge ruled that their land is already taken is not the Texas or American way of justice." San Juan Texas mayor San Juanita Sanchez added, "Giving the other side notice sounds pretty fair to me. The government is not even following what our justice system asks for" (William Ward, 2008, www.njeminentdomain.com/national-dont-fence-me-in-with-eminent-domain.html).

Up until the judge's ruling, the city of Eagle Pass thought the border patrol was consulting in good faith over an alternative to the border fence, which included clearing brush from the Rio Grande River to give the border patrol better sight of persons crossing the river (www.offthekuff.com/mt/archives/ 011017.html). According to Brownsville mayor Pat Ahumada, member of the Texas Border Coalition, "What the government is doing, it's like a police state. They are dictating to the citizens, it's very anti-American" (Ibid).

Texas Border Coalition v. Chertoff

By May 2008, Chertoff's actions threatened to destroy a way of life that had existed for hundreds of years. His disdain for local communities, townships and economic development zones greatly upset members of the Texas Border Commission (TBC).[14] Once it became clear to members of the Texas Border Coalition that DHS had no intention of negotiating in good faith with individual property owners, they figured that the least they could do was slow down DHS efforts to displace residents and destroy property. The courts were a last resort. Although it is very difficult to beat the government in court on eminent domain issues, it was hoped that a court challenge would buy enough time to allow TBC members to wait out the Bush administration and hope the next administration would reverse course.

Chertoff wanted to complete building the fence before Bush left office on January 20, 2009. Thus he needed to pack the planning and implementation process into this tight time-frame, which would prove impossible. Along the way, Chertoff tripped over many legal obstacles that were in place for the purpose of ensuring a fair and just taking process. Property owners who weren't rich or well-connected were treated pretty much the same way, and as a class they were treated differently than people who were wealthy and well-connected. As a result, hundreds of politically unconnected property owners of moderate means had the same legal grievance against Chertoff and the DHS.

These grievances comprised the formal complaint in the TBC class action suit, and consisted of the following: Chertoff failed to clearly define his interest in their property; failed to consult with the property owner; failed to work with the property owner to fix a price for the property; failed to establish fixed rules, guidelines, instructions or policies relating to the selection of properties to be taken or the process of negotiation or how the government will arrive at its position on a fixed price for the property (Texas Border Coalition v Chertoff 1:2008cv00848).

Native American Sovereignty

When it comes to the adverse effects of sovereign power under the Real ID Act, no people were adversely affected more directly than the Tohono O'odham in Southern Arizona. Many of the laws waived under Real ID forced the federal government to help protect the Tohono O'odham habitus. Executive Order 13175 recognizes the tribes' "inherent sovereign powers over their members and territory." This sovereignty zone was to protect the Tohono O'odham from the sort of incursions that DHS had planned for the reservation's 55 miles of border with Mexico. Such laws as the Wilderness Act helped preserve the tribe's sovereignty. The Department of the Interior acknowledged that its legal obligations under the Wilderness Act and other statutes prevented it from approving DHS' proposed border security infrastructure" (Norris, April 28, 2008). And yet Interior supported the waiver that would trump its commitment to Tohono O'odham sovereignty.

As former Tohono O'odham President Vivian Juan-Saunders put it, the O'odham nation was excluded from DHS planning for the border fence and border enforcement for "[t]he same reason that all tribes have experienced in years past. There's no respect for our tribal sovereignty, no respect for government-to-government consultations" (*Indian Country Today*, November 6, 2003). In 1853, as a result of the Gadsden Purchase,[15] the federal government pushed the U.S.–Mexico border south from the Gila River (south of

Phoenix). The new line divided the Tohono O'odham Indian territory placing some of it on the Mexican side and some on the U.S. side of the new U.S.–Mexico border. From 1853 until 2008, however, the Tohono O'odham were permitted to travel freely on their own territory, back and forth over the border.

In 1994, the Clinton administration began to tighten the immigrant flow at other crossing points on the border (Operation Gatekeeper; Operation Hold the Line), which pushed border-crossers onto this land. According to Saunders:

> Ever since efforts were taken to beef up security in other ports of entry in Arizona, Texas, New Mexico and California, that created a funnel effect where, because of the increase in security elsewhere, there was no other avenue of entry but the Tohono O'odham nation. I feel that as long as there's no attempt to secure the 75-mile-stretch that we have that is adjacent to Mexico, it will always continue to be in the state that it's in now.
>
> (*Indian Country Today*, November 6, 2003)

After squeezing border crossers into a bottleneck on the Indian reservation, the federal government then began militarizing the territory. Since 1994, ICE and the border patrol presence on the Indian Territory increasingly assumed the air of an occupying military force. The reservation has been inundated with military surveillance equipment, including helicopters and low-flying airplanes, unmanned aerial vehicles (Hermes 450s), electronic ground sensors, and remote video cameras.

DHS failed to consult with the Tohono O'odham about plans for the fence, which is nothing new considering that the Tohono O'odham were never consulted on the government plans to implement Operation Gatekeeper and Operation Hold the Line back in the 1990s (Norrell, November 1, 2006). The pattern and practice of ignoring the Tohono O'odham continues with the border fence. In addition, the fence initiative is in violation of the Native American Grave Protection and Repatriation Act, and the American Indian Religious Freedom Act, since the fence would quite literally plow through the burial places of their ancestors.

Conclusion

By December 2008, the CBP reported that 500 miles of fencing had been completed by December 12. Chertoff promised that about 600 miles would be completed by January 20, 2009 (*AP*, December 16, 2008). The fence will consist of about 370 miles of pedestrian fence and about 300 miles of vehicle fence (Winn, December 18, 2008). In the closing days of the Bush administration, a spokesperson to Rep. Duncan Hunter (R-Calif.) who was an architect of the Secure Fence Act of 2006, summed up Hunter's thoughts, "Mr. Hunter would certainly agree that the Department of Homeland Security missed an opportunity to get more accomplished in the time it had. Obviously, much more could have been put in place over the last two years" (Winn, December 18, 2008, www.cnsnews.com/Public/Content/Article.aspx?rsrcid=40972).

Nor did it matter that the incoming Obama administration voiced reluctance about completing the fence. As Matthew DeLong reported for the *Washington Independent*, "It would be difficult to imagine that completion of the planned 700 miles of fencing . . . will be very high on Napolitano's list of priorities" (DeLong, December 10, 2008). In December 2008, local politicians in El Paso, Texas sent a letter to President-elect Obama asking him to stop the fence because it was "ill conceived and an irresponsible expense" (*AP*, December 3, 2008). None of this mattered to DHS Secretary Chertoff.

Not only do such strategies as LIC and counterintelligence care little about lawless activity, but they have no qualms overriding the rule of law, which is where concern over sovereignty comes in. Once law authorizes the application of sovereign authority, the latter steps outside its restrictive parameters. When it comes to the border fence, the DHS used the law, the Real ID Act, to sidestep 36 federal laws. It also walked around the Secure Fence Act to forcibly take property from private and public owners without first consulting with them over just compensation. Finally, the DHS asserted sovereignty in the face of international law, which imposed human rights concerns on the debate over the fence construction.

The great menace left behind by construction of the pedestrian border fence is the combination of sovereign power and corporate control. These issues transcend the wall itself, because they have a negative impact on everyone. I say this because the deconstitutionalized zone created by the exercise of sovereignty at the border allows DHS to ignore the rights of border residents to be secure in their persons and property. This sovereignty claim conveys the message that the U.S. government can get away with almost anything. In the film *Malcolm X*, Spike Lee has Malcolm X saying that unlike the pilgrims who landed on Plymouth Rock, for black people, "We didn't land on Plymouth Rock. Plymouth Rock landed on us." Truer words could not be said of the situation at the border, again.

Chapter 7

The Federalization of Sovereign Control

Outsourcing Immigration Enforcement Authority to State and Local Officials

Introduction

Since 9/11 a great deal of attention has been placed on immigration enforcement as a pro-security tenet of the war on terror. In the months and years following the tragedy, the DHS lacked resources and was stretched thin by the demands the war on terror placed on its immigration agents. As a result, individual states and local law enforcement donned their ICE caps and began to enforce federal immigration laws, directly through 287(g) MOUs and indirectly though local anti-immigrant ordinances. This chapter addresses the controversy of federal preemption and immigration policy. Historically, immigration has been a federal matter. Since Proposition 187 passed in California, and more dramatically since 9/11, states and local governments have gotten themselves involved in regulating immigration. Both 287(g) authority and anti-immigrant ordinances are part of the post-9/11 wave of state and local control of immigration that was unleashed as a result of the April 2002 Bybee Memo, which heralded the "inherent sovereignty" of states to regulate immigration. Like the anti-immigrant ordinances, the Bybee Memo misreads the constitution and is bad policy. But it served as a catalyzing force among anti-immigrant forces around the country to mobilize against immigrants with the federal government's blessing.

In this chapter, I also argue that the federalization of immigration control follows the logic of a risk society, which relies upon the notion of preemption in its social, as opposed to legal sense (Amoore & de Goede, 2008). This logic suggests the legal order must be broken in order to preserve the social order (Amoore & de Goede, 2008, p. 16). Such federalization creates what Judith Butler refers to as "petty sovereignties," which denote the immigration officials, mid-level bureaucrats and private actors who render unilateral and unaccountable preemptive security decisions (Amoore & de Goede, 2008, p. 13). "Petty sovereigns abound, reigning in the midst of bureaucratic ... institutions mobilized by aims and tactics of power they do not inaugurate or fully control" (Butler, 2004, p. 56). I suggest that the federalization of immigration is a social risk strategy, that following Amoore and de Goede, "enables petty sovereigns to do their work and accords them a semblance of objectivity and scientific certainty" (2008, p. 13). This is done through the deployment of risk technologies. Risk technologies are deployed on the basis of following the logic of security rather than law. It permits state and local actors to engage in extra-legal activities that Richard Ericson refer to as "counter law" (2009). Hence, I shall argue that the federalization of immigration control, specifically in terms of the Bybee Memo, 287(g), the Alien Absconder Initiative and local ordinances provides incentives for local actors to act preemptively against immigrants, and to monitor and pursue them as prospective criminals.

In May, 2006, after more than 1 million undocumented immigrants and their supporters marched on America's streets as part of the "A Day Without" boycotts (see Chapter 8), hundreds of local and state anti-immigrant ordinances started being introduced in city councils and state legislatures around the country. And after attempts at comprehensive immigration reform failed in 2006 and 2007, state and local police along with ICE once again stepped up their raids on immigrant workplaces and neighborhoods. The federal government, it seems has deputized state and local governments as "petty sovereigns" when it comes to enforcing immigration law. Thus I also suggest that state and local interest in regulating immigration has served the larger immigration control objectives of the federal government.

In this chapter, I examine how federalizing immigration was an important tool in the construction of the immigration control regime. Specifically it extended executive enforcement power into local police departments and town halls. It also helped privatize risk, which is an integral part of the immigration control regime that I discussed in Chapter 1. Finally, the federalization of immigration control also established a racialized space[1] wherein Latinos and people of Middle Eastern descent were subordinated as other. After discussing the background of state powers of enforcement over immigration, and a brief historical look at how states have regulated immigration, I shall focus on specific policies, initiatives, and programs of the Bush administration that advances the basic tenets of immigration control on the backs of state and local government. In particular, I shall focus on the Alien Absconder Initiative; Bybee memo; 287(g) of the 1996 Immigration Act, and state and local anti-immigrant ordinances.

Throughout American history, states have frequently served as a laboratory for the government to experiment in social policy. Since 9/11, states have become a laboratory for the Bush administration to experiment with its specious thesis on unitary executive power, which augmented executive power while diminishing immigrant rights. Within short order, a federalization regime emerged, integrating attributes of sovereignty, neoliberal risk management, and now federalism.

Background

As discussed in Chapter 2, the federal government has plenary power over immigration, which gives it the power to prescribe rules as to which aliens may enter the US and which ones may stay and be removed. These powers of sovereignty originate with the federal government. The Congress has exclusive authority to prescribe procedures for determining the right of aliens in immigration proceedings, subject to the rights that aliens as persons enjoy under the Constitution. The recognition of federal plenary power over immigration leaves little wiggle room for states, unless you examine the authority to enforce immigration rules, which is not exclusive to the federal government.

As Congress has codified its own plenary power over immigration in the Immigration and Naturalization Act (INA),[2] it consists of both criminal and civil enforcement measures. Historically, states have possessed some authority to enforce criminal provisions of the INA, mostly in terms of cooperating with the federal government in criminal investigations. But enforcement of civil provisions has been an exclusively federal responsibility, with states playing a mere supporting role.

Local law enforcement can enforce federal laws under specific, limited conditions, most notably when there is a formal memorandum of understanding (MOU) between the DHS and the state and state and local police receive training. This procedure is known as a state's 287(g) enforcement authority, which I discuss below.[3]

Since mere illegal presence in the US is a civil offense, the federal government holds the responsibility to apprehend and remove deportable aliens.[4] In some circumstances, states and local governments may enforce criminal immigration laws that include smuggling and harboring of certain undocumented immigrants,[5] and re-entry after being previously excluded or deported.[6] This means that federal agents can identify, roundup, detain, and remove suspected undocumented immigrants. State police can arrest non-citizens they observe crossing the border for a second or more time.

The courts have supported the idea that states can enforce criminal immigration laws. In the Ninth Circuit case of *Gonzales v. City of Peoria*,[7] the court examined the city of Peoria's ordinance that authorized local police to arrest illegal immigrants for violating the criminal entry provision of the INA (8 USC 1324). The court held that local police officers may, subject to state law, stop or detain individuals when there was reasonable suspicion or, in the case of arrests, probable cause that such persons had violated, or are violating, the criminal provision of the INA.[8] In its opinion, the court established a clear demarcation between criminal and civil law enforcement, saying:

> We assume that the civil provisions of the Act regulating authorized entry, length of stay, residence status, and deportation, constitute such a pervasive

regulatory scheme, as would be consistent with the exclusive federal power over immigration. However, this case [Gonzales] does not concern that broad scheme, but only a narrow and distinct element of it—the regulation of criminal immigration activity by aliens.[9]

Since it is almost impossible to identify an individual as an "illegal alien" without actually observing him/her cross the border or some objective evidence, it is likely that police enforcement of civil immigration laws would bleed into racial and ethnic profiling. Incredibly, as the Alien Absconder Initiative and Operation Endgame discussed below, show, such racial profiling was at the heart of an immense effort at federalizing immigration control (Miller, 2005). In terms of the law, the query remains as to how local police have knowledge that someone standing on a street corning or living in a particular neighborhood in the past illegally crossed the border. In terms of risk management, however, this query opens the door to incredible opportunities for surveillance firms and military contractors.

The larger issue has to do with federal preemption and immigration. The general rule is that since immigration is a federal matter, states and local governments lack the authority to get involved. As the Supreme Court has said, the "[p]ower to regulate immigration is unquestionably exclusively a federal power" (*DeCanas v. Bica*).[10] At the same time, however, the court "has never held that every state enactment which in any way deals with aliens is a regulation of immigration and thus per se pre-empted" (*DeCanas* at 355). Still, issues of consistency, uniformity, effectiveness of enforcement and infringing upon federal laws and basic civil rights all place the burden on states and local governments to carve out very narrow exceptions to this basic principle. In nearly all instances, states and local governments have failed the challenge.

Brief History of State Anti-Immigrant Ordinances

The history of local communities and governments acting against the "alien other" goes back a long way in American history, and will not be recounted here in detail. Its roots touch Cotton Mather and the seventeenth century New England Puritans living side by side with Native Americans, inspiring Robert Bellah to say, ". . . Nowhere more than in America has a universal conception of man existed side by side with such harsh and brutal exclusions" (Bellah, 1992, p. 88). During the eighteenth century, anti-immigrant legislation—post independence—began with the 1790 naturalization law, which prohibited nonwhite immigrants from becoming citizens. Its purpose was to bar the naturalization of blacks and indentured servants (Daniels, 2004, p. 7). This was followed by the Alien and Sedition Acts of 1798, which increased the period of residency prior to citizenship to 14 years, authorized the President to deport any alien considered dangerous to domestic peace, and empowered the President to expel citizens of a country at war with the United States. The presumed enemy here were French supporters (naturalized Americans, Americans of French ancestry) of Vice[11] President Thomas Jefferson, who would oppose and then beat John Adams in the 1800 election. Michael Rogin described these examples "of a dominant strand of thought in the eighteenth-century America hostile to political liberty" (Rogin, 1988, p. 56).

During the nineteenth century, the federal government lacked the resources and infrastructure to control immigrant populations, and so the states had the chore of regulating immigrants at ports of entry and inside their jurisdiction. All the while, nativist groups targeted Irish Catholic and other immigrants, and when they could, involved local law enforcement and legislatures to add legitimacy to their nativist vision of a homogenous America. During the 1840s–1850s, American nativism enjoyed a string of electoral success spear-headed by such third parties as the American party, which had as its main platform the total rejection of the foreigner (LeMay, 1987, p. 31). In 1849, the Order of the Star Spangled Banner was founded in New York. This secret patriotic society soon became known as the Know Nothing party. An anti-immigrant, anti-catholic party, it found some electoral success in Massachusetts, Pennsylvania, Rhode Island, New Hampshire, Connecticut, Delaware, Maryland, Kentucky, and Texas. In 1856, the year, James Buchanan became President, the Know Nothings ran former President Millard Fillmore as their candidate (LeMay, 1987, p. 32).

The ferocity of Know Nothings and similar groups led to fits of intense anti-immigrant violence, which intimidated and devastated Irish and later Chinese communities, but this ferocity was not systematic. It wasn't until the 1850s and 1860s when state governments started enacting anti-immigrant ordinances that this ferocity began to translate into wholesale marginalization and exclusion. By the 1860s, Know Nothing candidates were being elected across the country. By the late 1860s, a Know-Nothing state Supreme Court judge in California ruled that Chinese were forbidden to testify against a white man. California became the incubator for anti-immigrant repression. In 1855, the California "foreign miner's tax," a $4 per month tax, effectively expelled Chinese immigrants from mining work camps. In 1862, the "anti coolie" Act taxed the labor of Chinese workers, requiring a $2.50/month work permit for all workers over 18 of the "Mongolian Race." Invidious legislation also included discriminatory labor laws, public health circulars, anti-miscegenation laws, and residential segregation laws. Chinese were expelled from public schools, forbidden to marry whites, and couldn't testify in court against whites (LeMay, 1987, p. 53).

The twentieth century, actually starting with the Haymarket Square Massacre in the late nineteenth century, offered up the idea of the radical scapegoat, typically an immigrant agitator committed to the overthrow of free and democratic institutions. Local anti-immigrant ordinances draw their normative weight from this tradition. The particulars of the state action were less important than the general mood it created, which led to the desired fear and intimidation. Thus the constitutionality of anti-immigrant ordinances mattered less than the fact that these ordinances further the anti-immigrant agenda.

As for the legality of state ordinances, it is clear that state and local anti-immigrant ordinances might have been found constitutional had they been enacted prior to 1850. Since 1849, however, the Court has been consistent about the principle of federal supremacy over immigration. But even though states like California, or only California, created an anti-immigrant regime that prevented immigrants from participating in civil society (marriage, home ownership, schools, and punitive taxes), local economies continued to exploit immigrants for their cheap labor.

Local and state governments enforced immigration policy as a matter of course largely because no federal state infrastructure existed to enforce federal policy. During these decades until the 1870s, the states were pretty much in charge of immigrants entering their ports of call. In the 1820s, several states imposed inspection, taxation and bond posting schemes designed to care for and later to deter immigrant paupers from entering the country. In 1824, for example, New York became the first state to fund programs for immigrant paupers, and pass the cost on to the immigrant. The state created a bond-posting scheme in which each vessel posted bond for each passenger on board unable to care for herself. Local and state authorities also required ship captains to pass along the passenger lists to local authorities to assist with record-keeping.

In *NY v. Miln*,[12] the Supreme Court upheld this practice by distinguishing between state and local policing power on the one hand, and the federal government's constitutional responsibilities over regulating foreign commerce. States could regulate immigration because it was a policing matter, not a matter of commerce (Koulish, 1996, p. 143). During the same period, other states introduced head tax schemes, which required each immigrant to pay a certain amount upon arrival at U.S. ports of entry. The tax funds were ostensibly to defray the costs of providing medical and other social benefits for arriving immigrants before they settled into their new homes and communities. A similar bonding measure required medical exams of each arriving immigrant aboard the vessel before disembarkation. Upon finding lunatics, idiots, maimed, aged or inform persons, the state imposed a bond on the ship's captain as insurance that these people wouldn't become public charges within ten years of arrival.

It wasn't until the late nineteenth century, when the federal government began to establish a federal infrastructure for immigration, that anti-immigrant nativism stood a chance of becoming systematic. The premise for the federal immigration infrastructure was that the nexus between immigration and foreign policy was too close to leave it to the whims of individual states. Since foreign vessels entering U.S. ports required a uniform response from the government, it was assumed that immigration would be considered a wholly federal matter. In a second series of cases to come before the Supreme Court, the court found that immigrants were to be treated as commerce as far as the law was concerned, and thus regulation of immigrants was a federal concern. In the Passenger cases (*Smith v. Turner and Norris v. City of Boston*) the court ruled that the state head tax and bonding schemes were in conflict with the Congress' "exclusive power to regulate commerce" (Passenger cases).[13]

At no time since 1849 has the court entertained the idea that regulating immigration was an inherent state power. That didn't stop the states from applying pressure on the federal government to assume control over immigration. In a manner not unlike the current situation, states initiated mostly symbolic gestures to spur the federal government into action. For example, in New York City, local authorities threatened to close Castle Garden, the foremost disembarkation center for immigrants in the country, unless the federal government enacted comprehensive immigration reform (Tichenor, 2002, p. 46). By 1875, and still more by 1882, the federal government had to develop an infrastructure capable of keeping track of incoming immigrants at ports of entry and final destinations. Over a century later, Proposition 187, again in California, the states once again would begin to jockey with the federal government over regulating immigration.

Before 2002, states were constrained by due process and equal protection when they interacted with immigrants. The general rule was that "the federal government alone controls immigration law, whereas states and localities may play at least some role, consistent with the Equal Protection Clause, in the regulation of non-citizens once they are in the country" (Huntington, 2008, p. 9). In fact, scholars distinguished between immigration law (a matter of national sovereignty), and immigrant law (dealing with immigrants within state and local jurisdictions), in order to emphasize the difference between the two sources of power. Immigrant law recognizes constitutional norms, which are nowhere to be found when the federal government wields sovereign power (Huntington, 2008, p. 7).

Since 1996,[14] but more specifically since 2001, Congress has extended the authority of states and local government to enforce civil provisions, which involve identifying and detaining immigrants for purposes of removal. But during this period, the Clinton Memo imagined that states could enforce federal law as long as they were not precluded from doing so by either the words or structure of federal regulatory interests. In other words, the states would be limited by the words or intent of the federal statute. Were a conflict to exist between federal and state interests, the former would prevail, such as in the case of having state and local governments enforce civil immigration law.

Alien Absconder Initiative

In December 2001, as part of its Alien Absconder Initiative,[15] the INS announced it would begin deporting an estimated 400,000 non-citizens within five years. Almost immediately it began sending names of thousands of non-citizens to the FBI's NCIC database,[16] which is available to state and local law enforcement and thus serves as a "force multiplier,"[17] and local law enforcement started detaining and deporting immigrants.[18] The Absconder Apprehension Initiative was followed by the federal government mandate, "Operation Endgame," that proposed to "remove all removable aliens" from the United States by 2012 (www.visalaw.com/04jun3/15jun304.html). Seeking to deport an estimated 400,000 non-citizens within five years in December 2003, DHS expanded its detention capacity by 8,000 beds, bringing the number of detention beds up to 30,000. To expand its detention capacity, DHS entered into contracts with CCA and Wackenhut, which then set about meeting the DHS demand (Miller, 2005).

If taken seriously, the Endgame challenge was immense. Since the federal government lacked the infrastructure and resources to remove 12–14 million undocumented immigrants, other government powers would have to be unleashed; the federal government's sovereign power over immigration would have to be somehow extended. The Operation Endgame mandate gave state and law enforcement a great deal of discretion with which to enforce federal immigration laws. When local officials overreached in terms of their pursuit of immigrants the federal government typically failed to rein them in or hold them accountable.

Bybee Memo

While Alien Absconder and Operation Endgame created the mandate to remove immigrants and gave state and local police access to information about immigrants, the Bybee Memo reinterpreted existing immigration federalism policy by recognizing the inherent authority of states to enforce immigration law. Since both the courts and Congress had been wary of recognizing state authority to enforce civil immigration law, the executive branch needed to find some creative justification for having local police help roundup and then detain some 12 million undocumented immigrants. This creative interpretation ignored judicial precedent and diminished congress plenary powers over immigration. Incredibly, it recognized in the states almost the same powers it had usurped for itself in the war on terror, inherent (sovereign) authority.

While the Bybee Memo never enjoyed the force of law, like a statute or court decision, its importance derives from its support across the Bush administration as a declaration of policy. More likely, it unleashed the state and local forces of counter law over immigrants (Ericson, 2008). The first public word of this memo came during a 2002 press conference by Attorney General John Ashcroft, who said:

When federal, state and local law enforcement officers encounter an alien of national security concern who has been listed on the NCIC for violating immigration law, federal law permits them to arrest that person and transfer him to the custody of the INS. The Justice Department's Office of Legal Counsel has concluded that this narrow, limited mission that we are asking state and local police to undertake voluntarily — arresting aliens who have violated criminal provisions of the Immigration and Nationality Act or civil provisions that render an alien deportable, and who are listed on the NCIC — is within the inherent authority of states.[19]

Soon after Ashcroft's news conference, then White House Counsel Albert Gonzales acknowledged the "inherent authority" argument that made the Bybee memo so controversial.[20] In other words the Bush team had coalesced around this misinterpretation of law.

On April 3, 2002, Jay Bybee, Assistant Attorney General, Office of Legal Counsel (OLC), issued an opinion that negated the Clinton administration reasoning regarding enforcement of civil immigration law. Soon after 287(g) was enacted, the Clinton administration's Assistant Legal Counsel issued a memo reinforcing the powers of state and local police to "enforce federal statutes where such enforcement activities do not impair federal regulatory interests. This general principle extends to state enforcement of the Immigration and naturalization Act" (Aleinikoff, 2002, p. 1020). The Clinton Memo also placed unambiguous restrictions on the states and local governments regarding enforcement of civil immigration law. Citing an earlier 1989 memo (from the OLC), the Clinton Memo said,

> We first expressed our belief that "the mere existence of a warrant of deportation for an alien does not provide sufficient probable cause to conclude that the criminal provisions (of the INA) have in fact been violated . . . Taking all these authorities into account, we conclude that state and local police lack recognized legal authority to stop and detain an alien solely on suspicion of civil deportability, as opposed to a criminal violation of the immigration laws or other laws (Aleinikoff, 2002).

restrictions

According to the Bybee Immigration Memo in 2002, individual states could *conditions* enforce federal civil immigration law if the following conditions were met: 1) actions taken by the state were authorized by state law, and 2) were not preempted by federal law. The Bybee Memo found inherent sovereign authority in the states' police power:

> We believe that the answer to this question rests ultimately on the State's status as sovereign entities. The Declaration of Independence proclaims that the States are "FREE AND INDEPENDENT STATES . . . and

that as FREE AND INDEPENDENT STATES, they have full Power to levy War, conclude Peace, contract Alliances, establish Commerce, and to do all other Acts and Things which INDEPENDENT STATES may of right do.

(Aleinikoff, 2002, p. 1021)

With this memo, Bybee ripped a huge hole in the federal government's supremacy over immigration matters. Such inherent authority recognizes a great deal of sovereign authority in states and local sheriff's offices to investigate, pursue, detain and remove immigrants. More than that, were it taken seriously, individual states would function like independent sovereigns—similar to Mexico or Canada enforcing U.S. immigration law while adhering to their own sovereign procedures, assuming such procedures exist (ACLU, 2005).

In other to justify his plan, Bybee manipulated several long held legal tenets of federalism. He drew on the tenth amendment for example, to describe such power as inherent:

The United States Constitution conferred on Congress only the powers "herein granted," U.S. Const. at 1 Sec. 1, and "reserved to the States respectively, or to the people, the "powers not delegated to the United States by the Constitution, nor prohibited by it to the States," (amd X). Thus, although the Constitution did not impose some disabilities on the States, it did not purport to confer, or otherwise be the source of their affirmative authority.

The inherent powers argument blurs the line between quintessentially state powers—such as police powers—and federal immigration powers. Were immigration powers actually an inherent power, then presumably New Mexico could build a fence at the border while Arizona did not; Texas could round up and imprison all border crossers, while New Mexico set them all free and gave them services and jobs. The implication is absurd. The inherent powers doctrine, as opposed to those that are the result of a deliberate act of delegation, would give states the power to define their own immigration enforcement agenda. The theory transcends immigration. States and local jurisdictions could claim authority to enforce any federal law—civil or criminal— that is, they could order arrests for civil infractions of federal statutes that do not call for such enforcement. Imagine local police hunting down suspected tax violators, or violators of environmental, food safety, or education statutes.

Bybee's argument subverts Article II, Section 3, of the Constitution, which says the President is obliged to ensure the responsible implementation of federal statutes. Unfettered state and local immigration enforcement authority simply does not comport with the President's obligation to "take care" that federal law is "faithfully executed" (the President, it says, "shall take Care that the

Laws be faithfully executed," (Article II, Section 3), personally and through officers whom he appoints (see ACLU Brief of Bybee Memo):

> The idea that each state and local jurisdiction could follow its own path executing federal law does not comport with the Constitution's Supremacy Clause, which gives the federal government the power to "preempt" any state or local immigration arrest authority.[21]

Quite the opposite; the logic of sovereignty for each state holds that the federal government could not preempt police enforcement of civil immigration laws, and under Bybee's interpretation, Congress "has not" preempted police enforcement of civil immigration laws.

In fact, Bybee's "discovery" of inherent state powers[22] actually extends the federal government's mandate over immigrants and immigration by other means. The states and local governments could now function as tentacles of federal power without the federal government assuming responsibility for the actions taken by these government units (Rodriguez, 2008, p. 1254). If the war on terror was a wholesale subversion of the constitution, as many scholars now argue,[23] and if memos coming out of the OLC during this period were providing legal justification for it, then perhaps Bybee imagined that state and local law enforcement would now think of themselves as federal agents. Gone would be the separate missions for federal agents and state and local police. Gone too would be the idea that local and state police were prevented by law from stopping someone on the street on the basis of mere appearance and inquiring about their citizenship status without first articulating an individualized suspicion of wrongdoing.

The "inherent sovereign authority" for states over immigration should be interpreted merely as another outsourcing opportunity, where the federal government both assumes power and abdicates responsibility by having another body do its dirty work. By recognizing the "inherent authority" of states over matters that previously had been almost universally considered to be federal jurisdiction, the Bybee memo created a new place for immigration enforcement to hide out, in county sheriff and local police offices.

Why would the Bush DOJ release states from Federal Supremacy and Article II, Section 3 constraints at a time when it was simultaneously seeking to enhance and consolidate federal executive power? The context during this timeframe was the "war on terror." The OLC was the office that provided legal justification for the "unitary executive theory," which the administration hoped, would provide it the powers to act with impunity against real and imagined enemies. Four months after issuing the Bybee Memo, Bybee co-authored and issued the notorious "Torture Memo" with Jonathan Yoo[24] Although the facts of the torture memo are dramatically different than the facts related to state enforcement of civil immigration law, the structure of the memos is similar. Both focus on inherent and sovereign powers that are unchecked by constitutional constraint. It is important to note that both memos develop an argument for sovereign power, and both dismiss the importance of constitutional checks on executive powers.

Thus it is not unreasonable to suggest that the April 3, 2002 Bybee Immigration Memo advances the Unitary Executive Power thesis of government, which helped the administration to justify torture in the name of liberty. It was part of a larger crusade to obviate constitutional constraints on executive power, remove the legislature from its constitutional role of checking executive power, and create the infrastructure of a police state, again in the war against terror. Bybee advances the idea that the Bush administration doesn't need to rely on the supremacy clause or Article II, Section 3 to exert its control over state and local police. Rather, it had the entire regime at its disposal, including a war on terror ideology, a wartime budget, intelligence-led policing, counterintelligence technologies and resources.

This is dangerous on several grounds. Although Bybee's memo did not refer to 287(g) by name, it changed how state and local law enforcement would interpret 287(g), with dangerous consequences: no more constitutional constraint when using state and local police power against immigrants. While it is difficult to imagine that Bybee really means to say that states possess such inherent powers, the ACLU and La Raza lawyers who successfully sued the DOJ to release the Memo suggest that this exactly is what the Memo infers.

IIRIRA Section 287(g)

Since much of this discussion about the federalization of immigration authority has to do with federal preemption, and Bybee's utter disregard for it, it is important to mention that few scholars challenge the validity of state authority over immigration when such authority is granted by an act of Congress, which is the case with 287(g) authority. In 1996, the Congress amended the INA to include section 287(g), which authorizes ICE to enter into agreements (memorandum of understanding, MOU/MOA) with state and local law enforcement agencies, thereby deputizing local police to act as immigration officers (Weissman, 2009; Aleinikoff, 2002, p. 1015). The 287g program is intended to target and remove undocumented immigrants convicted of "violent crimes, human smuggling, gang/organized crime activity, sexual-related offenses, narcotics smuggling and money laundering."[25]

Police authority under 287(g) allows law enforcement to engage in immigration functions related to identification, processing, and detention of immigrants, which includes the power to arrest and transfer, to investigate immigration violations, collect evidence, and assemble an immigration case for prosecution or removal (Kobach, 2005, p. 2). However, such authority was limited: "Police can only use 287(g) authority when people are taken into custody as a result of violating state or local criminal law"[26] (Aleinikoff, 2002, p. 1015). As an ICE fact sheet says, "[t]he 287g program is not designed to allow state and local agencies to perform random street operations," and "is not designed to impact issues such as excessive occupancy and day laborer activities" (ICE Fact Sheet, September 24, 2007). Many local communities were sold on 287(g) as a vehicle for targeting dangerous criminals, and violent repeat offenders (Fahim, 2007).

Although 287(g) is a provision of the 1996 law, the first 287(g) MOU was issued six years later to the state of Florida in September 2002.[27] By this time, the Bybee Memo had replaced the 1996 Clinton Memo as the guiding interpretive text, and expanded the scope and autonomy of a state's power to enforce immigration law. Since then, ICE has trained 951 state and local law enforcement officers in 67 agencies. As far as Bybee articulated the Bush vision, local and state authorities could enforce criminal and civil immigration laws with virtual impunity. The message to state and local law enforcement was that overly zealous enforcement and subsequent abuses would not be closely monitored, which turned out to be somewhat prophetic.[28]

In this regard, 287(g) must be interpreted as allowing the federal government to double-down on immigration enforcement inside the country's borders by deputizing state and local police to enforce federal immigration law. This localization of the criminalization of immigration must also be interpreted as a deliberate weapon in the federal government's "war on terror," which brings a panoply of technologies to bear against immigrants and places them in the hands of "petty sovereigns," who render unilateral and unaccountable preemptive security decisions (Butler, 2004, p. 56).

In many respects, 287(g) also functions as "counter law" (2008), which "flourishes in this political culture of precautionary logic and war on everything" (2008, p. 62). Considering the timing of the first 287(g) MOUs in 2002 coming closely on the heels of the Bybee Memo, it is useful to interpret the flourishing of 287(g) MOUs during this period in terms of "preemptive security," which Ericson says "is based on a precautionary logic that normalizes suspicion." Most of the local petty sovereigns who received 287(g) MOUs, applied for them on the basis of a perceived threat that immigrants brought to their communities. Although the perceived immigrant threat was described in terms of immigrant criminality, as Jonathan Simon notes, after 9/11, the line between the war on crime and war on terror had become blurred (2009). Ericson's argument is that a post-9/11 mode of risk sanctions a society where "the legal order must be broken to secure the social order" (Amoore & de Goede, 2008, p. 16).

In this section, I argue that 287(g) weakened the widely held belief in the preemption of federal immigration law. This set the stage for the 2006–2007 avalanche of local anti-immigrant ordinances introduced in local councils across the country.

Although 287(g) is intended to assist federal authorities enforcing criminal laws, the GAO in March 2009 reported that ICE has failed to provide state and local partners with clearly defined objectives for the program or to create a consistent system for supervising them.[29] As a result, it noted widespread confusion among 287(g) participants in terms of the purpose of the program (Aizenman, March 4, 2009).

According to a recent policy brief by the University of North Carolina and the ACLU, "the 287(g) program functions as a deportation program largely unrelated to crime or national security" (Weissman, 2009, p. 16). Rather than safeguarding against the violent repeat offender, data reveals that most undocumented immigrants caught as a result of 287 authority are charged with traffic infractions and low level misdemeanors (Tomsic, 2008). Further, many such traffic stops occur on roads that provide access into Latino neighborhoods and churches (Weissman, 2009). According to the GAO, one sheriff told the GAO that he understood his authority was that "287(g) trained officers could go to people's homes and question individuals regarding their immigration status even if the individual is not suspected of criminal activity" (Aizenman, 2009).

According to the UNC brief, ". . . MOUs are in actuality being used to purge towns and cities of unwelcome immigrants and thereby have detrimental effects on . . . communities" (Weissman, 2009, p. 8). Indeed efforts to purge towns of "unwelcome immigrants" are advanced by the conservative local politics that led to most of the 287(g) MOUs applied for in the first place.[30] In such places, like Maricopa County, Arizona, or Alamance County, North Carolina, for example, as Weissman documents, the 287(g) MOU gave local law enforcement license to target entire communities. As Deborah Weissman says:

> In some places in North Carolina, local elected officials, including those who have signed or supported 287(g) agreements, have contributed to nativist sentiment and have publicly expressed views that have denigrated immigrants regardless of their status based on racist stereotypes and baseless assumptions.
>
> (Weissman, April 2, 2009)

According to anthropologist Hannah Gill[31] who has studied the reactions to immigrant newcomers to Alamance County, North Carolina, Alamance County had a storied racist, anti-immigrant past before applying for a 287(g) MOU. For example, Alamance county politicians called for a moratorium on immigration to the county, referred to immigrant newcomers as "aliens and invaders who have taken over state agencies," and one county court interpreter resigned after "posting racist and anti-immigrant statements on the website of a white supremacist magazine"[32] (Weissman, April 2, 2009, p. 10). The pattern of anti-immigrant racism is repeated in other 287(g) venues.

The report finds that 287(g) has been implemented without proper regard for due process and the rule of law,[33] and impedes important interactions that local police need to have with residents in their jurisdiction.

The UNC/ACLU findings were reinforced and supplemented by recent hearings before the House Judiciary Subcommittee on Immigration,[34] which highlighted specific problems with 287(g). According to Mesa Arizona Police Chief George Gascon, who testified at the hearing, 287(g) fails because it does little to reduce serious, violent crime. House subcommittee member Jerry Nadler (D-NY) added that during the tenure of 287(g) agreements, crime actually increased in areas like Maricpoa County, Arizona[35] (Staff & Mahendra, 2009). In some significant part, crime increases because residents lose trust in police and fail to report crime.[36]

UNC law professor Deborah Weissman draws attention to this phenomenon using an example of domestic abuse crimes. She refers to a recent amendment in the INA that allows battered immigrant women to circumvent normal procedures for obtaining legal status, which is through the spouse.[37] In such instances, however, these women must rely on the police intervention and documentation of the abuse, which is then used in the process of obtaining legal status. Problems occur, and domestic abuse goes under reported, when local police also serve as deputized immigration officers. In this instance when local police responsibilities contract with 287(g) responsibilities, the victimization of battered women is intensified as women feel they must choose between further domestic abuse or deportation (Weissman, 2009).

As law professor David Harris further suggested:

> moving our state and local police into the business of immigration enforcement risks the gains we have made against crime over the last fifteen years, and creates significant new perils for the men and women who dedicate themselves to public safety.
>
> (House Hearings, April 2, 2009)

Another counter law example in 287(g) enforcement is racial profiling, which occurs when people feel they are being randomly pulled over because of the color of their skin. According to the ACLU:

> Available statistical data suggests that 287(g)-deputized officers are using race or Latino appearance to stop, question and arrest for immigration related offenses. Moreover, pending litigation, news reports and other reported evidence further suggest that 287(g) agreements are leading to racial profiling.
>
> (ACLU, March 4, 2009)

Perhaps nowhere are such targeted stops more prolific than in Maricopa County, Arizona, where Sheriff Joe Arpaio "disingenuously call(s) his roundups of Mexicans "crime suppression sweeps" (Stern, May 16, 2008). Typically, vehicle stops have targeted, stopped, interrogated, detained or arrested Latino persons based on their race, color and/or ethnicity, without probable cause or reasonable suspicion that they had committed any crime. In Maricopa County, deputies typically stop cars without articulating suspicion, and they come up with "probable cause" later on. According to a *Phoenix News Times* investigation, "Arpaio teamed up with (the local county attorney) to prosecute average illegal immigrants as smugglers, and deputies rounded up corn vendors and other run-of-the-mill illegals who happened to be driving dilapidated vehicles" (Stern, May 14, 2008).

Members of the House Immigration Subcommittee heard testimony from Julio Cesar Mora, a 19-year-old native-born U.S. citizen who told of how he and his father, a green card holder since 1976, were stopped in their car on the way to work, patted down, handcuffed and taken to a place where many workers were being held by officers in black uniform and ski masks. After several hours Julio and his father were released:

> To this day, I don't know why the officers stopped us out of all the cars on the road. Maybe it was because of the Campesina radio sticker on our bumper or maybe it was because my dad was wearing his Mexican tejana and thought we were illegal . . . They took away our pride.
>
> (Lemons, April 2, 2009)

In some instances local police get carried away all together. Once Maricopa County's MOU went into effect in January 2007, the Sheriff's Office (MCSO) transformed into a local law enforcement arm of ICE. Emboldened by his 287(g) authority, Sheriff Arpaio quickly embarked on an anti-immigrant campaign that included workplace and neighborhood sweeps, and which resulted in gross violations of law.

In one egregious example, in the middle of the night on October 16, 2008, Arpaio, along with thirty deputy sheriffs and thirty members of a volunteer posse, carrying weapons and wearing flak jackets, raided City Hall and the library in Mesa, Maricopa County, Arizona. Ostensibly, they were following through on a tip that illegal immigrants were inside the building working as janitors on a cleaning crew. The 60 heavily armed alien-busters, with dogs, arrested three suspected Mexicans employed to empty trashcans (Lacey, November 27, 2008). According to the Mesa Police chief, however, Arpaio's deputies had entered the city and the building without probable cause and without notifying his department of the pending raid, a situation that endangered public safety.

This raid in Mesa was merely one of many such raids that have been conducted on government buildings, amusement parks, workplaces and individual homes, in which Arpaio's deputies and his "posse" search for undocumented immigrants and people who look like them.

Finally, the MOA also gives states and local enforcement access to federal databases (NCIC). As it is argued, such access to national databases gives local police the ability to ascertain an individual's immigration status within a matter of minutes. Studies show it actually, "may take several days to figure out if someone is a citizen, depending on when born, when parents were born and what laws were in effect at that time" (Weissman, 2009). Thus the 287(g) MOU is not even an effective instrument for determining whether someone is lawfully in this country or who has immigration violation or what status of the case is.

Anti-Immigrant Ordinances

Not all anti-immigrant policies in small communities are the result of agreements with the federal government. Since 2006, more than 1,500 local anti-immigrant ordinances have been introduced in local and state legislatures around the country. These ordinances endeavor to create petty sovereignties where local governmental (police, department of motor vehicle clerks) and non-government actors (employers, landlords) come to exercise incredible powers over immigrants and force them to leave their communities (Butler, 2004).

These ordinances also function as "counter-law" (Ericson, 2008). The point that the ordinances are manifestly impractical and unconstitutional provides the "tell" to the "state of exception" (Agamben, 2005). The idea is to extend the post-9/11 security regime into the nooks and crannies of small town America using risk management technologies. Designed as these ordinances are upon Jay Bybee's designation of a state's inherent powers to enforce federal immigration law, the ordinances must be interpreted within the context of the larger political operations of spring/summer 2002 "war on terror" in the Bush OLC. The OLC was in the midst of issuing a series of "counter-law" memos that replaced legal logic (no torture), which in the immigration instance also includes federal preemption, with the logic of preemptive activities against prospective terrorists. Thus while seeming to relinquish federal control over immigration in the legal sense, anti-immigrant ordinances helped the federal government to extend its social preemption against immigrants in the security sense.

Most of the anti-immigrant ordinances seem poorly devised. They take Bybee's promise of "inherent powers" at face value and follow a template that blatantly violates the constitution; advances the right wing anti-immigrant agenda articulated by the anti-immigrant organization FAIR (discussed below); and is embraced by local moral entrepreneurs who readily scapegoat immigrants for their own short term political self-interest. They also place a huge amount of risk on the backs of politically powerful constituencies, ill advised to say the least, who inevitably oppose them in court; and are counterproductive to local economies that enact them. In other words, the ordinances almost seem like they were intended to fail, which they were in some sense.

After the May Day demonstrations of 2006, FAIR (Federation of American Immigration Reform), the hub of the country's anti-immigrant network, created an anti-immigrant ordinance template[38] that would be used as the basis for several hundred anti-immigrant ordinances across the country.

FAIR is a right-wing anti-immigrant non-profit organization. It was founded in 1979 by John Tanton, whose perspective on immigration is highlighted in a 1997 quote to the *Detroit Free Press*, which said that if U.S. borders are not secured, America will be overrun by people "defecating and creating garbage and looking for jobs."[39] Its stated mission is to "improve border security," to stop illegal immigration, and "to promote immigration levels consistent with the national interest," which means a national moratorium on legal immigration.

FAIR has easy access to local, state, and federal office holders. Although these anti-immigrant ordinances differ in terms of specific provisions they share the same basic anti-immigrant template, dealing with landlords employers, police, bureaucrats, and municipal clerks, in the following ways. They can make English the official language of the municipality, eliminate gathering places for day laborers, penalize employers for hiring undocumented immigrants, restrict undocumented immigrants' access to public benefits, and prevent undocumented immigrants from renting housing (Oliveri, 2009).

The anti-immigrant ordinances[40] were so poorly written that they threatened to punish landlords and business owners for lax law enforcement without defining it. In addition to being poorly defined, provisions were vague[41] and overbroad.[42] Finally, and perhaps most important, as suggested above, they make enforcement agents out of landlords and shop owners, people who have no training, and have taken no oath to uphold the laws and see the laws are faithfully executed. They impose fines on landlords who rent to illegal immigrants and deny business permits to companies that give them jobs, and place burdens on business owners and landlords to investigate the immigration status of their employees and tenants. Not only is such delegation of authority illegal, it also is grossly impractical and surprisingly naive.

In the rental-housing domain, for example, immigration law professor Aaron Schwabach, notes that "landlords would be taking a big risk in renting to anyone who might turn out to be ineligible."[43] Since "it is difficult (if not impossible) . . . to verify the immigration status of every potential tenant they encounter" (Oliveri, 2009). The obvious questions arise: How to verify a person's eligibility? What guidelines to follow and what about people who are legally in the US but ineligible to work— foreign students, or long term-tourists, or people that adjust their immigrant status?

This leads property owners who are not necessarily racist to reject applicants they suspect could have immigration issues. Because of this risk, according to Oliveri, "[t]hey are instead likely to resort to shortcuts, such as discriminating based on accent, surname, appearance, or other ethnic markers," which leads to discrimination against people who look or sound foreign, and violates federal (housing) law and constitutional standards of preemption (Oliveri, 2009). The landlord is "at risk of running afoul of 3604(c), of the Fair Housing Act, which prohibits making statements that evince discrimination based on protected characteristic ... Simply making a remark that indicates preference or discrimination is sufficient to violate the statute" (Oliveri, 2009).

In complying with the terms of the ordinances, landlords and employers usurp the immigration judge role, which places them in even greater jeopardy. Federal immigration law provides the immigrant with several opportunities to seek relief from deportation. Once apprehended, a suspected undocumented immigrant has the right to a removal hearing. At such a hearing, once the immigrant admits and concedes deportability, the immigration judge at her discretion can order the immigrant's "relief from deportation." The immigrant's right to a removal hearing is nullified, however, when immigrants are tossed from jobs, removed from their residence and expelled from their communities prior to a removal hearing.

Landlords and employers have the Hobson's choice of running afoul of the ordinance or an avalanche of federal laws. In addition to concerns about being in legal jeopardy, landlords and employers also were concerned that the ordinance's divisive nature would destroy the community's business climate, which it did.[44] As local business owners and landlords felt the unintended consequences of the ordinance, and came to regret the unreasonable responsibilities the new law had placed on them, they turned to pro-immigrant legal defense organizations for legal assistance.

As a result of the enormous risk the townships had exposed them to, they filed suit, in town after town. According to the ACLU, "Business owners and landlords decided to sue because they felt the law is difficult to comply with and exposes them to enormous risk.[45] It could require them to take unreasonable and expensive measures and possibly invade the privacy of their clients in order to comply, all at great detriment to their businesses" (www. aclu-nj.org/news/aclunjjoinslocalcoalitiont.htm). With such assistance at hand, the way out of the double bind quickly became obvious, as the federal court in the Hazleton case eventually concluded.

In *Lozano v. City of Hazleton*, Judge Munley referred to Justice Harry Blackmun's decision in *Plyer v. Doe* for guidance. According to Blackmun, "the structure of the immigration statutes makes it impossible for the State to determine which aliens are entitled to residence, and which are eventually deported."[46] Munley agreed that the Hazleton ordinance violated the Supremacy Clause and said:

> We cannot say clearly enough that persons who enter this country without legal authorization are not stripped immediately of all their rights because of this single act ... The United States Supreme Court has consistently interpreted the 14th Amendment to apply to all people present in the United States, whether they were born here, immigrated here through legal means, or violated federal law to enter the country.[47]

Thus, local ordinances that conflict with federal law are unconstitutional. When landlords and employers are forced to comply with local ordinances, they violate the rights of immigrants, regardless of status, to live in federally-funded rental housing (24C.F.R. 5.508(e)), and to work until their removal hearing (8CFR 274a. 12(c)(8)-(11),(14)).

As I suggested above, it seems as if the ordinances intended to fail. They pit the local moral entrepreneurs against local economic elites where the former may want to exploit anti-immigrant hatred and fear to advance their own short-term political career, but the latter are forced to protect their own economic interests. In some instances such as in Riverside, New Jersey the landlords and business owners use their influence to convince the town councils to reverse course, but it is more typical for them to turn to the courts. Interestingly, the fight has little to do with immigrants and more to do with local political power and economic interest. At the local level, moral entrepreneurs win for losing because of the publicity garnered, while the landlords and employers are eventually vindicated in court. At the national level, the spectacle itself achieves the intended result, which is national attention to the cause and a growing fear of immigrants. This fear in turn sparks similar ordinances in other towns and inspires the intrusion of risk industries and technologies into these small communities.

As for the spectacle of the ordinance, consider how the moral entrepreneurs exploit gross stereotypes instead of rely on facts. In Valley Park, Missouri, Mayor Jeffrey Whitteaker defines the immigrant problem in Valley Park as follows: "You got one guy and his wife that settle down here, have a couple kids, and before long you have Cousin Puerto Rico and Taco Whoever moving in . . ." (Hinman, February 27, 2007). In this instance, the resulting ordinance imposed fines on landlords who rented to undocumented immigrants, and suspended the licenses of businesses that hired them. Whitteaker pushed the ordinance through the local Board of Alderman without any debate or research to support additional claims in the ordinance that "illegal immigration leads to higher crime rates, and contributes to overcrowded classrooms and failing schools" (Hinman, February 27, 2007). The facts of the matter pale beside the power of the risk narrative that is being spread: communities are at risk of being overrun by immigrants.

In Hazleton, Pennsylvania, Mayor Lou Barletta justified his town's anti-immigrant ordinance with similarly specious claims. According to the Hazleton ordinance:

> That unlawful employment, the harboring of illegal aliens in dwelling units in the City of Hazleton, and crime committed by illegal aliens harm the health, safety and welfare of authorized U.S. workers and legal residents in the City of Hazleton. Illegal immigration leads to higher crime rates, subjects our hospitals to fiscal hardship and legal residents to substandard quality of care, contributes to other burdens on public services, increasing

their cost and diminishing their availability to legal residents, and diminishes our overall quality of life.

In this instance, it doesn't really matter that when placed under oath the moral entrepreneurs concede the apocryphal nature of the anti-immigrant tale. When he was on the witness stand, for example, Barletta was forced to admit that he could not substantiate such claims. At trial:

> Barletta admitted he did not contact the school district to ask about alleged overcrowding, call the hospital for statistics on the treatment of illegal immigrants or seek any data to back up any of the claims. . . . "So you had no data on hospital treatments or other health care?" asked Walczak, legal director of the ACLU of Pennsylvania. "No," Barletta said. He had no data on any other city services, from sanitation to fire calls that could prove his contention that illegal immigrants were draining city services and the budget, Barletta said. But he claimed he didn't need statistics to point out what was obvious to him and other longtime Hazleton residents.
>
> (*Morning Call*, March 15, 2007)

As it turns out, the entire basis for the Hazleton ordinance was a lie. The crime rate in Hazleton actually decreased per capita during the previous five years. Hazleton's economic reality emerged during trial. Part of its resurgence had to do with the arrival of thousands of Hispanics after 2000 (*Morning Call*). The new arrivals propelled Hazleton's population upwards and ushered in a renaissance, as Hispanics bought and rehabilitated shuttered buildings and opened roughly 60 businesses. Assessed property values rose three years in a row. The hospital that allegedly struggled to provide services to illegal immigrants turned a $4 million profit in 2006 (ACLU blog).

Again, it didn't matter because the spectacle created around the Hazleton ordinance met the desired objective. It inspired small towns to construct their ~~narratives~~ own risk narratives and to embrace the Bybee/Kobach argument about "inherent powers," a counter-law scenario that sabotages legal preemption for social preemption (Ericson, 2008). It incentivizes local politicians by helping to fast track political careers, while also spreading the national anti-immigrant ordinance movement. It also didn't matter that these ordinances were unconstitutional because legal authority was not the aim; rather the aim here was a "state of exception," where social authority replaces law. Thus it also didn't matter that these ordinances were practically ineffective and ran counter to the communities' own economic interests.

Consider Riverside, New Jersey. Its Brazilian community had been quite integral to the city's downtown economic revitalization. Before Brazilians started moving to the community, according to the *New York Times*, the once bustling textile mill town had been in decline (Capuzzo, 2006). "Three years ago this was a dead town . . . Now you see all the stores are open, the people are out . . ." (Capuzzo, 2006). According to the *Times* article, the Brazilians were largely responsible for revitalizing the local downtown economy, rehabbing and occupying vacant buildings, opening stores (hair and nail salons, corner shops) and cafes and restaurants on main-street and raising the real estate value of local properties (Capuzzo, 2006).

And yet, in 2006, shortly after the May Day protests, Kris Kobach helped the New Jersey township of Riverside draft one of the country's first anti-immigrant ordinances, which the town council passed that July.[48] The Riverside ordinance made it unlawful for locals to rent or hire persons who cannot verify they are legal residents.[49] Riverside's "Illegal Immigration Relief Act" was modeled after the ordinance that had just been passed in Hazleton, Pennsylvania. As in Hazleton, the ordinance stopped revitalization in its tracks. Within days, immigrants started leaving, and before long, many buildings and storefronts were boarded up and deserted.[50]

Klu klan

Chapter 8

Immigrant Resistance or Immigrant Control

The Technology Game is On

Introduction

When 4 to 6 million people turned out for the "Day Without Immigrants" General Strike and protest marches on May Day 2006, attention was turned to an immigrant rights movement that had heretofore never attracted much notice. There was something unusual about this day of immigrant marches. Even during the heyday of Cesar Chavez and the United Farm Workers, crowds this size never turned out as they did on this day, marching down streets in broad daylight. During the 1970s la Raza Unida Party of Texas tried mobilizing Hispanics at the border and found some success, but nothing like this.

The fervor that surrounded this day had placed the sovereignty/risk narrative on notice, or so it seemed. The authorities never saw it coming, which to say the least is a shortcoming for a risk management system. Further, according to the narrative, undocumented immigrants were not supposed to be active subjects. Nor were they supposed to assemble in such numbers in public spaces. Weren't they the subordinated other, lurking in the shadows, and huddling in hotel and restaurant kitchens and at construction sites? Indeed, immigrants were a difficult group to organize, and pro-immigrant activists had been difficult to locate outside of progressive places of worship and niche immigrant rights organizations at the border and in major urban areas where dense immigrant populations were present.

This chapter inquires how so many undocumented immigrants and their supporters turned out as they did, and how the State responded to the fact that "the sleeping giant is now awake." The bigger question is whether the May Day boycott made any difference in terms of legitimizing an alternative pro-immigrant-rights narrative. At first glance, the May Day message was simple: Americans awoke to consider what their work and consumer lives would be like in the absence of immigrant workers—without immigrants economies would buckle and collapse. This recognition of a pressing social reality certainly mattered; but did it make a difference?

May Day, 2006, unleashed a new generation of immigration politics if it is examined in terms of sheer turnout, enthusiasm, and organizing tools. With a simple message and newfound capacity, the events organizers disseminated the message on radio and over the web, reaching into homes, schools, community centers, and neighborhood bars and restaurants. Organizers marketed the event like no other immigrant event. They were able to entice the participation of large numbers of newbies to the movement who had never before participated in street marches or boycotts in no small part because of SEIU, which was instrumental to the success of the May 1, 2006 boycotts.

I will also examine the May Day Strike of 2006 in order to raise questions about the hegemony of immigration control. The strike was a direct response to pro-sovereign legislation, the Sensenbrenner Bill (HB 4437) that attempted to further criminalize undocumented immigrants. But seeds of opposition were evident within the sovereign and neoliberal narratives. For example, the strike was a response to neoliberal economic restructuring that indirectly had brought masses of undocumented immigrants over the border and to cities and small towns across America. Further, although deunionism is a key factor in neo-liberalism, an unintended consequence of relying upon undocumented labor is that immigrants now dominated the labor force in several post-industrial economic sectors, making them a ripe and eager constituency for the Service Employees International Union (SEIU).

At the same time, the strike also unleashed increasingly severe anti-immigrant ICE raids across the country. And so the battle was on, or so it seemed. I would argue that what seemed like another contested terrain was actually a spectacle that reinvigorated the state sponsors of the sovereignty narrative. Within months, state and local governments started passing anti-immigrant ordinances and statutes. At the national level, the DHS response to May 1, 2006 included the Boeing contract for SBInet. In other words, the boycotts never put a dent in the sovereign's exclusionary practices. Since 9/11, no other community in America has been treated as poorly and severely as immigrants. Even with organized resistance, or perhaps because of it, the immigration control narrative got stronger as state anti-immigrant practices grew more severe in 2006 and 2007. The post May Day response also strengthens the argument that change is unlikely until sovereign powers are curbed.

I also wish to examine the implications of the organizers' reliance on Web 2.0 technologies and other new media, which I hope to show, are both democratizing and repressive. In other words, Web 2.0 adds tension to the contested terrain.

The importance of Web 2.0 for the organizers of May Day 2006 cannot be overstated. Social networking and viral messaging were instrumental to organizing the event and encouraging immigrant resistance to the dominant immigrant-control regime. The user-generated content creates new democratic spaces for critical action and social change, and opportunities for the grass roots to reframe the debate by redefining problems and adding new perspectives that decision-makers have not considered. At the same time, however, these technologies provide additional opportunities for the government to surveil and control the undocumented community. Although many in the undocumented community escaped the billion-dollar gaze of SBInet, NSEERS, and US-VISIT, they risk being identified by the government in its effort to enlist such technology in its anti-immigrant regime.

In this chapter, I discuss the impediments to organizing immigrants generally, and then provide a brief case study of SEIU organizing the May 1, 2006 General Strike. Next I pinpoint the source of the tension caused by the immigrant community's increasing reliance upon Web 2.0 technologies and the sovereign's potential control over them. Specifically, I make brief mention of the "deep packet inspection" program, mentioned in Chapter 1, that combines the government and the telecoms in a surveillance practice that can put undocumented immigrants at great risk. I also analogize this struggle to the *Jewel v. NSA* case, which lays out the argument for the President's state secrets and sovereign immunity privilege that allows information of surveillance programs to be kept secret.[1]

Although *Jewel* is not an immigration case, the issues of sovereignty and surveillance are closely analogous to the immigration control issues I have discussed in this book. I argue that the only thing that separates the immigrant rights meme from the existing immigration narrative is the sovereign power that allows the executive to rule by whim. The challenge is to settle on a way to convince the sovereign to surrender his cape and decide to "deny the exception." In the *Jewel* case, "surrendering his cape" would suggest victims of illegal surveillance can litigate against the government. Once such allowance for redress is made, any victim of illegal wiretaps, including immigrants, may then have a fighter's chance at challenging abusive executive actions. Only then might the rule of law return. In the meantime, the sovereign narrative describes situations in which the executive has the power to preemptively observe, and in the immigration context, the same set of powers legitimizes mandatory detention and removal without first having some individualized suspicion of wrongdoing.

Factors Mitigating Effective Immigrant Resistance

Immigration is a difficult topic for people to rally around for many reasons. A big part of the problem has to do with inherent vulnerabilities within the immigrant community. The main vulnerability has to do with legal status. Immigrants are fearful that engaging in a public persona will attract the attention of CBP. Undocumented immigrants know they are only a phone call away from being imprisoned and/or forcibly removed from the country. Even some civil rights activists are loathe to consort with people connected to illegal activity, even so minor a civil offence as being in the US without documentation. The reason is that the stigma of undocumented immigration far exceeds the gravity of the legal offense. Since the 1960s, but particularly since

9/11, undocumented immigration has carried the baggage attached to it by the war on terror. Aliens are lawless invaders, enemy aliens, and potential terrorists. Of course they have been seen as "alien hordes" since the days of Chinese exclusion in the 1880s, but the ferocity of legal and extra-legal punishment has never been so great.

It is important to note that historically immigrants and labor unions have been perceived as competitors rather than allies. Labor unions historically have been strong allies of civil rights organizations, but have had conflicts with immigrants. Although the formative years of organized labor relied upon immigrant members and many labor leaders were foreign born, a tension still existed within organized labor that perceived immigrants as potential scabs. As Ruth Milkman documented, the typical attitude among unionists . . . was, "No, you can never organize those guys. You're beating your head against the concrete" (Milkman, 2006).

The antagonism in the relationship began to dissipate during the 1980s and 1990s, when organized labor's numbers dwindled to an all-time low as a result of neoliberal economic restructuring and deliberate deunionization efforts. Organized labor began to recognize immigrants as a natural constituency that could help fill their depleted ranks.

Ruth Milkman documented the growth of the immigrant/labor alliance in Los Angeles during the late 1980s. According to Milkman, the alliance coincided with workers centers and the Los Angeles Alliance for a New Economy's 'living wage movement'.

By 1990, the SEIU "Justice for Janitors" campaign celebrated its first major victory in Los Angeles. Undocumented immigrant janitors who had long been the backbone of this blue collar building industry in Los Angeles worked long hours for little pay in substandard conditions. The Justice for Janitors campaign resulted in a series of contracts that guaranteed improved wages and working conditions (Milkman, 2006).

SEIU is comprised mostly of immigrant workers. It is focused on uniting workers in three sectors: SEIU is the largest health care union, including hospitals, nursing homes, and home care; the largest property services union, including building cleaning, and security; and the largest public employee union (see www.seiu.org). It is an important union for immigrants because immigrants are quite prevalent in these sectors of the economy (Schiavone, 2008, p. 82).

During the 1990s, SEIU took the lead in organizing undocumented immigrants. It was at the heart of the organizing efforts in most cities. The SEIU claimed it "brought credibility to the demonstrations, making it safe for politicians and other community leaders to participate with grassroots groups they knew little about" (Schiavone, 2008, p. 82). According to Milkman, the SEIU organizing model provides a template for a possible revitalization of organized labor and for undocumented immigrant workers. First, it presumes the following conditions: 1) the existence of highly concentrated Latino immigrant communities around the country; 2) the existence of highly concentrated immigrant workers in service and construction related jobs, a result of neliberal economic restructuring away from manufacturing; 3) the SEIU's occupational rather than industrial focus. These conditions provide SEIU with organizing opportunities that do not exist elsewhere in the labor movement.

SEIU organizing excelled under such conditions. By 2006, SEIU claimed 1.8 million members. "Justice for Janitors" was one of several initiatives that also included such other priorities, such as health care and the public sector (Milkman, 2006).

In February 2000, due to the efforts of SEIU's Eliseo Medina, the AFL-CIO passed a resolution saying it would henceforth work on behalf of immigrants rather than seeing immigrants as a threat. Finally, it seems, organized labor had recognized that their own interests were served by forging alliances with nonunion organizations (Schiavone, 2008, p. 81). Indeed, this was the point when immigrant-rights organizations worked in alliance with SEIU to spearhead citizenship drives, voter mobilization drives, and coalition work with community groups. In this regard, undocumented immigrants were assuming the responsibilities of citizenship regardless of their immigration status.

Factors

The SEIU success story helps make sense of seeing millions of immigrants turning out for the "*Day* Without Immigrants," which was a response to several incendiary efforts by congress to clamp down on undocumented immigrant workers. Immigrants and their supporters had finally become fed up with the hubris of the White House and Congress. The last straw was the despised Sensenbrenner Bill (H.R. 4437) in the House of Representatives in December, 2005, which would have raised penalties for illegal immigration, criminalized people who provided shelter and services to undocumented immigrants (clergy, families, friends, educators, social service workers), and turned 12–24 million undocumented immigrants into felons. As Jesse Jackson described it in an important column in the *Chicago Sun Times* on May 2, 2006, "the insult turned to threat" (Jackson, May 2, 2006). The lack of proportionality struck many people as unjust and unfair. As Jackson said:

> Criminals? No. They are our mothers, fathers, aunts and uncles. Illegal aliens? No. They are our friends, teachers, church leaders, health care providers and business owners. Whatever differences we may have are dwarfed by our common struggle. So in April and on May 1, immigrants and their human rights supporters took to the streets, reigniting this era's civil rights struggle.

The Sensenbrenner Bill scared not just immigrants, but many who had been alarmed by the sovereign's abuse of power following 9/11. What would it mean for society to make felons out of the people who wash dishes, drive cabs, make hotel beds, and play an essential role in virtually every aspect of the service economy? It is likely the economy would buckle and crash.

This was the thinking behind the "Day Without Immigrants" General Strike. Coming exactly 120 years after Chicago's Haymarket Square massacre in 1886, an immigrant-led labor stoppage would again make the case to nativist lawmakers that immigrants play an essential role in the economy and should be treated with the respect and dignity they deserve. In 1886, the issues had to do with wages and living standards. These economic issues played a similar role in 2006, but added was the specter of making felons out of undocumented immigrants, and filling already overflowing prisons with undocumented workers who had committed no crime. The fear of wide-scale roundups of suspected undocumented immigrant workers proved too much to bear, and served as the catalyst for millions of people to risk taking to the streets.

Thus, on March 25, 2006 in Los Angeles, angry over Sensenbrenner's proposed legislation (H.R. 4437), 500,000 mostly Latino immigrant workers protested in downtown Los Angeles around city hall. The protestors not only argued against H.R. 4437, but also in favor of an alternate bill that would provide amnesty for undocumented immigrant in the country. The March 25 protests were repeated on April 10, 2006 when between 100,000 and 500,000 people assembled peacefully on the streets of 132 cities around the country. The protests culminated on May 1, 2006, with the General Strike, "Day without Immigrants" protests.

Although the perceived stakes for immigrant workers were quite high in spring 2006, due to the fear and anger stoked by HB 4437 and by hundreds of nativist organizations around the country, such high stakes still don't explain the immense turnout. It didn't hurt that the California State Senate voted to endorse the boycott of schools, jobs, and stores. It approved a resolution that called the May 1 protest the "Great American Boycott of 2006," and described it as an effort to educate Americans "about the tremendous contribution immigrants make on a daily basis to our society and economy" (Klatell, April 28, 2006).

Even more persuasive than a state senate resolution, however, was the hands-on and media/web-based organizing by SEIU locals in Los Angeles, Chicago, Detroit and elsewhere.

Protest organizers also disseminated their message by making full use of the media to educate and mobilize people by the millions. Organizers deployed low and high-tech communication technologies. Spanish language media helped counterbalance mainstream news coverage, by announcing protests and mobilizing people (Costanza-Chock, 2008, p. 6). San Francisco State researcher Garciela Orozco examined how organizers used Radio Bilengue, a local Spanish language radio station, to inform, encourage, and organize political action for the May Day protests. According to the study, "Radio Bilengue became an important organizational tool by bringing listeners together in a virtual space where they could feel united, empowered to express their values and opinions, and informed by the minute-by-minute information that they themselves were producing" (SSRC Research Hub, 2008).

Radio, and perhaps more importantly, online communication tools helped organizers involve undocumented immigrants without risk by having them camp out in public spaces (streets, sidewalks). Online communication technologies (photos, video, social networking) protect the identities of people who need to have their identities protected. The anonymity of online communication allows immigrants to engage in democratic participation without risking being identified by the expanding web of databases and counterintelligence technologies that target immigrant communities.

Blogosphere

SEIU organizers were supported by a nascent immigrant rights blogosphere that included such blogs as Immigration Prof.; MigraMatters: Progressive Immigration Reform;[2] Para Justicia y Libertad;[3] Border Line, and Blue Latinos, among others. Early on, Blogger Mickey Hingorani argues, the left blogosphere was less organized than the right blogosphere, and more disconnected from (progressive) power centers inside the beltway. But the right's lead in this regard evaporated as immigrant rights activists began to ride the wave of the democratic party resurgence in 2006, and then the Obama web-based juggernaut in 2007–2008. Hingorani refers to such organizations as Dreams Across America, as effectively creating coherent online strategies including blogs, social networking, and online video.

Web 2.0 Democratic Tool or an Orwellian Alternative?

The pro-immigrant blogosphere has benefited greatly from Obama's election on two fronts: first progressives gained a more sympathetic voice in Obama than in any previous administration in a long time, the Clinton administration included. Second, the progressive netroots both led and then rode the Obama wave in terms of developing and using Web 2.0 technologies. The Obama campaign was responsible for some of the most imaginative uses of social media ever. For example, they put up *mybarackobama.com*, which attracted millions of users trying to figure out how to help. The idea was to convene supporters rather than try to control them.[4] These two factors catapulted progressive netroots ahead of the rightwing counterparts.

Frank Sherry's *America's Voice: The Power to Win Common Sense Immigration Reform* provides some of the most sophisticated progressive Web 2.0 strategies. America's Voice is described as a "communications and rapid-response arm of a reinvigorated campaign to advance immigration reform" (ImmigrationProf, March 20, 2008). Its 2.0 website provides news, video, contacts, online communities, press, petitions, and fax writing requests to elected officials, while also providing a space, *Silent no More*, for immigrants to tell their own stories (www.americasvoiceonline.org/, consulted April 24, 2009).

The very manmade and natural catastrophes that can give cause to what Naomi Klein has referred to as "shock doctrine" politics (the Chilean coup in 1973 and more recently, 9/11) also open a window into democracy building possibilities (Klein, 2007).

Political activists (techno-geeks) can educate themselves on autonomous/ independent (non-corporate non-state) user generated tools and infrastructure, using Free and Open Source Software (FOSS) along with autonomous communication infrastructure, tools, and networks. The key for immigrant activists is finding infrastructure that won't track user IP addresses, and won't take material down on the basis of arbitrary requests from state officers.

Increasingly, this has become a game of cat and mouse between activists and the State, sometimes with lethal consequences and sometimes with liberatory ones. Let me suggest that the immigrant movement's use of Web 2.0 technologies would benefit from close examination of the democracy movements in China and Iran. Even America's Voice or SEIU's web potential is compromised by the fact that its servers can be coopted by the State and the phone companies. Indeed, the immigrant rights movement has moved beyond 2006 strategies, from blogging and websites to social networking. Consider the web-based organizing for the Dream Act and for comprehensive immigration reform in 2009.

This is the kind of thinking that is increasingly evident among immigrant rights organizers, particularly undocumented youth who are organizing support for the Dream Act.[5] Consider the following discussion of how young people organized for "Ideas for Change," an online campaign from the online community of undocumented students:

> Juan Rodriguez receives the message on the mailing list and forwards it out the Students Working for Equal Rights in Florida. Other Facebook groups follow suit with Greisa from Texas mass-messaging 11,000 people on the Facebook DREAM Act cause._Students from Philadelphia and Florida hit up every pro-migrant blogger on the Citizen Orange list with a personal narrative, getting alternative media exposure. __Thousands of miles away in LA County, an 18-year–old legal resident, Omar, calls the undocumented student helpline (1–800–596–7498) to volunteer his

services to the cause. Within a few hours, he gets connected to Dreams to be Heard at CSU Northridge, the Orange County DREAM Team, and the Underground Undergrads working out of UCLA. With the competition drawing to a close, Facebook profiles are reading: "Vote for the DREAM Act!" and close to a thousand people are signed up to vote at Change.org through a Facebook event. Some might even see the occasional Facebook ad that tells audiences: "DREAM Act 2009: Obama Supports the DREAM Act. Do you?" Welcome to Web 2.0 undocumented student activism. Youth in the usually-somber waiting rooms of history are bustling with renewed enthusiasm and energy. Trapped in marginal status, ignored by the mainstream media, with their backs to the wall and everything to lose, undocumented youth are emerging as leaders in their own movement for passage of the DREAM Act.[6]

Each also has its own Twitter feeds and hashtags that facilitate real time communication. Each campaign integrates interactive social media on websites with even more mobile and powerful tools such as Twitter. The difference between MySpace or Facebook on the one hand and Twitter on the other is that Twitter literally broadcasts messages to the public while the other are limited to friend categories (Grossman, 2009). Twitter is a highly mobile, fast, and very personal way to communicate messages in 140 characters or less. It is one thing for the state to censor information coming out of a political movement on Facebook; it is more difficult to censor Twitter.[7] Its one thing to write a blog for America's Voice; it's another to give real information in real time about interacting with immigration enforcement, about road blocks, and neighborhood and work place raids. For in this way, participants can gain the immediate real time support of potentially thousands of people who get pulled into the story, are affected by it, and in turn reach out to others to help observe, report, and provide support, and counsel.

As new media scholar Clay Shirky described the June 2009 street protests in Tehran:

> People throughout the world are not only listening but responding. They're engaging with individual participants, they're passing on their messages to their friends, and they're even providing detailed instructions to enable web proxies allowing Internet access that the authorities can't immediately censor. That kind of participation is really extraordinary.
> (http://blog.ted.com/2009/06/qa_with_clay_sh.php)

Under these conditions, participants on the street can communicate with each other (tweet), conveying tactical and logistical information about meeting places, where the police may be gathered, and so forth. In the meantime, once marchers send messages to Twitter, they receive messages back from persons around the globe, who become virtual participants. Further, the virtual participants can "retweet" their messages so that the numbers of persons experiencing the march and the issues related to it grow exponentially.

Although Twitter originated in 2006, it didn't come into its own until 2008–2009, when its potential to democratize street movements and safeguard the identities of marchers (read undocumented immigrants) became obvious during the June 2009 street protests in Iran following its stolen election. When "the whole world is watching," it is more difficult for local state and federal law enforcement to engage in abuse. And although repression is still a potent tool of social control, it becomes less palatable when its effects are broadcast in real time to thousands or millions of people, some of whom have the social capital capable of forcing policy makers to consider these abuses of power.

In addition, the use of Twitter and other similar social media, help personalize the political plight of undocumented immigrants. While following and responding to Twitter feed hashtags #iranelection and #iran9, I was drawn into this struggle, and felt an emotional pull when I changed the timeline on my own account to register as Tehran, something the protesters asked westerners to do. It is easy to imagine these technologies being using by the immigrant rights movement, and indeed it is.

Studies have shown that the American public is far more sympathetic to the immigrant neighbor who lives down the street than to immigration, a more abstract topic. In other words, polls have consistently shown that the public likes individual immigrants while opposing immigration in the abstract. New media has the opportunity to blur the difference and get the public behind pro-immigration issues through the lens of personal stories and tweets. That's how Twitter can be most effective. As Shirky says, "As the medium gets faster, it gets more emotions. We feel faster than we think. But Twitter is also just a much more personal medium. Reading personal messages from individuals on the ground prompts a whole other sense of involvement" (http://blog.ted. com/2009/06/qa_with_clay_sh.php).

Because of the precarious legal position of many of their members, however, online organizing and advocacy for pro-immigrant rights groups must be wary of putting too much stock in such social networking, and must be extremely wary of the potential for using Web 2.0 for surveillance and other forms of risk management.

Web 2.0 creates a rich stream of metadata for the State and individuals to use in tracking and monitoring Web 2.0 participants. For example, Flickr, which allows people to upload and share photographs and video streams, comes with geotagging of photos, which provides locational data associated with the images. In addition, facial recognition technologies allow interested parties to search for and identify a certain person's face on the image. As Michael Zimmer says, "For instance, law enforcement officials can simply search for all photos online matching location and timing of a certain political rally in order to broaden their ability to keep records of who was present" (http://idtrail.org/content/view/696/42/, 2007).

Further, tweets go out over two networks, the Internet and SMS, the network that cell phones use for text messaging. As Zev Grossman says, "it's technically relatively trivial for the state to take control of those choke points and block IP addresses delivering tweets through them. The SMS network is even more centralized and structured than the Internet, and hence even easier to censor" (Grossman, 2009).

It is one thing for individuals to use Web 2.0 technologies to track friends. It is quite another thing when the stalker is the state with its monopoly over the coercive use of force and growing web-based surveillance network. With sovereign powers and risk management technologies at its disposal, the state can track, identify, and locate undocumented immigrants who are organizing on the web.

Consider deep packet inspection technology, which goes way beyond blocking website access or severing Internet connections for activists and street protesters.[8] Deep Packet inspection, according to the *Wall Street Journal*, "enables authorities not only to block communication but to monitor it to gather information about individuals, as well as alter it for disinformation purposes" (Rhoads & Chao, 2009).

Sasha Costanza-Chock contends, "for many involved in social movement activity, surveillance and censorship are concerns that are at least as (if not more) important than the monetarization and value extraction realized through content licensing and advertising revenue" (Costanza-Chock, 2008, p. 8). Thus such commercial sites as Facebook, Twitter, Google, or YouTube can serve as a rich source of information for State officers looking for information about the political activism of immigrant-rights workers because, since 9/11, and as the *Wall Street Journal* has reported, this technology has strong anti-democratic currents.[9] According to the *Wall Street Journal*, "Deep packet inspection involves inserting equipment into a flow of online data, from emails and Internet phone calls to images and messages on social-networking sites such as Facebook or Twitter. Every digitalized packet of online data is deconstructed, examined for keywords and reconstructed within milliseconds" (Rhoads & Chao, 2009).

As science fiction writer Cory Doctorow warns, it is one thing for Amazon or Google to:

incrementally collect my searches, do lots of analysis on my email, cross-link my email with my search habits. Cross-link my search habits with my RSS reader, my photos, my social network and the rest of it. By all means, one after another, because all these things incrementally improve my life and my experience, until there's a terrible privacy breach resulting from it.
(Cory Doctorow, 2007)

Remove Amazon or Google from the picture or replace them with the likes of AT&T, or Verizon, then consider the privacy breach and you get the Jewel scenario, which deployed deep packet inspection-like practices. Now replace them with the likes of Unisyss, Accenture and so on, and consider the privacy breaches that might well result from using such interoperable dataveillance networks. Imagine making all this data available to Sheriff Arpaio, or the poorly trained border guard. For these reasons, the pro-immigrant netroots have reason for concern about Web 2.0 technology. As long as the State has the capacity to pick through the bones of user-generated information, the potential dangers for immigrant activists are extraordinary.[10]

Because of changes in NSA policy going back to 2000,[11] the executive order that President Bush issued in October 2001 to establish a program of dragnet surveillance, could easily be deployed against suspected undocumented immigrants and immigrant-rights activists. Since shortly after the executive order was issued, AT&T and the federal government started engaging in eavesdropping on specific communications, and since then have "indiscriminately intercepted the communications content and obtained the communications records of millions of ordinary Americans as part of the Program authorized by the president" (*Jewel v. NSA*).[12]

According to the complaint filed in *Jewel v. NSA* (September, 2008):

> The core component of the Program is Defendant's nationwide network of sophisticated communications surveillance devises, attached to the key facilities of telecommunications companies such as AT&T that carry Americans' Internet and telephone communications. Using this shadow network of surveillance devices, Defendants have acquired and continue to acquire the content of a significant portion of the phone calls, emails, instant messages, text messages, web communications and other communications, both international and domestic, of practically every American who uses the phone system or the Internet . . . in an unprecedented suspicionless general search through the nation's communications networks.
>
> (Complaint, *Jewel v. NSA*)

The close ties between the telecommunications industry and the White House and NSA since 9/11 continue to hold great dangers for the immigrant community. As discussed in the next chapter, the Obama administration's position on *Jewel* adds to the concern.[13] The kinds of communications that have been intercepted (domestic-international communications) come largely from the country's immigrant population. Further, undocumented immigrant activists who avoided US-VISIT and Real ID databases may be outed by NSA-ATT monitoring their communications, or by their own participation in Web 2.0.

Unless undocumented immigrants stop being perceived as a threat to national security, and the tyranny of immigration control is reversed, then the May Day protests and Dream Act campaigns may provide little more than fascinating examples of symbolic politics.

Ultimately, this next phase of immigration control politics will indeed pit the power of the State and private telecom firms against young computer geek immigrant advocates. While it is not clear that the state would win, history tells us not to underestimate it. In the meantime, immigration control is transformed into a contested terrain between two sets of risk managers representing much different immigration discourses. The first set of risk managers, of course, consist of the status quo state and private firms that reap political dividends and financial benefits from immigration control. On the other side, increasingly are the immigrant advocates, undocumented immigrants, and computer hackers and geeks. The game of cat and mouse ensues in which the voices, text, and images of undocumented immigrants become increasingly visible on Flickr, YouTube, and Twitter, while the immigrants and their advocates deploy increasingly sophisticated resistance strategies to hide the identity of the thousands and millions of participants who might be harmed, incarcerated or deported were their identities to be revealed.

As Zev Grossman reports on Twitter and the Iranian protests:

> It's technically relatively trivial for the state to take control of these choke points and block IP addresses delivering tweets through them. The SMS network is even more centralized and structured than the Internet, and hence even easier to censor.
>
> But there are counter-countermeasures to this kind of censorship. Sympathetic observers outside Iran have set up "proxies"—servers that relay Twitter content into Iran through network addresses that haven't been blocked yet. When the Iranian authorities discover such a proxy, they block it too. It's an arms race crossed with whack-a-mole. Protesters are also organizing denial-of-service attacks against government websites—coordinated efforts to shut down their servers by flooding them with traffic.
>
> (Grossman, 2009)

Chapter 9

President Obama's New Emphasis on Immigration Control

Introduction

During the campaign, there were few hints that the Obama administration's first important announcement on immigration would be Barack Obama extending some of President Bush's most excessive immigration control policies at the border. And yet, on March 24, 2009, that's exactly what the Obama White House did. The White House announced that it would, in effect, double down on immigration control: doubling the size of border enforcement task forces and violent criminal alien teams; tripling the number of intelligence analysts along the border; and quadrupling the number of border liaisons working with Mexican law enforcement officials (Thompson, March 24, 2009). This includes security teams that combine local, state and federal officers, 16 new DEA positions at the border, 100 officials from the ATF, and possibly the National Guard.

In summer 2008, Obama's vote in support of the Merida Initiative was a subtle endorsement of Bush border militarization policies. The Merida Initiative, signed into law by President Bush on June 30, 2008, authorized $400 million to help Mexico deal with unchecked drug trafficking and violence. Plan Merida is a security cooperation between the United States and Mexico. It is designed to combat the threat of drug trafficking, transnational crime, and money laundering. According to the State Department:

> This multi-year program demonstrates the (U.S.'s) commitment to work in partnership with governments in Mexico, the nations of Central America, the Dominican Republic and Haiti to confront criminal organizations whose illicit actions undermine public safety, erode the rule of law, and threaten the national security of the United States.
>
> (www.state.gov/p/inl/merida/index.htm)

The final aid package was for a total of $1.6 billion over three years for security purposes that would implement counter-narcotics, counter-terrorism, and border security measures.

Plan Merida provides the framework, then, for examining Obama's initial position on intelligence-led immigration control. It also places Obama's efforts squarely within the same immigration control narrative that his administration has criticized, but which perpetuates the neoliberal/neoconservative approach to border control. According to its critics, "the initiative contains fatal flaws in its strategy. Its military approach to counter-narcotics work will escalate drug-related violence and human rights abuses, and result in an inability to achieve its own goals" (Carlson, July 10, 2008). According to one critic, "it funda-mentally . . . recasts economic and social problems as security problems and militarizes Mexican society" (Carlson, July 10, 2008).

The origins of the Merida Initiative can be found in the March 2005 creation of the Security and Prosperity Partnership (SPP), which was intended to be an extension of NAFTA between the US, Mexico, and Canada. The SPP intended to "link economic integration of the three countries to U.S. security needs . . . and to provide a privileged—and institutionalized—role for trans-national corporations in continental deregulation" (Sciacchitano, February 2008).[1] This is the real reason to be concerned about Obama's new approach to immigration control. Perhaps the most anti-democratic aspect of SPP is that it was negotiated in secrecy. As *Dollars and Sense* reported, "it is not a treaty and will never be submitted to the U.S., Mexican, or Canadian legislatures. Instead it attempts to reshape the North American political economy by direct use of executive authority" (Sciacchitano, February, 2008).

Since SPP provides the policy foundation for the Merida Initiative, as well as for the Obama border control policy, and itself is a creation of the sovereignist impulse, it highlights a new Obama policy that nonetheless perpetuates the sovereign exception at the border. Like the Merida Initiative, Obama's plan has a supply-side focus that emphasizes security and military assistance to the exclusion of social and economic needs at the border. A good deal of the funds allocated from Merida was directed towards Mexico's military and security forces. This places the administration squarely within the sovereignty and risk management sides of the immigration control Bermuda triangle.

The Obama Plan has already drawn criticism from the human rights organization Witness for Peace. In a letter signed January 8 to President-elect Obama, Witness for Peace stated that "instead of spending billions in a failed 'supply side' strategy that funds human rights abuses, destroys the environment, and fuels a decades-long armed conflict, end military aid and invest in real alternative development abroad and drug prevention and treatment at home" (Witness for Peace, 2009).

Few people question the severity of the violence in northern Mexico. This crisis has produced 6,500 deaths caused by warring drug cartels in northern Mexico. According to Napolitano, "Mexico right now has issues of violence that are a different degree and level than we've seen before." According to

Mark Koumans, Deputy Assistant Secretary for International Affairs, "the sustained levels of violence that we observe in Mexican border cities like Tijuana, Ciudad Juarez, and Nogales threaten private citizens, tourists, workers, and businesses alike. The approximately 6,000 drug-related murders in Mexico last year were more than twice the previous record . . ." (Testimony House Appropriations Committee, March 10, 2009).

But how should the United States respond in a way that doesn't continue the disdain for the rule of law, and the human rights abuses that have occurred at the border for the past eight years? As Yolanda Chavez Leyva wrote for *Progressive Magazine*:

> But do I want troops sent to the border in the name of protecting me?
> No.
> For more than twenty years, those of us who live on the border have witnessed the increasing militarization of the border. The border wall is a daily reminder of this, as are the helicopters that fly over our neighborhoods, the checkpoints manned by the border patrol and the local law enforcement, as well as the daily harassment of the citizens who happen to have darker skin. We are frequently the target of various "wars"—against undocumented migration, against terrorism and now against drugs. I am tired of living in a war zone.
> (www.progressive.org/mag/mpleyva032309.html, 2009)

But the Obama administration is indeed planning to send the National Guard to the border as part of a $350 million initiative to "expand the military's role in the drug war" (Sheridan, Hsu & Fainaru, April 25, 2009).

On Inauguration Day, few would have imagined that Witness for Peace and Leyva would have felt compelled to register such a plea with Barack Obama. In his Inaugural Address, Obama announced that he would return the country to the rule of law. The new President's language left the listening world spellbound and on notice that the false choice between security and liberty had been banished and the constitution had returned:

> As for our common defense, we reject as false the choice between our safety and our ideals. Our Founding Fathers, faced with perils we can scarcely imagine, drafted a charter to assure the rule of law and the rights of man, a charter expanded by the blood of generations. Those ideals still light the world, and we will not give them up for expediency's sake. And so to all other peoples and governments who are watching today, from the grandest capitals to the small village where my father was born: know that America is a friend of each nation and every man, woman, and

child who seeks a future of peace and dignity, and that we are ready to lead once more.

> (www.whitehouse.gov/blog/inaugural-address/)

Similarly:

> Recall that earlier generations faced down fascism and communism not just with missiles and tanks, but with sturdy alliances and enduring convictions. They understood that our power alone cannot protect us, not does it entitle us to do as we please. Instead they knew that our power grows through its prudent use; our security emanates from the justness of our cause, the force of our example, the tempering qualities of humility and restraint.
>
> (www.whitehouse.gov/blog/inaugural-address/)

The sovereignist approach was finished. Such power is doomed, Obama opined, because it is in discord with the "justness of our cause, the force of our example." Nothing less than the integrity of our institutions was at stake.

In keeping with his inspiring rhetoric, in its opening months the Obama administration reversed much Bush neoliberalism with budgets promising neo-Keynesian reforms and executive orders pulling the country back into the realm of the rule of law. Early proposals called for jobs, infrastructure, and public works programs, sounding a lot like the New Deal. The President also announced that he would close Guantanamo in part to help restore America's commitment to law and justice. Quickly, it seems, the new president reimagined the role of the federal government in American life as a tool for rebuilding the economy and creating social change.[2] If George Bush used the shock of 9/11 to change course to a draconian neoliberalism, Obama, it seemed, was willing to use the economic crisis of 2008–2009 to shift course again.

On the immigration control front, it was a sign of a new course that the Obama administration ordered a review of the first workplace raid taken under the new watch at DHS. Almost immediately after ICE conducted a raid on February 24, 2009 at a manufacturing plant in Bellingham, WA, Secretary Napolitano ordered the review to see if due process protections had been violated. Perhaps it is telling, however, that Napolitano did not also issue a moratorium on all future workplace raids pending the outcome of the review. In fact, that evening, in Obama's address before both chambers of Congress, he ignored immigration altogether.

Five weeks later, the *New York Times* attacked the new President and his Secretary of Homeland Security in an editorial entitled "Who's running Immigration.?":

> But if he and the homeland security secretary, Janet Napolitano, are making a clean break with the Bush way on immigration, we haven't seen it yet. That shambling machinery lurches on . . . So, a question:

Are Mr. Obama and Ms. Napolitano in charge or not? Let them show it by ending the raids and Sheriff Arpaio's abuses. Something has to be done about immigration, but it has to be smarter than this.

(March 3, 2009)

The *Times* addressed the larger question of whether the Obama administration would redirect the Bush course on immigration control. Where were the signs that the new administration was going to move to reform Bush's repressive immigration control regime regarding workplace raids, the border fence, SBInet, 287(g), Real ID, EZ Pass, mandatory detention, and deportation policies?

As it turns out, Obama was moving deliberately towards the March 24 response to escalating drug cartel violence at the border, which announced Obama's plans regarding immigration control. Legalization, which the administration also announced it is interested in pursuing, is a positive thing for immigrants, but has little relation to the immigration control narrative, which consists of sovereignty, neoliberalism, and risk management. Legalization fits both inside *and* out of this narrative structure. The March 24 announcement showed the administration's hand on many of the issues that rely on the immigration control narrative (sovereignty, neoliberalism, and risk management). It suggested a rhetorical shift in emphasis, with little difference in terms of resource allocation and deployment of anti-immigrant technologies from the previous administration. As the *New York Times* reported, the shift is "from the homeland security priorities of the Bush administration, targeted mainly at the threat of Islamic terrorists overseas and illegal immigration at home. While the new President has vowed to maintain counter-terrorism efforts, the addition of fighting Mexican drug trafficking as well as human smuggling networks represents a new emphasis" (Hsu & Sheridan, March 22, 2009). Still, the reality of the Bush border regime remains: military intervention, beefed up border patrols; increasing federalization and public/private intelligence gathering and sharing, and state of the art surveillance techniques.

In this chapter I suggest that Barack Obama is not the immigrant rights advocate that some of his supporters chose to believe he was. Rather, his position on important structural issues, like Presidential power and state of the art technologies, shows a history of being enamored with the uses of executive power. He is also fascinated by technology and surveillance, which of course are creatures of the military-industrial complex. He shares of some sovereignist and free marketer tendencies that have quickly translated into policy that is not as different from the immediate past as many would like to see.

Obama the Sovereignist?

In this section, I am going to focus on issues related to Obama's position on the Bush administration's abuse of executive power in condoning torture.

I do so to draw an analogy to immigration control. I believe that Obama's position on executive power informs his commitment to the sovereignty narrative as it is applied to immigration control.

Perhaps the most egregious Bush-era abuse is the policy condoning torture against suspected terrorists. Former Vice-President Cheney admitted that the administration engaged in torture, and the International Red Cross recently concluded as much following an investigation that was released in 2009. And yet, as much as President Obama has spoken against torture and declassified Bush torture memos, he has done almost everything in his power to prevent Senator Leahy's Truth Commission, which would unravel the mysteries surrounding Bush war crimes, from becoming reality. He has also prevented a criminal investigation into war crimes during the Bush years.

On February 5, 2009, the *Guardian* reported that the Obama White House desired the UK to suppress evidence about the torture of British resident Binyam Mohamed when he was detained at Guantanamo Bay (Norton-Taylor, February 5, 2009). On February 9, the Obama administration announced that it would maintain the Bush position in *Mohamed et al. v. Jeppesen Dataplan, Inc.*, the case in which victims of extraordinary rendition sued the Boeing subsidiary that flew them to secret CIA camps for illegally aiding the CIA. Both administrations said they would rely on a "state secrets privilege" under which "the executive branch claims it has the power to make an unreviewable decision that allowing this case to continue would jeopardize national security" (ABCnews.com, February 9, 2009).

Also in February 2009, the Obama White House invoked the "state secrets privilege"[3] in a suit filed by two former lawyers of the Al-Haramain Islamic Foundation (now defunct), which was the target of government surveillance (Kravets, February 13, 2009). In this instance, the Bush White House apparently had accidentally released a document to defense attorneys showing that these two men had in fact been illegally wiretapped. The charity is now suing the government. The Bush DOJ and then Obama AG Attorney General Holder asked U.S. District Court Judge Vaughn Walker to throw the case out on the grounds "that the government shouldn't be forced to divulge classified information in a civil case and argued that the judge has no authority to force the government to disclose such information to defense attorneys" (Ambinder, March 25, 2009; Kravets, March 6, 2009). At issue here, according to Marc Ambinder, is not the classified information, but rather that:

> Absent of concrete justice for those wronged by the Bush administration's legal errors/sins of commission is much less important to the Obama administration than the correct application of the rule of law in the present. They seem to be worried that any concession to the principle of disclosure in these cases would jeopardize information that is and ought to be properly protected. This isn't an easy explanation to swallow, but it's the one the administration has settled on.
>
> (Ambinder, 2009)

One of the more troubling aspects of Obama's seeming shift to the right during the Presidential campaign before the democratic convention was when he sided with the Bush administration's desire to give immunity to the telecom industry for illegally spying on Americans. Civil libertarians thought that once he was elected and had a chance to examine "the bones" of the Bush doctrine his DOJ would renounce telecom immunity, and side instead with the rule of law that would permit the courts to interpret the legality of executive branch decisions granting telecom immunity in individual cases.

Instead, the Obama administration once again continued Bush policy, this time confirming the Bush administration's view of the "state secrets" privilege while introducing a broader and new post-Bush "sovereign immunity" privilege. In 2005, the Bush administration admitted that it ordered the NSA to intercept messages between American citizens and suspected foreign terrorists without seeking the approval of either the courts or Congress. In summer 2008 Obama voted for legislation, which became law, that authorized the wiretap program, and was intended to dismiss lawsuits against companies, which had cooperated (Egelko, February 27, 2009).

Given his first chance to reverse Bush on telecom immunity, the Obama administration instead defended immunity for telecoms that were accused of illegally sharing customer information with intelligence agencies (Oswald, February 26, 2009). The Obama administration relied on Bush's "state secrets" privilege and asked the federal judge to uphold the telecom immunity law that candidate Obama supported, and which covers companies that cooperated with the Bush administration (Oswald, February 26, 2009).

As regrettable as that was, Obama took Bush one step further when his DOJ claimed a "sovereign immunity privilege" in the Electronic Frontier Foundation's lawsuit against Bush administration officials. The Electronic Frontier Foundation (EFF) had taken Senate leaders like Jay Rockefeller at their word when they promised that even with telecom immunity, public officials could still be held accountable, and sued for illegal wiretapping (Rockefeller, October 31, 2007). Thus, in October 2008, the EFF filed suit against the National Security Agency (NSA) and other government agencies on behalf of AT&T customers "to stop the illegal, unconstitutional, and ongoing dragnet surveillance of their communications and communications records."[4] The Obama DOJ demanded the dismissal of the Jewel lawsuit, citing the Bush "state secret" doctrine as well as the "sovereign immunity" privilege, a new kind of government immunity that not even Bush lawyers had dared roll out. As writer and lawyer Glenn Greenwald describes it:

> The Obama DOJ has now invented a brand new claim of government immunity, one which literally asserts that the U.S. Government is free to intercept all of your communications (calls, emails and the like) and—even if what they're doing is blatantly illegal and they know it's illegal—you

are barred from suing them unless they "willfully disclose" to the public what they have learned.

(Greenwald, April 6, 2009)

"Sovereign immunity" means the sovereign (the king) is too elevated to be sued by his subjects and is therefore immune. Within a constitutional republic, the concept means the government cannot be dragged into court by citizens unless it agrees to waive in advance its sovereign immunity. In American law, Congress enacted legislation after the Church Committee investigation of executive power abuses that waives sovereign immunity for the President. As applied to this particular case, however, the Obama administration is saying "the Patriot Act bars any lawsuits of any kind for illegal government surveillance unless there is "willful disclosure" of the illegally intercepted communications" (Greenwald, April 6, 2009). In a keen bit of reporting for Salon.com, Greenwald analyzed Obama's claim to "sovereign immunity" and concluded:

> Every defining attribute of Bush's radical secrecy powers—every one—is found here, and in exactly the same tone and with the exact same mindset. Thus: how the U.S. government eavesdrops on its citizens is too secret to allow a court to determine its legality. We must just blindly accept the claims from the President's DNI that we will all be endangered if we allow courts to determine the legality of the President's actions. Even confirming or denying already publicly known facts—such as the involvement of the telecoms and the massive data-mining—would be too damaging to national security. Why? Because the DNI says so.
>
> (Greenwald, April 6, 2009)

This is the clearest signal yet that the Obama administration is committed to using sovereign powers in some situations. Further, the EFF case signals that when such powers are being invoked, constitutional norms take a back seat to the notion that "the King can do no wrong." It is even more troubling that Obama seems to have no qualms about invoking sovereign immunity when dealing with citizens, with the obvious implication that sovereignty issues concerning non-citizens are even less likely to be reversed or dramatically reformed.

The Obama administration also sided with the Bush administration to kill a lawsuit filed to recover millions of missing emails from the Bush EOP (Executive Office of the President). During its first term, the Bush White House failed to install an electronic data recovery system, resulting in millions of emails "getting lost." When the problem was discovered in 2005, the Bush administration "rejected a proposed solution." Regrettably, as Anne Weismann, chief counsel for Citizens for Responsibility and Ethics in Washington, said, "The new administration seems no more eager than the last" to deal with the issue (Yost, February 21, 2009).

Another egregious Bush abuse has to do with the former President signing statements in which he blurred the "separation" part of separation of powers by selectively saying which provisions enacted by Congress he would implement, and which he would not. Given the opportunity to reverse the Bush trend toward imperial powers, President Obama called on his own officials to refer to AG Holder before "relying on any of them [Bush signing statements] to bypass a statute" (Savage, March 9, 2009). "But Mr. Obama also signaled that he intended to use signing statements himself if Congress sent him legislation with provisions he decided were unconstitutional" (Savage, March 9, 2009). On March 11, 2009, he issued his first signing statement, including a provision about whistle blowers that makes it more difficult for Congress to check and balance the powers of the executive.

It is much too early to suggest that these instances support the idea that President Obama is as enamored of executive power as Bush. Most signs, particularly the President's efforts to restore the rule of law suggest otherwise. But efforts to call off the courts by referring to "state secrets" and "sovereign immunity" cannot be interpreted as anything other than the acts of a sovereignist.

Obama the Free Marketer?

When he was running for President, Barack Obama relied on the Democratic Center for American Progress (CAP) for many of his ideas and advisors. In November 2007, CAP issued a 21-page report on immigration policy that has served as a guide for Obama and his team during and since the campaign (Principles for Immigration Reform, CAP).

Highlights of the CAP report include a strong enforcement and neoliberal agenda. It calls for "robust enforcement": "Comprehensive immigration reform must make enforcement—at our borders, ports of entry, and work-place—a priority" (CAP, p. 5). The report also highlights neoliberal goals of employment and free trade, not human rights or civil rights. As the website *StatesWithoutNations* points out, "once in office, Obama's Veteran's Administration (VA) briefly flirted with the idea of privatizing veterans' health benefits. According to the plan, which the administration revoked, the VA would have charged injured veterans private health insurers to supply needed treatment to wounded vets" (*Washington Post*, March 18, 2009). Further, his Education Secretary spent much of his tenure as CEO of Chicago's Public Schools, privatizing about 20 per year (Sharkey, December 18, 2008).

Is Obama a neoliberal with a civic conscience? Perhaps. Such an approach promises to soften the hard edges in Bush policy, while retaining the Bush frame of sovereignty and free markets. Advanced liberalism implies a gentler and kinder neoliberalism that makes full use of the sovereign's discretion, for example, but deploys it as often as an act of mercy as a punitive act.

Obama Transition Team

When Obama chose Stanford University Professor Mariano-Florentino (Tino) Cueller to run his transition team on immigration, Cueller's professional focus on managing complex systems gave some indication of Obama's immigration agenda. Rather than overhauling or replacing the existing regime, Obama seemed committed to "repairing it." This is what Cueller does; it's his expertise. As Cueller noted on December 9, 2008, in an interview with *Azteca America*: "What we are working toward in the transition is to present certain options for the President-elect and his new administration that take into account the commitments that he made during his campaign to repair the immigration system" (PR Newswire, December 10, 2008).

Cueller's professional expertise has to do with the way organizations cope with the legal responsibility of managing complex criminal justice, regulatory, and international security problems. He's a systems guy, someone who can look at a bureaucracy and make it run more effectively and efficiently. During the Clinton administration, he worked as a senior advisor to the undersecretary for enforcement on efforts to improve border coordination and anti-corruption measures. Thus, it makes sense to assume the Obama administration will produce a better functioning, less abusive immigration control regime.

Obama Appointments

By most accounts, Obama made an inspired choice in Arizona Governor Janet Napolitano for Secretary for the DHS. Napolitano was a border governor, showed courage and integrity in representing Anita Hill against Clarence Thomas before an all male Senate Judiciary Committee in 1991, and demonstrated her political savvy in becoming Arizona Governor.

Napolitano, however, fits comfortably within the sovereignist approach to immigration control. She was the first governor to support state employer sanctions; a state guest worker program; to broker a 287(g) agreement; and declare a state of immigration emergency and call for the (Arizona) National Guard deployment at the border. By all accounts she is an aggressive advocate of immigration control. She is at ease around law enforcement issues. According to the *LA Times*, ". . . Napolitano . . . signed into law the nation's harshest penalty for employers who knowingly hire illegal immigration, a measure that would take away their business licenses for a second violation" (Savage, November 23, 2008). According to Napolitano, speaking at the National Press Club in 2006:

> As U.S. Attorney I supervised prosecution of more than 6,000 immigration cases. As attorney general we wrote the law that breaks up human smuggling rings by seizing their assets. And as governor I have worked closely with Arizona's border communities to address illegal immigration

head on. We've cracked down on human trafficking by increasing the penalty for illegal immigrants who commit crimes in the United States. And we've disrupted dozens of criminal syndicates involved in human smuggling though our fraudulent id task force. We've redesigned Arizona's ports of entry to better detect illegal cross border activities and we have utilized new technology to detect stolen vehicles that transport illegal immigrants and drugs on our highways. We fought to increase the presence of National Guard on the border at federal expense.[5]

(www.c-spanarchives.org/library/index.php?main_
page=product_video_info&products_id=
196855-1&showVid=true)

Although Napolitano bears much of the challenge for immigration control, Obama also selected Hilda Solis to be his Secretary of Labor. Solis is an immigration advocate. She favors a path towards citizenship and has opposed guest worker programs and is likely to champion programs that mitigate the exploitation of undocumented labor in the agricultural, roofing, and construction fields, as well as in the service industry. Indeed Obama also opposed guest worker programs in 2007, precisely because he sees them as undermining efforts to secure basic rights for immigrant workers.

Solis seems to be a lone voice for immigrant rights, which stands outside the immigration control narrative. In addition, Obama named Cecilia Munoz, former Senior Vice President of the National Council of La Raza to be his director of Intergovernmental Affairs. Among her responsibilities, Munoz will deal with issues related to the federalization of immigration control. The more powerful Napolitano, however, does not promise much movement outside the dominant immigration control narrative.

We are left with the familiar ring of border fences, SBInets, privatization, and national guard-laden militarization. Perhaps Napolitano's past decisions will be used as a holding pattern for the new President while he reviews the past administration's record from the inside. Perhaps they are a harbinger of things to come. In the meantime, the Obama framework borrows sovereign and free market tones from the recent past. For background, it is important to note that as the Obama administration begins, the war on terror continues, as does the new executive branch's commitment to sovereign power and outsourcing. Dramatic change is likely in terms of Bush era criminalization. Obama is likely to remove from the books draconian Bush and Chertoff practices that were responsible for reducing complex economic and social phenomena to punitive black and white crime control.

Border Fence

When Barack Obama made his speech in Berlin near the Brandenburg Gate in Germany, July 2008, he said, "The walls between the countries with the most and those with the least cannot stand . . . The walls between races and tribe; natives and immigrants; Christians and Muslims and Jews cannot stand. These now are the walls we must tear down" (Lillis, April 6, 2009). Indeed, Barack Obama's election to the Presidency was hailed in the immigrant community, particularly at the border. The Hispanic community turned out in record numbers for this son of a Kenyan citizen, whose memoirs are replete with references to the immigrant story. In fact, Latino voters tipped the balance for Obama in Virginia, New Mexico, Nevada, Colorado, and Florida. Almost immediately local politicos in Texas started asking Obama to tear down the wall.[6] They had grand expectations that the new President would declare an end to the war on terror against them and demilitarize the border, and perhaps also finally, after more than a century, replace sovereign controls with constitutional controls.

In March, 2009, the administration stopped using the term "war on terror," but also stepped up efforts to militarize the border. Once again, a close reading of Obama's recent past in the Senate shows that his continued support for border militarization is not surprising. Obama voted for the Secure Fence Act. It was only after hearing horror stories about the fence during the campaign that he recently said he wants to evaluate whether to continue building the fence (www.cnsnews.com/Public/Content/Article.aspx?rsrcid=40972). During the spring 2008 Democratic Party debate in Austin, Texas, then candidate Obama made the following comments about the border fence: "There may be areas where it makes sense to have some fencing. But for the most part, having the border patrolled, surveillance, deploying effective technology, that's going to be the better approach" (Glantz, November 3, 2008).

As for Janet Napolitano, she told the Senate during her confirmation hearings that she believes the border fence is a necessary component of an overall border security plan, as "it helps prevent those who are crossing illegally from blending immediately into a town population." At the same time, on numerous occasions Napolitano has said, "show me a 50 foot wall and I'll show you a 51 foot ladder." She doesn't like the fence, but she had no qualms about complying with efforts to build it. In fact, after then-Governor Napolitano called out the state's National Guard to the border, she ordered them to do work that supported construction of the fence.

Early moves in the new Obama administration suggested it might reject the Bush "cookie cutter" approach to fence construction and its draconian—no consultation—components, and instead deploy a more locally-based approach. At least, that is what local city officials in Brownsville, Texas, hoped for when they recently proposed that Brownsville become "a center of excellence," "where alternative border surveillance technologies would be tested in lieu of a U.S.–Mexico border fence" (Tillman, 3 May 2009).

Brownsville would replace the border fence, which officials suggest would devastate its local economy, with a river-walk and dam project. The dam would broaden the Rio Grande separating Brownsville and Matamoros, making it

more difficult for undocumented immigrants to cross the river, and making
the river capable of supporting border patrol boat patrols, which would also
help deter undocumented crossing. In addition, the river walk would beef up
the tourism side of this border economy. Thus, the new model would replace
fences with securitized tourism.

Along other stretches of the border, for example Arizona's T'ohono
O'odham reservation, the administration has indicated it will consult with the
tribe and construct security measures that accord with the unique characteristics
of this border culture (Capriccioso, March 13, 2009). According to Napolitano:

> For tribes that are on the borders of Mexico and Canada, we need to work
> together in a special way because we have tribes and families on both sides
> of the borders . . . As we tighten up requirements to show lawful presence
> and immigration status and the like, we need to take into account how
> tribes will be a bit different. We need to build that into the consultation
> policy from the outset.

But, as spring 2009 came and went, the Obama administration still had not
halted construction of the border fence. In fact, as the *New Mexico Independent*
reports:

> Hundreds of miles of border fence dividing the United States and Mexico
> are going up as planned. Despite pleas from some Democrats, environ-
> mentalists and local communities to halt construction . . . the Department
> of Homeland Security . . . has so far maintained the same border fence
> policies as the DHS under President Bush—a position reminiscent of the
> Obama's continued support of certain controversial Bush terrorism
> policies.
>
> (Lillis, April 6, 2009)

Even more alarming is the Obama administration's failure to reinstate the
dozens of laws that Michael Chertoff waived with the sovereign powers given
him under the Secure Fence Act of 2005. Apparently the waivers "(will) stay
there, officials say, at least until the 670-mile long first phase of fence
construction is complete" (Lillis, April 6, 2009).

With more than 600 miles of the fence already built, a CBP official has
guessed the fence will be complete by the end of 2009. Once the fence is
complete, Obama is much less likely to order it be taken down, and the human
rights abuses against Eloise Tamez and the 121 other border residents currently
involved in lawsuits against the federal government will be much more difficult
to address (del Bosque, February 6, 2009). Although Napolitano had
previously mocked the border fence, it may well be part of her legacy, as she
now seems set on institutionalizing Bush-era immigration control mistakes,

perhaps hoping to make them "more effective and efficient." In addition, her enhanced border enforcement platform consists of militarizing the border with virtual technologies, beefed up border patrol, the federalization of local law enforcement and the military. To Napolitano, doing it the right way consists of using advanced security technology as a law enforcement and counterintelligence tool (Frank, December 29, 2008).

SBInet

Three days after Obama's election on November 4, the GAO issued yet another scathing critique of SBInet, saying the project was mismanaging its technology (Lipowicz, September 12, 2008). According to Rey Koslowski, associate professor at the University of Albany, "A new Administration and Congress may think twice about dedicating billions of dollars to a program that has been difficult to deploy and has yet to prove itself in the field" (Lipowicz, September 12, 2008). Yet once in office, Obama made it clear that SBInet would not soon be vanquished. Quite the opposite; it's growing. On May 8, 2009, the administration announced the "no kidding, real SBInet system," which SBInet drector Mark Borkowski said would be completed within five years (Lipowicz, May 8, 2009). Although Secretary Napolitano referred to SBInet as being "problematic" during her nomination hearing before the Senate Homeland Security and Governmental Affairs Committee, she also insisted that technology was an integral part of any border protection system. Napolitano said she thought SBInet "could hold great promise and we want to keep pushing the issue of technology because these borders are vast and manpower alone is not going to do it. You need to be able to augment manpower with technology, keep pushing that technology fencer as it were" (Biessecker, January 16, 2009). As governor, Napolitano supported virtual surveillance systems and chastised the federal government for delays in deploying the virtual fence. The odds are that SBInet will continue to play a significant role in Obama immigration control policy.

In March 2009, the USCBP issued a formal request to hire a project management contractor to help it meet its goals for the project (Lipowicz, March 12, 2009). By late March, SBInet became an early and unexpected beneficiary of the Obama stimulus package. With $100 million in funding from the American Recovery and Reinvestment Act (ARRA) of 2009[7] for SBInet, another $100 million for "non-intrusive inspection technology and $60 million for tactical communications equipment and radios," and with $770 million appropriated from the FY 2009 federal budget for fencing, infrastructure and technology, the question for Napolitano has to do with where to allocate the money, not whether to allocate it (McCarter, April 8, 2009).

In late March, Napolitano announced that of the $100 million in ARRA funding, $50 million was to go to SBInet "to accelerate deployment of surveillance technology and associated command and control technologies in Arizona, including deployment in Nogales and Sonoita stations," and $50 million to pay for tactical communications modernization for the El Paso and Rio Grande Valley Sectors" (DHS, April 1, 2009).

Also in March 2009, Mark Borkowski,[8] Executive Director of SBI Programs, told the House Appropriations Committee's Homeland Security Subcommittee that SBI would oversee construction of a permanent operational system for a 53-mile segment of virtual fencing in Arizona. Borkowski said a decision was pending "on whether to deploy the same system along the entire Arizona/Mexico border" (Lipowicz, March 10, 2009). Borkowski added that "Boeing likely will continue working on SBInet for an unspecified period of time after its initial contract expires in September 2009" (Lipowicz, March 10, 2009). Finally on May 8, 2009, Borkowski announced a $6.7 billion dollar chain of "tower mounted sensors and other surveillance equipment over most of the 2,000 mile border in the next five years" (Lipowicz, May 8, 2009).

Real ID

As Senator, Barack Obama voted for Real ID, but so did everybody else in the Senate because the program was appended to Hurricane Katrina relief funding, which received a unanimous vote. The only other time Real ID came up for a vote, Obama was out campaigning. During the campaign, Obama voiced opposition to Real ID, focusing on how the program would be funded. According to Obama, "I do not support the Real ID program because it is an unfunded mandate, and not enough work has been done with the states to help them implement the program" (www.nilc.org/immspbs/DLs/resrc_guide/DLRG003.htm).

For her part, as Governor, Janet Napolitano supported the concept of Real ID but opposed the law because it was an "unfunded mandate." She referred to the estimate that Real ID will cost at least $4 billion to implement, and that the federal government has only allocated $90 million to help the states comply with the law (*SecureIDNews*, December 1, 2008). She signed into law the Arizona's refusal to comply with Real ID, making it one of 11 states to do so. But at the same time, Arizona was one of the nation's first states to comply with Real ID requirements. Arizona also is scheduled to issue EDLs, which have an embedded RFID ID number that corresponds to the cardholder's personal information (*SecureIDNews*, December 1, 2008).

In early spring 2009, Napolitano participated in a working group with some of the nation's governors, established by the National Governors Association, to review Real ID. According to Napolitano:

> What they're looking at is whether statutory changes need to be made to Real ID . . . They are looking at whether some version of an enhanced driver's license that perhaps creates options for states would be feasible.

They're looking at what the fiscal impact would be particularly given that states have no money right now.

(Strohm, March 3, 2009)

For Obama, as well as Napolitano, the real concern over Real ID has to do with funding. Napolitano never opposed Real ID's counterintelligence, law enforcement, and neoliberal mission. Nor has she ever spoken out against its intrusions on personal privacy. According to *NextGov*, Napolitano is said to be giving consideration to "allowing all states to issue an 'enhanced' driver's license to comply with the law" (Strohm, March 3, 2009). Regrettably too, as Obama perpetuates Bush EDL policy, there seems to be little concern for personal privacy issues, which is surprising given his commitment to issues related to personal privacy. Napolitano has been a strong proponent of surveillance cameras (known in Arizona as "janetcams"). In fall 2008, Arizona announced plans to deploy a new photo enforcement web, "mobile camera units that will eventually grow into 100 mobile and fixed devices—believed to be the nation's first such statewide deployment" (Davenport, September 26, 2008). The idea was for the state to raise revenue by issuing more driving tickets on the back of individual privacy. Napolitano hopes that virtual technologies will replace pedestrian fences at the border primarily because she doesn't think walls or fences will deter undocumented entries.

E-Verify

When she was Governor of Arizona, Janet Napolitano was convinced that E-Verify worked and worked well. "Some of the arguments that are made about how it works or does not work don't carry much water with me. I've already used it for several years," she said. "It works" (Berry & Chebium, March 31, 2009). Thus, when it came time to take a position on extending E-Verify past its scheduled expiration date of September 2009, she did so without hesitation. "It's all about who gets to work and making sure they're legally present in our country. And to do that nationally E-Verify becomes a key component," she said. "It certainly needs to available, effective and as inexpensive as possible and that employer needs to use it as a tool" (Berry & Chebium, March 31, 2009). The only question, Napolitano suggested, was whether to make E-Verify mandatory for all employers (Berry & Chebium, March 31, 2009).

Fusion Centers

Obama's budget includes $260 million to expand state and regional "fusion centers," which will pay for thousands of state and regional intelligence analysts. The people working in these centers will implement the Obama priority of intelligence-sharing among law enforcement offices at the local, state, regional and national levels. Indeed, Secretary Napolitano reported to the

House of Representative during the last week of February, 2009, "she planned to make intelligence-sharing with state and local authorities a priority and wanted to focus on the more than 50 state and local intelligence fusion centers around the country" (Bain, March 2, 2009).

Fusion centers facilitate efforts to coordinate the federalization of immigration control between local and state law enforcement. Such efforts, among other things, help local and state law enforcement to implement the 287(g) policy, which in effect deputized local sheriffs to enforce federal immigration laws. According to Napolitano, at the House hearing, "The fusion of information between the federal, state and local levels is what makes the intelligence gathering process critically valuable to preventing threats from materializing . . . information sharing is also what makes response efforts effective" (Bain, March 2, 2009).

287(g)

By 2009, 67 state and local law enforcement agencies in 23 states had signed 287(g) agreements with ICE to federalize immigration enforcement. All these agreements came during Bush's second term. Although 287(g) was a creation of the 1996 Immigration Act, it had zero participants as of 2002. Perhaps no individual personifies 287(g) more than Sheriff Joe Arpaio, who stuck his 287(g) powers in the face of the new President by organizing a spectacle on February 4, 2009 in Maricopa. According to a press release he issued inviting the press to watch, Arpaio ordered "approximately 200 illegal aliens to be chained and marched" from the Durango Jail to a segregated area of his "Tent City" incarcerated complex (Press Release, February 3, 2009). The GAO had Arpaio in mind when in January 2009 it issued a report that condemned the 287(g) program, finding that 287(g) failed to root out violent felons and instead deported immigrants "who have committed minor crimes, such as carrying an open container of alcohol" (Archibald, March 3, 2009).

It is difficult to fathom how Janet Napolitano ever thought it a good idea to attach herself to Sheriff Joe Arpaio on the 287(g) program, but that's what she did, even after she oversaw the investigation of Arpaio for his brutal treatment of persons jailed in his "tent city" style jails. Napolitano watched from the sidelines while Arpaio's deputies and posse turned their 287(g) authority into illegal dragnets of the Hispanic community. In 1996, the U.S. DOJ investigated Arpaio after registering concerns that he had "willfully violated the constitutional rights of prisoners in his jail" (Lacey, November 27, 2008). This was followed by an official complaint from Janet Reno's DOJ in 1997, which was signed by Deval Patrick, then Assistant U.S. Attorney General in the Civil Rights Division. Napolitano said nothing, and when she was preparing to run for Arizona Attorney General, she appeared with Arpaio at a press conference and declared the federal investigation and complaint a "technicality" (*Phoenix New Times*, November 24, 2008). Arpaio then supported Napolitano's candidacy.

When Napolitano signed Arizona's 2005 anti-smuggling legislation into law, she de facto made Arizona into the only state in the country to treat undocumented entries as felons. Arpaio's Maricopa County played home base to the new law, as the Maricopa County Attorney Andrew Thomas issued an opinion that all "illegal aliens," not just smugglers, would be prosecuted under the statute (*Phoenix New Times*, November 24, 2008). Although Napolitano finally cut $1.5 million from Arpaio's budget in 2008, which she said was wrongly allocated to anti-immigrant raids, it seems she had no real problem with his earlier abuses over some dozen years. Now that she is head of DHS, she has ordered a review of 287(g).

Workplace Raids

In February 2008, in his debate in Austin Texas with rivals for the Democratic Party nomination, then-Senator Barack Obama said he would consider suspending workplace raids were he to be elected President. In July 2008, presumptive democratic nominee Barack Obama spoke before the 40th annual conference of the National Council of La Raza and said that "when communities are terrorized by ICE immigration raids . . . when nursing mothers are torn from their babies, when children come home from school to find their parents missing, when people are detained without access to legal counsel, when all that is happening, the system just isn't working, and we need to change it" (Lucas, 2008).

During his acceptance speech in Denver, in August 2008, nominee Barack Obama again spoke of the harsh effects of immigration raids on immigrant families. When the election was over, President Obama's transition website said: "Immigration raids are ineffective: Despite a sevenfold increase in recent years, immigration raids only netted 3,600 arrests in 2006 and have placed all the burdens of a broken system onto immigrant families" (www.barackobama. com/issues/immigration/index_campaign.php).

And yet, in late February 2009, when Janet Napolitano issued a review of the ICE workplace raid at Bellingham, what she didn't say is as important as what she did say. Although orders for such reviews are a rarity at ICE, the order focused on due process violations as opposed to the policy that generated the raid. As it turns out, under Napolitano's orders, the workers arrested in Bellingham were quickly freed and given work authorization after the initial review (Turnbull, March 31, 2009). Still, it seems that perhaps DHS is more concerned with how raids are performed as opposed to whether they should be performed. Such an approach may contradict positions Obama has taken, but it would coincide with statements Napolitano has made that she is not opposed to cracking down on illegal immigrants.

Regrettably, as the *New York Times* laments:

> More than two dozen people were arrested at a family-run company that rebuilds car engines. They were charged with the usual paperwork offenses.

The company said it was blindsided, and so was Ms. Napolitano. She said she had not known about the raid in advance and promised an investigation.

Americans who might applaud any crackdown on illegal immigrants, particularly in a recession, should know that scattershot raids and rampaging sheriffs are not the answer. The idea that enforcement alone will eliminate the underground economy is a great delusion. It runs up against the impossible arithmetic of mass expulsion—no conceivable regime of raids will wrench 12 million illegal immigrants from their jobs and homes.

The country is not a safer or better place because one more business and two dozen more families are torn apart outside Seattle. The system under which illegal immigrants labor, without hope of assimilation, is not any less broken (*NYT* editorial, March 3, 2009).

By the end of March 2009, the administration issued protocols to "ensure more consistent work-site investigations and less 'haphazard' decision-making (Hsu, March 29, 2009). The message seems to be that the Obama administration will continue with worksite raids, but will use them in a more consistent fashion, adhering to basic norms of due process. The alternative, of course, would have been to shift policy away from worksite raids all together.

Employer Sanctions

Perhaps the major shift in Obama's immigration policy comes in the new administration's focus on employer sanctions. As the *LA Times* reported, ". . . Napolitano will direct federal agents to focus more on arresting and prosecuting American employers than the illegal laborers who sneak into the country to work for them . . ." (Meyer & Gorman, March 31, 2009). While it remains to be seen what DHS will ultimately decide to do with the workers at plants that are forced to close because ICE has just arrested the employer, it is evident that the continued border militarization, beefed-up staffing, national guard and so forth provide an awful lot of "leverage to play to the fear and uncertainty in immigrant communities, as they promote new immigration reform as a kind of cure-all" (Rome & Frickey, 2009).

Immigrant Detention

Although Napolitano had stated that she planned to detain 100,000 additional immigrants in 2009, a series of events early in her tenure helped compel a reexamination of mandatory detention policies. In March 2009, the AP issued a special report that showed most immigrant detainees are not criminals (Roberts, March 15, 2009). The Inter-American Court for Human Rights held a hearing on immigrant detention conditions in the US. And, perhaps more than any other single event, two high-profile detainee deaths in Rhode Island

and Virginia called attention to the treatment immigrants receive in detention. Guido R. Newbrough, German-born and U.S. resident for 42 years,
died of a bacterial infection that affected his heart. His worsening condition
was ignored by prison guards, despite his pleas for help in the days before his
death. Abdoulai Sall from Guinea died of kidney failure in December 2006,
but a recently-released report obtained by the ACLU said the jail "has failed
on multiple levels to perform basic supervision and provide for the safety and
welfare of ICE detainee (. . .) The medical health care unit does not meet
minimum ICE standards" (Roberts, March 15, 2009).

After taking office, Napolitano ordered a review of many operational
aspects of the immigration and border control system. She ordered a
review of the detention standards used and the ICE's compliance with them.
In addition, she also created a new post Special Advisor on ICE and Detention
and removal, and hired Dora Schririo, her former state corrections chief
in Arizona.

It remains quite possible that the Obama administration will dramatically
reform immigration policy. The more important issue, however, is whether
Obama will lead the country towards a new immigration narrative. To the extent
that he continues to perceive immigration through the lens of sovereignty
and neoliberalism, and defines it in terms of homeland security and the need
for cheap labor, then even such dramatic reforms as legalization, which is
currently being discussed, would merely reproduce the existing power asym-
metry between immigrants and the State. The more dramatic change would
consist of bringing the constitution back into administration of immigration, and human rights dignity back into the discussion of migration and social
displacement. By recognizing that the constitution and human rights law,
as opposed to the doctrine of sovereignty, provides the guiding values in
immigration matters, the President would introduce basic constitutional norms
of due process and separation of powers that would establish a benchmark for
holding immigration officials accountable for their actions. Such a move would
begin the process of contending with important social realities of the
immigration experience that have heretofore been ignored.

Chapter 10

Conclusion

Considering that both sovereign controls and free market ideologies germinate in spaces that are inhospitable to democracy, there is no better place for experimenting with privatizing federal policy than immigration, a policy area that historically has been isolated from America's commitment to the rule of law. Immigration policy has been one of this country's most racist and least democratic areas of federal policy. It is also one of the few public policy areas in which stakeholders (foreigners) have no voice in the political or policy process. With such conditions in tow, 9/11 presented a "perfect storm" situation for immigration control. Hopefully, this book has provided some new insight into the extra-constitutional and unconstitutional practices of governance that can be generated under such unusual conditions.

As I have argued in this book, the Bush era was responsible for blending three overlapping and reinforcing strains in the immigration control discourse: sovereignty, neoliberalism, and risk management. No real political space exists for immigrants within this discourse. Rather the main beneficiaries were the industries of immigration control that designed and built walls, virtual fences, private prisons, surveillance, and data mining technologies. This insidious part of immigration control was designed to monitor and instill fear in immigrants for profit rather than actually remove them. The fear that was generated by this system was in turn responsible for heightening the demand in society for more preemptive policies and risk management techniques.

Of course, as discussed in Chapter 2, immigration control has been aligned with sovereignty long before Bush, but the Bush administration strengthened the discourse by connecting it with neoliberal policy and risk management technologies. In the long period between the notorious *Mezei* and *Knauff* decisions and mid-1990s, the executive branch rarely articulated a theory of sovereign authority over immigrants, or citizens for that matter. Since the Warren Court era of the 1960s, it was considered politically incorrect to suggest that a population of people in this country would not be treated in accordance with constitutional norms or, since the 1990s, human rights, immigrants included. But as discussed in Chapter 2, the courts persevered in applying the doctrines of sovereignty and plenary powers to immigrant cases. The words changed over time but the meaning of these doctrines remained constant overall: the courts defer to the political branches on immigration matters, even as Congress, petty sovereigns in the executive branch and private firms refuse to recognize immigrants as juridical subjects and treat them instead as homo sacer.

The discourse continued to supplicate immigrants, even with progressive policy reforms such as the 1965 Immigration Act. The 1965 Act placed a hemispheric ceiling on permanent resident visas from Mexico and Latin America. Its implementation limited the number of immigrants who were permitted across the border with Mexico, but not the number of persons who actually came across the border. This led to the beginning of what has become known as the undocumented immigration problem.

This was an important moment in the development of immigration control because the issue of undocumented immigration could have been framed in terms of a human rights crisis, and/or third world economic crisis, or as an "illegal immigration" problem. The Carter and then Reagan administrations chose the last option and framed the issue as a problem that cast blame upon the individuals crossing the border. This brought about the "illegal immigration" discourse, which emphasized metaphors of individual law-breaking at the border and which along the way stigmatized and criminalized border crossers. Over time, as Tim Dunn has documented, the criminalization discourse began using military and war metaphors, as the militarization of the border soon followed during the 1980s and 1990s (1996, 2009).

As international economic pressures shifted towards free trade under NAFTA in the 1990s, and as demand grew within NAFTA industries for cheap economic labor, the numbers of undocumented immigrants coming into the US increased. Along the way, the demand for social control of immigrant labor, a.k.a. "illegal aliens," grew as well. The double demand for immigrant labor and social control proved tantalizing to the fledgling risk management industry, and soon, the narrative had shifted from depicting immigration as an economic issue, to imagining it in terms of risk, as part of a war against "illegal enemies" and drugs. These fictional wars were soon portrayed as matters of life and death, and set the stage for the Bush administration's war on terror at the border, and for the securitization of immigration.

As imaginary wars at the border gained currency, the sovereignty doctrine reminded the President of the plenary powers at his disposal to fight any perceived enemy of the nation state, even those individuals who crossed the border seeking jobs.

During the Bush administration, immigrants were homo sacer; they were non-persons, had no rights, and were considered little more than fodder for the development of gargantuan military and risk management contracts. Indeed immigrants were the lynchpin for the development of the immigration control industry. Their presence was required to fill beds in private detention centers, and to serve as "lab rats" for experiments in surveillance technologies.

Further, their bodies helped respond to the economic demand for cheap labor in the growing service economy of the early twenty-first century.

It didn't matter that almost all the Bush-era experiments (SBInet; US-VISIT, the border fence) were colossal failures that wasted billions of taxpayer dollars while also running roughshod over the property rights and civil liberties of families residing at the border and across the country. Neither did it matter that the immigration control discourse dehumanized immigrants, turned them into suspects, and preemptively criminalized them. All that mattered, it seems, was that an industry had developed because of immigrants, and thus immigrants were needed, in large numbers, to keep this industry growing.

The gist of a risk management regime is to allocate billions of dollars to build an industry around securing the country from some unknown future source of terror. Until that uncertain moment arises, however, immigration control technologies will endeavor to identify trends among immigrants that make them high risk for some future uncertain act. Their identities, including information about schools, family, backgrounds, interests, purchases, and so forth, shall be analyzed, sliced and diced in myriads of ways so as to generate fear and thus justify continuing the risk management discourse. In the meantime, the following is certain: 1) risk management techniques will continue to invade the privacy of immigrants and travelers; 2) the culture of anti-immigrant fear will continue; 3) risk management will continue to be growth industries; 4) the specifics of future illegal acts of any sort will continue to be unknowable. With high levels of fear being generated, the salience of the security meme will continue. That's the point of this costly exercise.

Under Bush, risk management extended into the nooks and crannies of different immigrant communities, appearing to preempt future wrongdoing by identifying already existing facets in the immigrant identity. SBInet, for example, endeavors to deter potential illegal border crossers from making the attempt and predict illegal border activities before they occur; Real ID requires and then stores a lot of personal information in state and national databases; and US-VISIT and ATS continue to deconstruct the personal profiles of international travelers. These programs are scheduled to continue under Obama, albeit with some revisions, despite the fact that these programs had been thoroughly trashed and critiqued by the GAO and congressional investigation.

One of the most important points of critique against Bush immigration control is that it failed on its own terms: it failed to deter terrorists and it failed to catch terrorists. Not one terrorist was detained or removed from the country because of these immigration controls. The country is no safer for this immigration control industry. Quite the opposite, as many political commentators have noted, when the executive branch, telecoms and risk management firms embark on risk management practices that run counter to the rule and spirit of law, the strength of American democracy comes into question, both domestically and internationally.

One of the lessons of the Bush administration is that government simply cannot afford to incarcerate all the undocumented immigrants present in this country. Federal, state and local jails have been overwhelmed by Bush mandatory detention policies. Even though private detention is a boom industry, there remain too many immigrants in too few private detention centers. Legalization, or regularization, would relieve pressure on jails and detention centers, which during the 2009 financial crisis have been releasing nonviolent offenders back into the general population. Common sense would suggest releasing non-criminal aliens as well, particularly those who violate no criminal law.[1]

The risk management alternative to building new prisons and jails is surveillance, and this is one place where you are likely to see some significant difference between Obama and Bush. Although both Bush and Obama allocated funds for such high tech failures as SBInet, Obama is more likely to support the soft touch of technology as opposed to the harsher touch of mandatory detention and removal policies. Obama's 2009 stimulus package allocated hundreds of millions of dollars to private firms to develop additional surveillance and database technologies for border and immigration control. The plan seems to be to regularize undocumented immigrants and then manage the risk, with surveillance technologies.

Similarly, whereas Bush and Obama policies seek to penalize persons who they each say "fail to play by the rules," Bush endeavored to round them up, detain and forcibly remove them, while Obama seems more inclined to forcing them to the end of the line to regularize their status. While Bush targeted undocumented immigrant laborers in the workplace, Obama seems more inclined to focus his attention on employers. Thus whereas both Presidents favor employer sanctions, for Bush it was merely one piece in a larger anti-immigrant network of practices, whereas for Obama employer sanctions seems likely to have a more strategic role to play.[2]

Thus similarities and differences between plans for comprehensive immigration reform under Obama and previous regularization policies, like IRCA (1986), become obvious. First are the similar efforts to combine legalization with punitive sanctions. IRCA contained both legalization and employer sanctions. As it turned out, amnesty and sanctions were merely flip sides of the same neoliberal coin, aimed at adjusting the balance between the supply of immigrant labor and demand and the supply of immigrant prisoners and demand. The difference between 1986 and 2009/2010 is that in 2009 immigration reform is well defined within a risk management discourse that endeavors to socially control immigrants through risk management techniques.

One of the lessons of the IRCA legalization provision is not so much that it gave legal status to large numbers of undocumented immigrants; rather the importance was in how immigrant status was regularized. Immigration attorney and scholar Lucas Guttentag in the Daily Kos blog[3] inquires about the process of legalization. Guttentag focuses attention not on legalization per se, but on the mechanics of reform, the laws, regulations, and rules that will determine *how* to recognize immigrants (not *whether* to recognize or legalize).[4] His attention is on due process and the role of the courts, asks whether Obama will reverse a decade of court stripping and encourage courts to hold Congress, ICE and CBP accountable to the rule of law:

> There is one fundamental due process principle that is usually forgotten and will get lost in the shuffle unless we put it front and center. The issue is the role of the courts and judicial review. . . . It means that every person, including immigrants, must have an absolute right to go to court to enforce the law and the Constitution.
>
> (Guttentag, 2009)

The Future of the Immigration Control Regime

The immigrant community was not alone in hoping Barack Obama would reverse course on Bush immigration control policies. Neither was it alone in its chagrin over Obama's early steps in the immigration control field. Few people expected that the new administration would continue the Merida Initiative at the border, announce a "border czar," and include hundreds of millions of dollars in the 2009 Stimulus package to help jumpstart the failing SBInet project. Fewer still would have expected that President Obama would establish a "sovereign immunity" privilege that expands the powers of the executive over citizens and immigrants alike.

Instead supporters expected an announcement that the President was serious about comprehensive immigration reform in his first years in office. They hoped he would appoint someone like Cecilia Munoz, the former Senior vice president for the National Council of La Raza, in the new administration. And so it heartened his supporters to hear Munoz, President Obama's director of Intergovernmental Affairs, announce in mid April, that Obama's immigration reform proposals would include a regularization package for undocumented immigrants.

The question arises for Obama that is similar to the one that arose during Bush's first year in office: how to make sense of such dramatic apparent contradictions in militarization and regularization. In this book, I have endeavored to make the case that the Bush contradiction was more fantasy than reality and that the reality of Bush immigration control policies pitted the sovereign powers of the U.S. government in its entirety against individual immigrants who are stripped of rights and dignity. The guest worker programs that Bush and Fox negotiated on September 5, 2001 and the INS custody list coincided within a discourse that was intended to advance an immigrant risk society. They are merely two sides of the same coin.

Although it is too early in his administration to know for sure, Obama seems to be following a similar pattern (sovereignty + neo liberalism = risk management-based immigration control techniques).

When making an initial assessment of Obama's immigration control policy, it is important to examine the President's early policy moves, administrative appointments, and past statements as a guide. Indeed, the early indication is that Obama's approach will fall within the same immigration control triangle, and perhaps most firmly in line with the risk management strategies that provide justification for neoliberal/sovereign-based decisions.

Obama's fondness for technological panaceas suggests a soft but repressive touch, and advances the administration's reliance on private firms for surveillance, data collection, and management. It remains to be seen whether the administration will compel Congress to enact legislation that covers immigrants within crucial privacy protections.

At the same time, some tactical shifts under Obama have already extended government regulation to areas that were deregulated under Bush. The first obvious shift, according to DHS Secretary Napolitano, has ICE shifting emphasis from workplace raids to enforcing employer sanctions. This shift in focus keeps a campaign promise to stop workplace raids. It also promises to end the inhumane practice of separating families. Perhaps more importantly, though, this tactical shift reveals a larger strategy. The tradeoff is between heightened enforcement at the workplace for legalization. It stands to reason that Obama's early emphasis on employer sanctions, which is more humane than workplace raids, will lead to an even more humane policy of legalization/amnesty. This isn't a bad way for the Obama administration to start, but it doesn't escape the confines of the existing narrative.

There is nothing in these practices, however, that remove Obama from the dominant immigration control discourse, which is where immigration control is likely to remain in the absence of a concerted effort to change the terms of debate.

And so I suggest the following. It is important for the Obama administration to add immigration to the universe of constitutional norms and remove it as an exception to the rule of law. It is also important for it to embrace international human rights law as the basis for immigration decisions. International human rights law, perhaps even more than constitutional norms, can challenge the sovereign basis of immigration law. Whereas the survival of the nation state is the sine qua non of sovereignty, and everything else is secondary, the survival and dignity of the human being is the first order principle under a human rights regime. Human rights challenges sovereignty in its profundity and simplicity because "human rights are the rights that one has because one is human" (Donnelley, 2003).[5] Also important is that because it transcends the territorial limits of the nation state, human rights law also removes the exception in the sovereignty discourse. As David Cole notes, "Because they are predicated on one's status as a human being, rather than on one's affiliation with any particular nation state, international human rights are both the most relevant to, and most tested by, the treatment of foreign nationals" (2006, p. 2). Whereas Cole argues for making human rights the underpinning of immigration law, he concedes the obstacles that the present system, which is based on sovereignty and plenary powers, presents for those who would like to see the incorporation of such a change. I would suggest this is precisely why the change need begin at the level of discourse. Were the terms of the debate to change to implicitly acknowledge that basic human rights precede sovereignty, the hegemony of the sovereignty discourse falls away.

Since civil liberties and adherence to constitutional norms comprise this country's version of human rights, America's adherence to human rights in the international context is likely to play out in the field of constitutional rights, which also includes larger structures of separation of powers and other accountability mechanisms. Finally, immigrants, even undocumented immigrants, would be treated as juridical subjects rather than as homo sacer, which will play out in the micro politics of immigration proceedings. In terms of separation of powers, a new narrative could open the way for congress to restricting the President's "prosecutorial discretion" over immigration enforcement (Sarat & Clarke, 2008; Cox & Rodriguez, 2009). Further, constitutional due process has a role to play especially in expedited removal hearings. Bringing the constitution into the immigration control discourse would also help foster dialogue about regulatory society in which government once again assumes responsibility for its actions and for the social welfare of the people living within its boundaries. This marks a different approach to sovereignty as delimiting government responsibility instead of delimiting government power. Along with such features of a new discourse is a narrative that ceases to demonize immigrants as "alien-other."

This means applying constitutional checks and balances and separation of powers to immigration and immigrants. It means establishing and implementing strong protections for immigrant privacy when it comes to data mining. It means according due processes to legal proceedings at the border, however expedited the removal process, and making sure immigration officers as well as any state and local officer enforcing immigration law reconcile their actions with the fourth and fifth amendment. It means treating the civil offense of unauthorized entry as other civil offenses are treated. The criminalization of immigration contradicts the values associated with such a new narrative. It also means shifting away from the neoliberal paradigm that blames individuals for their own hardships in life. This in turn means adopting a language of immigration that internalizes the norms of human rights law and that considers the full subjectivity of immigrants as human beings as opposed to some alien other or commodity. Several other changes would follow from recognizing the humanity of immigrants. Immigrants would no longer be associated as some abstract risk to national security and to the market.

As obvious as it sounds, the fact remains that the sovereignty narrative does not recognize the human dignity of immigrants. By recognizing the subjectivity of immigrants, a thread is pulled from the narrative. Once this occurs, neighborhood and workplace raids become intolerable; and automatic removals, forced separation from families, mandatory detentions, and subhuman conditions of confinement become more difficult to ignore. In short, as constitutional norms emerge, real political opportunities can follow. Once the veil is lifted, a credible debate might occur about the government's responsibility for the social welfare of these important members of the community as well as for temporary visitors who are here legally or in violation of civil laws.

The new discourse could take several forms, as indeed there exist multiple ways to define the immigration politics of control. For starters, I would suggest playing with the political space that is created when the sovereignty, neoliberal, risk management "triangle" is replaced by its opposite. For example, I would recommend a narrative structure that is created around the following concepts: constitutional norms instead of sovereignty; social welfare instead of neoliberalism; and asset analysis in place of risk management, which identifies deficits in the immigrant identity. The political space would be inclusive as opposed to exclusive. Further, these concepts would support the idea of the institutional integrity of America's decision-making entities as well as human dignity for the immigrants coming into contact with these institutions. Constitutional norms would apply specifically to individual encounters that immigrants have with law enforcement as well as to judicial/administrative proceedings. The values associated with constitutional norms would establish the idea that all decision-makers and adjudicators are accountable to the rule of law and that immigrants have a place with which to redress grievances. It also suggests that executive bodies must treat immigrants with the idea that their behavior is subject to judicial review. Finally, the appearance of constitutional norms would replace the secrecy of many immigration procedures with transparency and accountability.

Next, the notion of social welfare recognizes the need for government intervention in the market and more particularly, that the government has responsibility for the well being of human beings as well as markets. It follows that once the government again is recognized as having social responsibilities for its people, individuals stop being automatically blamed for the social problems that might plague them in society. The idea here is not to return to the social welfare system that was taking shape as a result of the New Deal and Great Society programs of the 1940s and 1960s. But it does suggest that persons, regardless of immigration status, also possess social rights.

The shift from risk management to asset management would provide a response to the obvious questions that follow from recognizing the social rights of immigrants. These questions derive from the belief that undocumented immigrants, for example, are not members of society, and that the amount of rights they can claim, should reflect this fact. But, if the discussion about undocumented immigrants is reframed in terms of the benefits they bring to society, then it makes sense that rights and privileges would follow, if nothing else, from a sense of gratitude for the contribution they make. This indeed, is the larger message behind the "Day Without Immigrant" boycotts on May 1,

2006. It was a plea for gratitude as much as it was a demand for rights and justice. The purpose was to show how dependent society is on this particular class of neighbors and community members.

If the undocumented immigrant issue were framed in terms of providing an important economic, social, and political asset[6] as opposed to being immoral or being a threat to security, the government's response would be forced to be compassionate as opposed to punitive. Indeed, this would be a fine legacy for the Obama administration to leave behind.

Notes

I Introduction

1 PENTTBOM is an acronym for the Pentagon-Twin Towers-Bombing.

2 At least 762 were placed on what became known as the INS Custody List. See Office of Inspector General Report, The September 11 Detainees (April 2003), which also says that Chertoff gave instructions "to hold these people until we find out what is going on." According to Chertoff's deputy, Alice Fisher, this meant, "the Department was detaining aliens on immigration violations that generally had not been enforced in the past."

3 See relevant book excerpt at http://archive.salon.com/news/feature/2003/03/31/brillexcerpt1/index1.html.

4 According to the *New York Times*, "One technique the CIA officers could use under the circumstances without fear of prosecution was strapping a subject down and making him experience a feeling of drowning" (January 29, 2005).

5 See website for The Harry Walker Agency, which features this quote advertising Michael Chertoff for public speaking events. See website: http://74.125.45.132/search?q=cache:aHYfMfMf480J:www.harrywalker.com/speaker/Michael-Chertoff.cfm%3FSpea_ID%3D1183+Chertoff+Patriot+Act&cd=7&hl=en&ct=clnk&gl=us&client=safari.

6 Chertoff was nominated to become Secretary of Homeland Security in January 2005, after Bernard Kerik declined Bush's offer in late 2004. The Senate confirmed on February 15, 2005.

7 President Bush nominated Chertoff to the U.S. Court of Appeals on March 5, 2003. The Senate confirmed him on June 9, 2003.

8 It is important to note that OIC head Jay Bybee who signed off on the torture memo and worked closely with Chertoff was similarly promoted to the Court of Appeals. It is apparent that someone in the administration recognized that what they had done was wrong, and did their best to remove these individuals from the line of fire.

9 In 2005, Michael Chertoff replaced Tom Ridge to become the second head of DHS.

10 See Theimer (2002). According to the AP, Ridge owned stock in several corporations registered to lobby for federal defense related contracts, including Avaya, EMC Corp., General Electric, Merk & Co., Unisys, and Oracle.

11 Arthur Schlesinger Jr. coined the term "imperial presidency" in his book of the same name to describe executive power that was out of control.

12 See Naomi Klein (2006) who reports that Donald Rumsfeld was an acolyte of Milton Friedman, a neoliberal who had hoped Nixon during his first term would repeal the Keynesian economics of the welfare state. Although Friedman was disappointed

when Nixon demurred, he settled for exporting his neoliberal agenda to Pinochet's Chile after the 1973 coup (Klein, 2006).

13 As a growing body of literature documents, risk management has to do with the new brand of governmentality, or how government power is deployed through governmental and nongovernmental organizations and actors (Amoore, 2008). In many ways, this brand of governmentality, a term coined by Michel Foucault, runs counter to the rule of law and often subverts it.

14 According to Michael Jackson, the former Deputy Director of the DHS, DHS used Rumsfeld's plans for reforming the military as a model for immigration control, which makes Rumsfeld an important early figure in this discussion (Bigelow, May 18, 2006).

15 Chertoff ostensibly was delegated this power by the 2006 Secure Fence Act.

16 It is important to note that even with sovereign powers, Chertoff couldn't help Boeing meet its contractual obligations.

17 Please note that while some immigrants who become naturalized can then vote, my discussion of immigrants refers to non-citizens.

18 This observation is not meant in any way to be disparaging against the incredible work being done at the grassroots level by immigrants, many are undocumented, or their non-immigrant supporters. Rather, I speak of disempowerment and political marginalization in structural terms, which I shall examine in more detail along with successful resistance strategies in Chapter 7.

19 See Maurice A. Roberts, *Proposed, A Specialized Statutory Immigration Court*, 18 San Diego Law Review.

20 See note 169 in Koulish (1992). See also Gordon & Mailman, 72.04(4)(a). The testimony of a hearing is generally not transcribed unless there is an appeal or a transcript is requested.

21 See note 173 in Koulish (1992) 8 C.F.R 242.15.

22 For discussion of appeals and non final orders, see for example, http://bulk. resource.org/courts.gov/c/F3/383/383.F3d.62.02–2702.html

23 In *Reno v. AADC*, the INS attempted to deport eight non-citizens on account of their affiliation with the Popular Front for the Liberation of Palestine (PFLP), which the government described as a terrorist organization.

24 As William Walters puts it, "the most immediate institutional expression of this fusion (of migration and security) is surely the abolition of the Immigration and Naturalization Service and the transfer of its functions and units into the Department of Homeland Security" (Walters, 2008, p. 158).

25 Notable exceptions included the ACLU, the Center for Constitutional Rights (CCR), and the privacy organization EPIC who documented government abuses and filed many lawsuits against the government. Journalist Deepa Fernandez also covered this story and wrote the book *Targeted* (2007), which documents the outsourcing of border control.

26 See Harvey (2005, p. 2) for the definition of neoliberalism that I rely upon in this book. David Harvey defines neoliberalism as follows:

> Neoliberalism is in the first instance a theory of political economic practices that proposes that human well-being can best be advanced by liberating individual entrepreneurial freedoms and skills within an institutional framework characterized by strong private property rights, free markets, and free trade. The role of the state is to create and preserve an institutional framework appropriate to such practices. The state has to guarantee, for example, the quality and integrity of money. It must also set up those military, defense, police, and legal structures and functions required to secure private property rights and to guarantee, by force if need be, the proper functioning of

markets. Furthermore, if markets do not exist (in areas such as land, water, education, health care, social security, or environmental pollution) then they must be created, by state action if necessary. But beyond these tasks the state should not venture. State interventions in markets (once created) must be kept to a bare minimum because, according to the theory, the state cannot possibly possess enough information to second-guess market signals (prices) and because powerful interest groups will inevitably distort and bias state interventions (particularly in democracies) for their own benefit.

27 For example, neoliberals consider contract law and property law to be sacrosanct.

28 For a brief cogent discussion of these aspects of sovereignty see the Stanford Encyclopedia of Philosophy at, http://plato.stanford.edu/entries/sovereignty/.

29 See Levi & Wall, cited by Amoore & de Goede, 2008, p. 9, who refer to data-veillance in terms of "the proactive surveillance of what effectively become suspect populations, using new technologies involves the classification, compilation and analysis of data."

30 For discussion of privatizing risk in historical context, see Hacker (2006). Hacker briefly argues that the era of privatized risk is contrasted with the welfare state era risk was social; paid for with taxes to cover nearly everyone. In the era of privatized risk, risk becomes an elite commodity, like private police and boutique health care. It becomes a privilege for the wealthy few. The public paid taxes that financed law enforcement for everybody. The criminal system focused less on individual blame and causation and more on insuring subjects against extreme misfortune. See also Paul Passavant who says,

> In order to achieve security against misfortune for its subjects, risk societies rely on a notion of solidarity that enables the socialization of risk to produce social security. We must not understand one as a guilty or evil others, but as bearing a degree of responsibility for unfortunate events, and we must trust our fellow members of society that they will govern themselves such that they will take normal precautions against accidents.
>
> (Passavant, 2005)

31 The good citizen, for example, is on the ready for catastrophe, "by keeping emergency kits, being aware of . . . risks and taking everyday precautions like not opening post that has no return address" (Amoore & de Goeda, 2008, p. 12)

32 See Amoore & de Goede (2008).

33 Deep Packet Inspection sifts through data as it flows through a network searching for keywords in the content of e-mail and voice transmissions www.wired.com/threatlevel/2009/06/wsj-nokia-and-siemens-help-iran-spy-on-Internet-users/.

34 See Ngai (2004) for discussion of how the quintessential "alien other" in immigration culture is the Mexican laborer. Ngai discusses how the undocumented Mexican laborer is the "prototypical illegal alien," as well as how the equation between latino/a identity and illegality persists.

35 See John Higham's seminal work, *Strangers in the Land: Patterns of American Nativism* for discussion about his highly charged emotional idea about a defensive kind of nationalism that dislikes internal minorities on the ground of their foreign connections.

36 John Higham famously documented the history of nativism. In his book, *Strangers in the Land*, Higham provides a description of nativism that speaks to the movement's ferocity:

> Here is the ideological core of nativism in every form. Whether the nativist is a workingman or a Protestant evangelist, a southern conservative or a northern reformer, he stood for a certain kind of nationalism. He believed— whether he was trembling at a catholic menace to American liberty, fearing

an invasion of pauper labor, or simply rioting against great English actor William Macready—that some influence originating abroad threatened the very life of the nation from within. Nativism, therefore, should be defined as intense opposition to internal minority on the ground of its foreign connections.

(Higham, 1955, p. 4)

37 Nativism is the ethnocentric belief that non-native Americans are inferior beings. Nativism was evident in Benjamin Franklin's perception of German immigrants in Pennsylvania. As a political movement it was first popularized by the "Know Nothings" during the 1850s.

38 Walters suggests that since 9/11 "Arabic or Muslim" identity is constituted as the dominant racial marker of insecurity in the age of terror (p. 172).

39 CointelPro is an acronym for a series of FBI counterintelligence programs that officially existed from 1956–1971. Its purpose was to neutralize political dissidents and target radical political organizations. For more see Donner (1981). See also Paul Wolf at www.icdc.com/~paulwolf/cointelpro/cointel.htm.

40 Although the Obama administration has discontinued use of the term "war on terror," it continues many of practices of the Bush administration.

41 According to Suskind, "Even if there's just a 1 percent chance of the unimaginable coming due, act as if it is a certainty. It's not about 'our analysis,' as Cheney said. It's about 'our response.' . . . Justified or not, fact-based or not, 'our response' is what matters. As to 'evidence,' the bar was set so low that the word itself almost didn't apply."

42 See also http://trac.syr.edu/immi, gration/reports/178/ (2007).

43 See also, Borradori, 2004; Thomassen, 2005.

44 The police are trained and regulated and instructed to adhere to the rule of law. When in pursuit, the police must still adhere to the rule of law and the fourth amendment of the constitution. The cop needs individual suspicion of wrongdoing in order to stop and question.

45 To be clear, I am not suggesting that sheriffs have inherent sovereign powers. Rather, I suggest a culture of plenary powers. The discourse since the Bybee Memo legitimates the behavior of sheriffs and local police to *act as if they had* sovereign powers. Federal officials fail to hold sheriffs accountable should they overstep the limits of the rule of law.

46 Although immigration law has developed outside the constraints of the Constitution, of course changes in the law reflect in some important ways larger changes in legal culture, which in turn have influenced immigration law. For example, the INA no longer excludes Chinese, and national origins quotas were similarly aborted. The more important point here is that such changes are the result of the political branches acting for political/policy reasons, as opposed to the courts intervening and forcing change.

47 The Minutemen Project describes itself as a "citizens neighborhood watch on our border." It is a vigilante group, co-created in 2005 by Jim Gilchrist and Chris Simcox, to patrol the border.

48 FAIR is the largest anti-immigration group in the US. The founder of FAIR is John Taunton, who is an outspoken anti-Latino critic who espouses a belief in eugenics.

49 CIS was founded in 1985 as a think tank to provide "academic" support to the activist FAIR.

50 Although there is no explicit mention of immigration in the Constitution, which is my point, Article I Section 9 does mention "the migration or importation of such persons."

51 A RFID is a radio frequency identification device that can be applied to or embedded within a passport, drivers' license, or even under the skin for the purpose of identification and tracking radio waves.

52 Biometrics is a method of identifying people on the basis of physical or behavioral traits, such as finger print, iris recognition, or DNA.

2 Framing "Illegal Aliens": Sovereignty, Plenary Powers, and Discretion

1 The CBP at the border need give no reasons for reading the content of a border crosser's laptop. They can read email and search through digital snapshots. See www.wired.com/threatlevel/2008/08/border-laptop-s/.

2 See Chapter 1 at p. 1.

3 See Calarco & DeCaroli, 2007. Whereas law denotes a juridical subject who has rights and thus safeguards against state power, in this exceptional space sovereignty bears down on the "bare life," of an individual.

4 An interesting example of the self-regulating subject in the immigration context has to do with "Operation Scheduled Departure," a program that allowed undocumented immigrants without a criminal record a chance to "self deport" by turning themselves into agents. The program was scrubbed after three months. See http://mypetjawa.mu.nu/archives/193473.php.

5 See Justice Jackson's dissent in ex rel Mezei, 345 U.S. at 219.

6 As Agamben says, this phrase originates with the German political philosopher Carl Schmitt.

7 The National Security Entry-Exit Registration System (NSEERS) established a national registry for temporary foreign visitors. For more, see DHS Factsheet: Changes to National Security Entry-Exit Registration System (NSEERS), 1 December 2003.

8 The Real ID Act of 2005, imposed security procedures on state issued drivers' licenses and state ID cards.

9 E-Verify is an Internet-based system operated by the DHS.

10 See for example, Jonathon Turley, "Camps for Citizens: Ashcroft's Hellish Vision," *LA Times*, August 14, 2002.

11 It is important to my argument to recognize that Sarat and Clarke (2008) analogize between prosecutorial discretion and Agamben's notion of sovereignty as "the exception."

12 7 Cranch 116, 3 U.S. (L. ed) 287.

13 2 Black 635, 670 (1863).

14 It should be noted that in the Prize Cases sovereignty had to do with the notion of equality among nation states. 2 Black 635, 670 (1863).

15 I wish to acknowledge a correspondence with Daniel Levin about the Prize Cases.

16 *United States v. Curtiss-Wright Export Corp.* 299 U.S. 304 (1936) is famous for declaring the existence of inherent executive power in the field of foreign affairs. Specifically the case had to do with whether congress could more broadly delegate powers to the executive branch in foreign affairs than in domestic affairs. For an interesting application of *Curtiss-Wright* to the Bush Presidency, see Louis Fisher, "The Scope of Inherent Powers," in George C. Edwards and Desmond S. King, *The Polarized Presidency of George W. Bush* (2007).

17 The Chinese Exclusion cases refer mostly to *Chae Chan Ping v. United States*, 130 U.S. 581 (1889)

18 See Saito (2003), who says, "Plenary simply means full or complete. The Supreme Court has used this doctrine to say that in certain substantive areas such as immigration law the courts will not intervene because Congress and the executive— the political branches of government—have complete power." Saito (2003) and Cleveland (2002) also note that plenary powers are also the cornerstone for federal

law governing Indian nations and external colonies such as Puerto Rico and Guam. Thus the use of plenary powers is unusual but not unique to immigration.

19 For an interesting discussion about Chinese Exclusion, see Tichenor, (2002). See also Saito (2007).

20 130 U.S. 581 (1889).

21 142 U.S. 651 (1892).

22 See *Fong Yue Ting v. United States*, 149 U.S. 698 (1893).

23 Justice Gray writing for the Court in *Fong Yue Ting* rejected equal protection claims based on the racial restrictions of the certificate.

24 Id. At 733–34.

25 See *United States v. Curtiss-Wright Export Corporation*, 299 U.S. 304 (1936).

26 According to legal scholar David Cole, after years of litigation challenging the fairness of relying on secret information, "it came out that the confidential information against Knauff was nothing more than rumor and hearsay sparked by a jilted lover of her husband" (Cole, 1991).

27 345 U.S. 206 (1953).

28 342 U.S. 580 (1952).

29 See Martin's "Due Process and membership in the Political Community" (1983).

30 430 U.S. 787 (1977).

31 727 F. 2d 957, 968 (11th Cir. 1985); see also Saito (2003), nte 36.

32 533 U.S. 678 (2001).

33 727 F. 2d 957, 968 (11th Cir. 1985).

34 Antiterrorism and Effective Death Penalty Act of 1996, Pub L. No. 104–132, 110 Stat. 1214, 1996.

35 70 F.3d 1045 (CA9 1995).

36 525 U.S. 471 (1999).

37 See http://papers.ssrn.com/sol3/papers.cfm?abstract_id=869634.

38 548 U.S. 557 (2006).

39 542 U.S. 507 (2004).

3 Criminalizing Immigration

1 The AEDPA added 17 additional types of crime to the category of aggravated felony, which was grounds for deportation. The IIRIRA added four more types of crime to the aggravated felony definition and lowered certain threshold requirements. According to the HRW Report, *Forced Apart*, before 1996, "theft offenses and crimes of violence were aggravated felonies only if the term of imprisonment was five years or more; IIRIRA reduced the term of imprisonment provision to a one-year threshold" (July, 2007).

2 See HRW Report, "Forced Apart, July 2007, which says "In their statements, members of Congress continually made such connections explicitly or implicitly to non-citizens involved in crime, no matter how petty the offense or how distinguishable from terrorism."

3 See CBP.gov, Septwmber 14, 2005. Under the law, according to DHS, immigration can expeditiously return non-Mexican illegal aliens to their country of origin as soon as circumstances will allow. Individuals in ER proceedings are not released into the United States.

4 www.humanrightsfirst.org/refugees/reports/due_process/due_pro_ap1.htm.

5 According to the NPI study, "The NFOP budget has soared over 23-fold in recent years, from $9 million in fiscal year 2003, its first year of operation, to more than $218 million in FY 2008. Moreover the program has experienced a 1,300 percent growth in personnel since its inception."

6 According to the Bush administration, both NFOP and Operation Streamline were outgrowths of its counterterrorism strategy. "Bush administration officials say the government's focus on immigration crimes is an outgrowth of its counterterrorism strategy and vigorous pursuit of immigrants with criminal records" (Moore, 2009). This was a lie.

7 According to immigration lawyer and blogger David Bennion, "What the government won't tell you is that the category 'immigrants with criminal records' includes those who have shoplifted, sold counterfeit DVDs, or been caught smoking pot" (Bennion, 2009).

8 See Sampson, 2008. Research shows that immigrants—even "illegal" ones—are associated with lower crime rates, and immigration tracks with broad reductions in crime since the 1990s.

9 The charges included falsely using criminal documents for employment. Typically such charges of fraud and identity theft are reserved for cases involving the theft of someone's identity for the purpose of robbing them. It is almost unheard-of to bring such charges against an individual who allegedly used false papers for employment.

4 Neoliberalism, Risk, and Immigration Control

1 It should be noted that many New Dealers at the time were unaware of Keynes' work.

2 The real Friedman acolyte was Donald Rumsfeld, a keen observer under Nixon who served as Nixon's special assistant and was then special envoy under Reagan before being named Bush's Secretary of Defense.

3 See the following that discusses ACLU lawsuits against the private immigration jail in Tyler, Texas. http://mexfiles.net/2007/03/22/hutto-is-child-abuse-and-can-be-reported/.

4 www.corpwatch.org/article.php?id=14333.

5 Privatization of Immigration Control

1 According to Rumsfeld, "The adversary's closer to home. It's the Pentagon bureaucracy. Not the people, but the processes. Not the civilians, but the systems. Not the men and women in uniform, but the uniformity of thought and action that we too often impose on them."

2 See Chapter 8 for discussion of the significance of the May 1, 2006 protests.

3 (9th Cir. 2008) For discussion of the case, see Electronic Frontier Foundation (EFF) website at www.eff.org/cases/us-v-arnold.

4 www.eff.org/files/filenode/US_v_arnold/arnold_amicus.pdf.

5 Parts from this section can be found in "Blackwater and the privatization of Immigration Control" (Koulish, 2008).

6 See www.pbs.org/frontlineworld/stories/mexico704/history/timeline.html.

7 http://archives.cnn.com/2001/ALLPOLITICS/09/04/bush.fox.visit/index. html; http://georgewbush-whitehouse.archives.gov/news/releases/2001/09/ 20010905.html.

8 http://usinfo.org/wf-archive/2001/010130/epf203.htm.

9 www.alipac.us/ftopicp-907017-.html.

10 www.dhs.gov/xnews/releases/pr_1165414188787.shtm.

11 www.nilc.org/immlawpolicy/removpsds/removpsds120.htm.

12 In September 2006, Boeing was awarded the SBInet contract from DHS.

13 The connection between privatization, sovereignty and profiteering has to do with the absence of accountability, which is part and parcel of sovereignty and privatization in the immigration context.

14 www.quno.org/geneva/pdf/economic/Discussion/BP-GATS-Mode4.pdf.
15 www.slate.com/id/2171747/.
16 www.adc.org/PDF/nseerspaper.pdf.
17 Immigration and Customs Enforcement, www.ice.gov/pi/news/factsheets/nseersFS120103.htm.
18 According to one study, "Many non-immigrants subjected to NSEERS program did not understand the details of the program, as the rules were unclear and public outreach and notice were insufficient" (Penn State University Dickenson School of Law Center for Immigrant Rights, March 31, 2009, p. 6).
19 www.gao.gov/new.items/d07248.pdf.
20 www.heritage.org/press/commentary/ed081904c.cfm.
21 www.gao.gov/new.items/d07378t.pdf.
22 The Unisys contract is just the latest contract with Bush family members from an administration that has been eager to reward financial contributors and supporters with lucrative government contracts. Unisys' relationship to the Republican Party dates back to when former DHS Secretary Tom Ridge was Governor of Pennsylvania. According to *Government Executive* magazine, "Tom Ridge is an old friend of the Blue Bell, Pennsylvania Company from his days as Pennsylvania governor (Unisys chairman and CEO, Larry Weinbach, met with Ridge not long after the September attacks)." Thus it is no surprise that in 2002 Unisys was recipient of a lucrative TSA grant. In 2004, it worked with Governor Jeb Bush's One Florida Mentor Protégé Program, and in 2008, Unisys was tapped to be the IT provider to the 2008 Republican Party Convention. The WHTI contract is just the latest in this train of government contracts despite the fact that Unisys has received less than stellar marks for its previous work.
23 It will be interoperable with the ADIS, IDENT, POE, IBIS, TECS, APIS, AIDMS, CCD, SEVIS systems.
24 According to the GAO (February 2008, p. 5), "As the prime contractor, Boeing is responsible for acquiring, deploying, and sustaining selected SBI technology and tactical infrastructure projects. In this way, Boeing has extensive involvement in the SBI program requirements development, design, production, integration, testing, and maintenance and support of SBI projects. Moreover, Boeing is responsible for selecting and managing a team of subcontractors that provide individual components for Boeing to integrate into the SBI*net* system."
25 The SBInet procurement process relies upon a system-of-systems approach, a lead system integrator, and indefinite delivery, indefinite quantity (IDIQ) contracts.
26 At the same hearings, Dennis Kucinich raised similar questions about the ideological bias inherent in the LSI procurement approach: "We have seen that privatization has meant profit for a few at the expense of the many, the many being the taxpayers of the United States, but also at the expense of (BBP). The contractors having control and influence over Government acquisition has meant that the financial interests of the contractors are regarded (http://64.233.169.132/search?q=cache:z0WINmRZpM4J:oversight.house.gov/documents/20071114143600.pdf+Kucinich+SBI+procurement&hl=en&ct=clnk&cd=6&gl=us&client=safari).
27 According to David Walker, GAO chief, in testimony to Congress: "Along with this greater discretion comes the need for more government oversight and an even greater need to develop well-defined outcomes at the onset" (Brodsky, Phillips, & Peters, August 15, 2007).
28 Each tower includes radar (MSTAR), infrared cameras and other sensors, and data processing and communications equipment.
29 COP is supposed to provide uniform data through a command center environment to border patrol officers in the field and all DHS agencies, and to be interoperable

with stakeholders external to DHS, such as local law enforcement (GAO, February, 2008, p. 4).

30 See GAO-08–508T February 2008, p. 13, which says that "SBI program officials reported that Project 28 was designed to be a demonstration project, rather than a fully operating system."

31 L-1 Identity Solutions (NYSE: ID) is the trusted provider of advanced technology products and solutions that protect and secure personal identities and assets. Formed in 2006 from the merger of industry powerhouses Visage and Identix, the L-1 Identity Solutions companies have a 20-year history of developing technologies to solve the world's most challenging identity-related problems. These include cutting-edge technologies and services from Integrated Biometric Technology, SecuriMetrics, and Iridian Technologies, to name a few.

32 Real ID also includes provisions to strip the federal courts of jurisdiction over immigration matters, which creates a damning tilt toward unfettered executive power over immigrants. Further squirreled away in the Act is Section 102, which grants sovereign authority to the Secretary of DHS to waive 36 federal laws related to constructing the border fence.

33 Emergency Supplemental Appropriations Act for Defense, the Global War on Terror, and Tsunami Relief, 2005.

34 505 U.S. 144 (1992).

35 According to the final regulations, verifying documents consists of two procedures: inspection to see if the document is genuine, and checking to see that the identity data on the document are valid (EPIC Report, p. 9).

36 See EPIC Report May, 2008, p. 8, which refers to reviews of similar databases that reveal millions of incorrect records belonging to U.S. citizens.

37 See EPIC Report (EPIC, 2009, p. 10) which says, "The Privacy Act of 1974 applies to the entire national identification system under guidelines set out by the Office of Management and Budget ("OMB") and the Department of Homeland Security itself." The OMB guidelines explain that:

> the Privacy Act "stipulates that systems of records operated under contract or, in some instances, State or local governments operating under Federal mandate 'by or on behalf of the agency . . . to accomplish an agency function' are subject to . . . the Act."
>
> (Office of Mgmt and Budget Privacy Act implementation: Guidelines and Responsibilities, 40 Fed, Reg. 28, 948, 28, 951 (July 9, 1975))

38 The alternative address is a "dummy" address created by the government. It forwards to the actual address and is the only address that is encoded on the bar code of the card, which means anyone who "swipes" the card has access to limited information.

39 According to its website, Digimarc is a "leading provider of driver license issuance solutions" (https://www.digimarc.com/govt/realidsect_wp.asp).

40 See H.R. 1645 and s. AMDT 1150.

41 Privacy Impact Assessment for the US-VISIT Dec ember 22, 2005, DHS: http://74.125.45.132/search?q=cache:RKlw3M44odsJ:www.dhs.gov/xlibrary/assets/privacy/privacy_pia_usvisit_update_12—22—2005.pdf+US-VISIT+data+mining&hl=en&ct=clnk&cd=1&gl=us&client=safari.

6 Race, Class, and the Border Fence Fiasco

1 According to a working group study at the University of Texas Rapoport Center, "DHS has published no comprehensive maps of planned construction. Selected maps displaying specific segments of the planned wall were originally available on a CBP

website as part of the draft environmental impact statements the government prepared before the environmental laws were waived. However, government officials repeatedly stated that those maps were outdated without providing newer maps. The maps have now been removed from the website and are no longer available" (www.utexas.edu/law/academics/centers/humanrights/publications/Background_and_Context.pdf, p. 7).

2   It should be noted that the Real ID Act waiver authority does not extend Chertoff's sovereign powers to the virtual fence, forcing DHS to issue environmental impact statements and so forth in areas set aside for the virtual fence.

3   There is no evidence that decisions were made based on an analysis of national security concerns.

4   See UN Human Rights Committee, General Comment No. 18 Non-Discrimination 10/11/1989, at section 82, citing Inter-American Court on Human Rights, Compulsory Membership in an Association Prescribed by Law for the Practice of Journalism.

5   CNN, Chertoff to Hunter: Border Fence "Overly Simplistic" (July 1, 2007); the *New York Times*, Homeland Security Stands by its Fence (May 21, 2008).

6   The Act's delegation of discretion consists of a general requirement to construct barriers, "along not less than 700 miles of the southwest border where fencing would be most practical and effective and provide for the installation of additional physical barriers, roads, lighting, cameras, and sensors to gain operational control of the southwest border" (P.L. 110–161).

7   The DHS Secretary is not *required* to install: "fencing, physical barriers, roads, lighting, cameras, and sensors in a particular location . . . if the Secretary determines that the use or placement of such resources is not the most appropriate means to achieve and maintain operational control over the international border at such location."

8   See Nedderman working group for more details. See also the following for details on alternative options: United States Government Accountability Office, Testimony before the Subcommittees on Management, Investigations, and Oversight, and Border, Maritime and Global Counterterrorism, Committee on Homeland Security, House of Representatives, Secure Border Initiative: Observations on Selected Aspects of SBInet Implementation, Wednesday, October 24, 2007. Available: www.gao.gov/new.items/d08131t.pdf.

9   Current U.S. immigration law authorizes the Secretary of DHS to contract for and buy any interest in land adjacent to or in the vicinity of the international border when the Secretary deems the land essential to control and guard the border against any violations of immigration law. It also authorizes the Secretary to commence condemnation proceedings if a reasonable purchase price cannot be agreed upon. See Illegal Immigration Reform and Immigrant Responsibility Act, section 102. 5 P.L. 110–161.

10   The expedited condemnation proceeding violated the terms of the IIRIRA that directed DHS to not use the DTA in acquiring land for border protection (IIRIRA 102(b)(2) and (d)).

11   See Pub. L 110–161, 121 Stat. 1844 (2007), Sec. 564(2)(c)(i).

12   See National Network for Immigrant and Refugee Rights website, which reports, "The court rejected Dr. Tamez's argument that if she and the Department of Homeland Security are unable after negotiations to agree on a fixed price for the right of temporary access to her land, that the government may only proceed to condemn her land under a federal law that grants her a right to a jury trial. The decision states that if the parties are unable to negotiate a fixed price for the interest the Government seeks in Dr. Tamez's land, then the Department of Homeland Security may seek to condemn the land under an expedited procedure known as

the Declaration of Taking Act" (www.nnirr.org/news/index.php?op=read&id=130&type=8).

13 DHS "shall consult with . . . States, local governments, Indian tribes, and property owners in the United States to minimize the impact . . . for the communities and residents located near the sites (where) fencing is to be constructed."

14 TBC's member cities are Laredo, Rio Grande City, Mission, Hidalgo, Harlingen, Alamo, Eagle Pass, San Juan, Brownsville, Roma, Edinburg, Mercedes, El Paso, Pharr, McAllen, Port Isabel, Del Rio, La Joya, Weslaco. TBC's member counties are Cameron, El Paso, Hidalgo, Starr, Webb, Dimmit, Maverick, Val Verde, Zapata, and Terrell.

15 The Gadsden Treaty was signed in 1853. It was ratified in 1854.

7 The Federalization of Sovereign Control: Outsourcing Immigration Enforcement Authority to State and Local Officials

1 The idea of a racialized space considers hegemonic social relations between people of color and dominant groups and institutions within particular communities that adopt anti-immigrant programs.

2 INA 8 USC 1101.

3 A second instance of state enforcement power is temporary and occurs following a mass influx of non-citizens, which requires an immediate response from the government, and the federal government receives the state's consent to empower its police to assist the DHS.

4 Civil provisions here include any civil offense under the INA.

5 See 8 USC 1324.

6 See 8 USC 1325(a).

7 722 F. 2d 468, 476 (9th Cir. 1983).

8 Gonzales, 722 F. 2d at 475.

9 Gonzales, 722 F. 2d. at 474–5.

10 424 U.S. 351 at 354.

11 Another view is that the target was the French government agents trying to persuade America to declare war on Britain to support Revolutionary France.

12 3b U.S. 102 (1837).

13 48 U.S. 7 HOW. 283 283 (1849).

14 See Antiterrorism and Effective Death Penalty Act (AEDPA; P.L. 104–132; Sec. 439); and IIRIRA (P.P. 104–206; Sec 133 and 372).

15 See Memorandum from Deputy Attorney General for Commissioner of INS, January 25, 2002, at http://news.findlaw.com/hdocs/docs/doj/abscndr012502 mem.pdf.

16 NCIC is a computerized index of criminal justice information (criminal record history information, fugitives, stolen properties, missing persons), and is available to federal, state and local law enforcement. Many people criticize NCIC databases for inaccurate data and for not being responsive to changing data. For more information see, www.fas.org/irp/agency/doj/fbi/is/ncic.htm.

17 See http://74.125.45.132/search?q=cache:C6Q1_yJda-AJ:www.ice.gov/pi/dro/index.htm+Absconder+Apprehension+Initiative&cd=5&hl=en&ct=clnk&gl=us&client=safari.

18 See www.aclu.org/safefree/general/17211res20030609.html.

19 Federal News Service, Press Conference With U.S. AG John Ashcroft and James Ziglar, Commissioner, INS, Re: Tracking of Foreign Visitors, June 5, 2002.

20 See CRS Report at http://74.125.47.132/search?q=cache:BivPQeBTZF8J:www.mnllp.com/CRSenforce11mar04.pdf+immigration+law+1252+(c)&cd=4&hl=en&ct=clnk&gl=us&client=safari, note 26, which says "In June 2002, White House

Counsel, Alberto Gonzalez, acknowledged the 'inherent authority' conclusion from the 2002 OLC opinion in a letter to the Migration Policy Institute (which requested information about the new policy) available at: Bender's Immigration Bulletin, vol. 7, p. 965 August 1, 2002."

21 The doctrine of preemption is based on the principle that the U.S. Constitution and U.S. laws are the "supreme law of the land," pursuant to the Supremacy Clause (Art. VI, cl. 2 of the U.S. Constitution). According to *Martinez v. Regents of the University of California*:

> (S)tate law is pre-empted . . . in three circumstances. First, Congress can define explicitly the extent to which its enactments pre-empt state law . . . Second . . . state law is pre-empted where it regulates conduct in a field that Congress intended the federal Government to occupy exclusively . . . Finally, state law is pre-empted to the extent it actually conflicts with federal law.

22 Some conservative legal scholars have attempted to justify Bybee's notion of inherent powers for states to enforce immigration. See, for example, Kris Kobach (2005).

23 See Mayer, 2008; Wax, 2008; Ball, 2007.

24 For an excellent critique of the torture memos, see Dean, March 6, 2009.

25 See United States Immigration and Customs Enforcement, Partners, available at www.ice.gov/partners/287g/Section287_g.htm.

26 According to an ICE fact sheet:

> [t]he 287g program is designed to enable state and local law enforcement personnel, incidental to a lawful arrest and during the course of their normal duties, to question and detain individuals for potential removal from the United States, if these individuals are identified as undocumented illegal aliens and they are suspected of committing a state crime.
>
> (Fact Sheet, September 24, 2007)

27 As of June 2009, 63 law enforcement agencies have entered into 287(g) MOUs with ICE. See www.ice.gov/partners/287g/Section287_g.htm.

28 See GAO Report (09–109), Immigration Enforcement: Better Controls Needed of Program Authorizing State and Local Enforcement of federal Immigration Laws, (January, 2009) which criticizes the 287(g) program for lack of federal oversight, http://www.gao.gov/products/GAO-09-109.

29 See GAO-09–381T Immigration Enforcement: Controls over Program Authorizing State and Local Enforcement of Federal Immigration Laws Should Be Strengthened.

30 It is important to note that about 95% of local municipalities nationwide have never applied for a 287(g) MOU. Of those who discussed the matter, many local jurisdictions rejected the idea of applying for a 287(g) MOU because 1) they would receive almost no resources from the federal government aside from initial training and access to national databases, and 2) concern over public safety outcomes if they were to be seen by their communities as "la migra." In turn, many applications for 287(g) MOUs are the result of political (anti-immigrant) as opposed to policy (law enforcement) motivations. For more discussion on this issue see Monica Varsanyi (2008).

31 See Weissman congressional testimony, which refers to Gill's work.

32 Weissman's testimony refers to Hannah Gill's new book, *North Carolina and the Latino Immigrant Experience* (forthcoming).

33 According to the UNC policy brief (2009 at p. 13), state and local law enforcement officers may be failing to comply with:

• Federal constitutional law by not complying with equal protection, as a result of racial profiling and harassment of foreign nationals.

- The Civil Rights Act of 1964 by discriminating against individuals based on their race, color, or ethnicity.
- Department of Justice Guidelines that were developed "for Federal officials to ensure an end to racial profiling in law enforcement."
- Federal criminal procedure law by hurrying undocumented immigrants through the system.
- International treaty law by failing to communicate with consular officers from the detainees' countries of origin in a timely matter, as required by Article 36 of the Vienna Convention on Consular Relations.

34 April 2, 2009, Committee on the Judiciary Subcommittee on the Constitution, Civil Rights, and Civil Liberties and the Subcommittee on Immigration, Citizenship, Refugees, Border Security, and International Law, United States House of Representatives Joint Hearing on the "Public Safety and Civil Rights Implications of State and Local Enforcement of Federal Immigration Laws."

35 www.americasvoiceonline.org/blog/entry/local_immigration_enforcement_hearing_highlights/.

36 For example, see one poll in North Carolina taken after implementation of 287(g) MOU, at James H. Johnson, Jr. et al., A Profile of Hispanic Newcomers to North Carolina, Popular Gov't, Fall 1999.

37 See u-visa remedy—get three year visas if cooperate with local law enforcement in investigation and prosecution of crimes; get certification from local police.

38 For more information see Mary Bauer, 2006. According to Bauer writing for the Southern Poverty Research Center, "A 'model' ordinance has been making the rounds of various cities around the country. What it proposes to do is to punish people who hire, rent to, or sell to so-called 'illegal aliens.' www.splcenter.org/intel/intelreport/article.jsp?aid=682.

39 See Anti Defamation League (ADL) website.

40 Mayor Lou Barletta who drafted the Hazleton ordinance claims he copied much of the language from a similar ordinance proposed in San Bernardino, California.

41 According to the formal complaint, *Riverside Coalition of Business Persons and Landlords v Township of Riverside*, at www.aclu-nj.org/downloads/Riverside Complaint.pdf, "[t]he Riverside ordinance is so vague that plaintiffs and those interacting with plaintiffs will be unable to comply with or apply it in a consistent manner" (at p. 17). Moreover it violated Article 1, Paragraph 1 of the State of New Jersey Constitution for vagueness. For example, the ordinance fails to define the term, "illegal immigration;" creates fines and penalties for "aiding and abetting" "illegal immigrants," but again fails to define the terms.

42 According to Elliot Mincberg, Vice President and Legal Director for People, For the American Way Foundation, one of the legal organizations representing the Coalition, "This ordinance is so vague and overbroad that it's virtually impossible to obey and appears to ban a large amount of innocent conduct." See www.aclu-nj.org/news/aclunjjoinslocalcoalitiont.htm.

43 See http://74.125.47.132/search?q=cache:eSbOhWnMze0J:www.tjsl.edu/node/555+Hazleton+ordinance+landlords+risk&cd=3&hl=en&ct=clnk&gl=us&client=safari.

44 See press release by PRLDEF, September 17, 2007, at http://74.125.47.132/search?q=cache:kPeN3CG5pYcJ:www.prldef.org/civil_rights/Riverside/Riverside%2520Rescinds%2520Local%2520anti-immigration%2520ordinance.pdf+anti+immigrant+ordinances+risk&cd=2&hl=en&ct=clnk&gl=us&client=safari.

45 According to the legal complaint, it places landlords, employers and business owners in the untenable position of being obligated, without any standards, to demand proof of status for every suspected illegal alien to avoid the risk of imprisonment, fines and loss of municipal businesses, or alternatively, to deny services

to lawful residents as a precaution to avoid transgressing the Riverside ordinance, thereby risking violation of federal and state anti-discrimination laws" (at www. aclu-nj.org/downloads/RiversideComplaint.pdf, p. 3).

46 457 U.S. 202.

47 496 F. Supp. 2d 477.

48 See http://74.125.47.132/search?q=cache:wkttl-m1E0UJ:sites.google.com/site/ transborderproject/immigration-index/immigration-reform-law-institute+ FAIR+immigration+Riverside+NJ&cd=7&hl=en&ct=clnk&gl=us&client=safari.

49 Under the ordinance, employers and landlords would be fined one thousand dollars for each incident of renting to or hiring an undocumented immigrant. Business would be denied business permit or renewals and barred from receiving grants or township contracts for five years. According to the complaint "Violations of the ordinance result in fines of one thousand to two thousand dollar; a term of imprisonments or period of community service not exceeding 90 days; denial of approval of a business permit or non-renewal of a business permit, or Township contracts or grants for a period of not less than 5 years from the last offense." See complaint at www.aclu-nj.org/downloads/RiversideComplaint.pdf. See also www. nytimes.com/2006/07/28/nyregion/28ban.html?_r=1.

50 According to local business owner David Verduin, the negative effect on the community was almost immediate, having "scared off" about one-third of the immigrant population, causing some businesses to close and others to see declining sales. www.aclu-nj.org/news/aclunjjoinslocalcoalitiont.htm.

8 Immigrant Resistance or Immigrant Control: The Technology Game is On

1 The doctrine of sovereign immunity says the federal government is immune to civil lawsuits for monetary damages unless Congress waives that immunity by statute that specifically authorizes such lawsuits.

2 Migra Matters put out a bilingual call announcing the May 1, 206 Boycott. It also provided a list of activities and events, and posted public meeting times and locations across the country. http://migramatters.blogspot.com/2006/04/great-american-boycott-2006-events-for.html.

3 This blog provided a live stream of events as they were occurring throught the day. For example, see http://xicanopwr.com/2006/05/may-day-el-gran-boicot-live-blogging:

> "For the biggest news. The boycott at Los Angeles Harbor."
>
> 8:40 AM Mr. A is reporting that the truckers have successfully shut down 90% of Los Angeles Harbor. So far only 5 trucks have shown up.
>
> 9:05 AM The traffic at LA harbor is usually 100 trucks per hour, but so far today only 5 trucks showed up in the last few hours.
>
> [Update] hosted by and the in solidarity with the May 1st General Strike/Walkout/Boycott in the U.S. and actions for Freedom of Movement taking place all over Europe on May 1st, 2006.
>
> [] Hundreds of Mexican union members took to the streets of central Mexico City early Monday to support Mexican migrants living and working in the United States and to boycott U.S. goods in what was dubbed a "A Day Without Gringos."
>
> At the U.S. Embassy in Mexico City, there were about 50 police officers recalled because of the arrival of the Zapatista leader, Subcomandante Marcos, he has been very vocal in supporting the Mexican boycott.
>
> [RE:RE:Update] is reporting that Puerto Rican schools, government offices close because the government ran out of money Monday, forcing Puerto Rico

to close public schools and shut down government offices, putting almost 100,000 people out of work.

It is the first-ever partial shutdown of the government in island history and it happened on May Day, how strange.

4 For an excellent discussion of the Obama campaigns use of Web 2.0, see Clay Sharky lecture (filmed May, 2009) at www.ted.com/talks/clay_shirky_how_cellphones_twitter_facebook_can_make_history.html.

5 The Dream Act would provide certain undocumented immigrant students who graduate from U.S. high schools, are of good moral character, arrived in the US as children, and have been in the country continuously for at least five years prior to the bill's enactment, the opportunity to earn conditional permanent residency. The students will obtain temporary residency for a lapse of six years. Within the six year period, a qualified student must attend college, and earn a two year degree, or serve in the military for two years in order to earn citizenship after the six years period. If student does not comply with either his/her college requirement or military service requirement, temporary residency will be taken away and student will be subjected to deportation.

6 http://news.newamericamedia.org/news/view_article.html?article_id=13a66cc 162790c5ae097e0a548ccbb7c.

7 While anyone's Facebook page can be censored by the owners of Facebook, tweets can only be censored if the government were to block the entire twitter network.

8 http://online.wsj.com/article/SB124562668777335653.html#mod=rss_whats_ news_us.

9 http://online.wsj.com/article/SB124562668777335653.html#mod=rss_whats_ news_us.

10 Of course some of these concerns could be mitigated by acts of Congress. The challenge, however would be to get congress to include immigrants in its privacy requirements.

11 In June 2000, the National Security Agency (NSA) announced it was pursuing a "government-industry partnership for information technology infrastructure services" (Truthdig.com). On September 1, 2001, *Government Executive* magazine published an investigation of the privatization of the NSA:

> Beginning in November (2001), hundreds of National Security Agency technology specialists will walk out the doors . . . ending their careers as federal workers. But nearly all will return the next day to do the same jobs they did before, as contractors under the largest outsourcing ever conducted by an intelligence agency . . . One of the largest IT outsourcing pacts in government, NSA's Project Groundbreaker contract reflects a growing recognition by agencies that private companies can provide better IT support at lower prices than federal workers can, www.truthdig.com/dig/page2/20070809_inside_the_data_mine/.

12 www.docstoc.com/docs/5379095/Jewel-Complaint.

13 See Chapter 9 for analysis of the Obama administration on the *Jewel* case.

9 President Obama's New Emphasis on Immigration Control

1 According to Laura Carlsen, it is a "common front that would assume shared responsibility for protecting the United States from terrorist threats, promoting and protecting the free-trade economic model . . ." (Carlsen, 2008).

2 For further evidence of this, see the President's Lincoln Day Dinner speech in Springfield Illinois, February 12, 2009.

3 By claiming "State secrets," the Bush administration endeavored to put executive power and secrecy above the constitution.

4 See www.eff.org/cases/jewel that describes the lawsuit *Jewel v. NSA*.
5 According to her National Press Club speech, here are the main points for a Napolitano immigration policy:

*   Innovative, technology-driven border control between the ports of entry.
*   Reform the visa system and streamline the visa process.
*   Institute a temporary worker program with no amnesty.
*   Employers who knowingly hire illegal immigrants should be held accountable and penalized.
*   Modernize our border infrastructure so that enforcement does not hinder the flow of legitimate travel and commerce.
*   A pathway to citizenship that involves a substantial fine, learning English, having no criminal history, keeping a job, paying taxes, then getting in the back of the line and waiting your turn.
*   Address the root causes of illegal immigration by engaging directly with Mexico and Latin America.

6 According to Angelica Salas, director of the Coalition for Humane Immigrant Rights of Los Angeles, "We voted in the millions, and now we're going to demand progress in the millions" (Aizenman, November 11, 2008).
7 Public Law 111–5.
8 Mark Borkowski replaced Gary Giddens as head of SBInet in September, 2008.

10 Conclusion

1 Since under the Obama regulation plan, undocumented immigrants would "get to the back of the line" in terms of being able to apply for citizenship, risk management strategies would likely be tailored to this new reality of having millions of formerly undocumented immigrants going through the rigors of regularizing their status.
2 An underreported but obvious point here is that immigrant laborers are quite likely to endure the brunt of effective enforcement of employer sanctions. It is unlikely that ICE, for example, would enter the workplace and arrest the employer while leaving the undocumented workers behind.
3 www.dailykos.com/story/2009/4/15/720361/-Obama-AdministrationTakes-on-Immigration-Reform.
4 The downfall of legalization under IRCA (1986) was that the Regan administration cared not one whit about applying constitutional norms to immigration. As an outcome, the design for legalization was sabotaged. As Guttentag says, ". . . sadly, we know from long experience that our immigration agencies . . . are more likely to restrict or even undermine a legalization program than implement it generously and fairly. Whether by instinct, or because it is overwhelmed, incompetent or downright hostile, we cannot depend on DHS to police itself" (www.dailykos.com/storyonly/2009/4/15/720361/-Obama-AdministrationTakes-on-Immigration-Reform).
5 See the following website for resources on human rights as the field pertains to immigration. www.energyofanation.org/7d00b32b-a738-4a71-9ccf-2117fc9bbb64.html?NodeId=.com.
6 John McKnight reminds us to frame the debate in terms of the assets that immigrants bring to America rather than on deficits and constructed fear. I think this is where the change begins, with the terms of the debate. From there the courts need to recognize the nexus between immigrants as persons under the constitution whether at the border or within the country's interior. Neither does the issue of immigration control end by recognizing due process and separation of powers, but it is here through which the larger struggle must pass because from this point forward immigrants gain access into the larger political debate in myriads of possible forms.

Bibliography

ACLU. (1999). Analysis of immigration detention policies: Support fair detention policies. Retrieved September 2, 2009, from www.aclu.org/immigrants/detention/1177lleg19990818.html.

ACLU. (2007). Immigration expert: Hazleton went too far. Retrieved May 12, 2009, from http://aclupa.blogspot.com/2007/03/immigration-expert-hazleton-went-too.html.

ACLU. (2008). *REAL nightmare*. Washington, DC: ACLU.

ACLU. (2009). ACLU testimony submitted for the house homeland security committee hearing titled, "the role of state and local law enforcement in immigration law." Retrieved September 2, 2009, from http://74.125.113.132/search?q=cache:9REPlkVLxc0J:www.aclu.org/immigrants/gen/39062leg20090304.html+ACLU+march+4+2009+287+g&cd=2&hl=en&ct=clnk&gl=us&client=safari.

Agamben, G. (1998). *Homo sacer: Sovereign power and bare life*. Stanford, CA: Stanford University.

Agamben, G. (2005). *The state of exception*. Chicago: University of Chicago.

Aizenman, N. C. (2009). Conflicting accounts of an ICE raid in MD. *The Washington Post*, February 18.

Aizenman, N. C. (2009). Report cites problems in ICE training program. *The Washington Post*, March 4.

Aleinikoff, A. (1998). A multicultural nationalism? *American Prospect, 36*, 80.

Aleinikoff, A. (2002). *Semblances of sovereignty: The constitution, the state, and American citizenship*. Cambridge: Harvard University Press.

Aleinikoff, A., & Martin, D. (1985). *Immigration: Process and policy*. St. Paul, MN: West.

Aman, A. C. (2006). Law, markets and democracy: A role for law in the neo-liberal state. *New York Law School Law Review, 51*, 801.

Ambinder, M. (2009). State secrets privilege invoked again. *The Atlantic*, March 25. Retrieved September 2, 2009, from http://politics.theatlantic.com/author/marc_ambinder/.

Amnesty International. (2009). *Jailed without justice: Immigration detention in the USA*. Washington, DC: Amnesty International.

Amoore, L., & de Goede, M. (Eds.) (2008). *Risk and the war on terror*. New York: Routledge.

AP. (2008). O'odham: Border fence would cause damage. *Tuscon Citizen.Com*, April 14.

AP. (2008). Lawmakers get hostile reception at border fence hearing. *Dallas Morning News*, Monday, April 28.

Aradau, C. (2001). *Migration: The spiral of (in)security.* Rubikon International Forum of Electronic Publications, March.

Arce, L., & Van Auken, B. (2008). New York city cops arrest immigrant day laborers. www.wsws.org/articles/2008/oct2008/immi-o29.shtml.

Archibold, R. C. (2009). Report questions immigration program. *The New York Times*, March 3.

Arenson, K. W. (2004). In protest, professor cancels visit to the U.S. *The New York Times*, January 17.

Bacon, D. (2005). *Illegal people: How globalization creates migration and criminalizes immigrants.* Boston: Beacon Press.

Bain, B. (2009). DHS secretary discusses department's IT programs. *Federal Computer Week*, February 25.

Barry, T. (2009). Imprisoning immigrants for profit. *Counterpunch*, March 13/15.

Bellah, R. (1992). *The broken covenant: American civil religion in time of trial.* Chicago: University of Chicago.

Bennion, D. (2009). Immigrant rights, July 1, 2009, from http://immigration.change.org/.

Benson, L. B. (2006/07). Making paper dolls: How restrictions on judicial review and the administrative process increase immigration cases in the federal courts. *New York Law School Law Review*, 51, 37.

Bernstein, N. (2009). Another jail death, and mounting questions. *The New York Times*, January 27.

Bernstein, N. (2009). Target of immigrant raids shifted. The *New York Times*, February 3.

Berry, D., & Chebium, R. (2009). DHS chief supports E-Verify. *Daily Record*, March 31.

Biessecker, C. (2009). Technology important for border security, Napolitano says. *Defense Daily*, January 16.

Bloom, R. (2008). Border searches in the age of terrorism. *Mississippi Law Journal*, 78(2), 295.

Borradori, G. (2004). *Philosophy in a time of terror: Dialogues with Jurgen Habermas and Jacques Derrida.* Chicago: University of Chicago.

Brenner, N., & Theodore, N. (2003). *Spaces of neoliberalism: Urban restructuring in North America and Western Europe.* New York: Routledge.

Brill, S. (2003). *After: The rebuilding and defending of America in the September 12 era.* New York: Simon & Schuster.

Brodsky, R., Phillips, Z., & Peters, K. M. (2007). Big contracts, big problems. *Government Executive* Magazine, August 15.

Brulliard, K. (2008). Crackdown on illegal immigration quiets soccer fields. *The Washington Post*, March 12.

Butler, J. (2004). *Precarious life: The power of mourning and violence.* London: Verso.

Calarco, M., & DeCaroli, S. (Eds.) (2007). *Georgio Agamben: Sovereignty and life.* Stanford, CA: Stanford University.

Calavita, K. (1992). *Inside the state.* New York: Routledge.

De Canas v Bica. (424 U.S. 351 1976).

Capriccioso, R. (2009). Homeland security chief promises consultation. *Indian Country Today*, March 13.

Capuzzo, J. (2006). Town battling illegal immigration is emptier now. *The New York Times*, July 28.

Carlsen, L. (2008). A primer on Plan Mexico. Retrieved September 2, 2009, from http://74.125.113.132/search?q=cache:pTDlhZNF0ZgJ:www.narconews.com/Issue53/article3093.html+Carlson+july+10+2008+militarize+mexican&cd=2&hl=en&ct=clnk&gl=us&client=safari.

Carroll, S. (2009). ICE raids mostly nab non-criminals. *The Houston Chronicle*, February 4.

Chae Chan Ping. (130 U.S. 581 1889).

Chavez Leyva, Y. (2009). We shouldn't militarize the U.S.–Mexico border. *The Progressive Magazine*, March 23.

Citizens for Responsibility and Ethics in Washington (CREW) (Ed.) (n.d.). *DHS: Five years of government mismanagement. Citizens for Responsibility and Ethics in Washington.* Retrieved September 2, from www.homelandsecurityforsale.org.

Clayton Jr., W. E. (1995). Our border can be controlled. *The Houston Chronicle*, June 1.

Cleveland, S. H. (2002). Powers inherent in sovereignty: Indians, aliens, territories, and the nineteenth century origins of plenary Power over foreign affairs. *Texas Law Review*, *81*, 1.

Cole, A. (2008). Virtual fence for Mexico border is put off. *The Wall Street Journal*, September 10.

Cole, D. (1991). Don't let white house order secret trials. *The New York Times*, June 2.

Cole, D. (2003). *Enemy aliens: Double standards and constitutional freedoms in the war on terror.* New York: New Press.

Cole, D. (2006). The idea of humanity: Human rights and immigrants' rights. *Columbia Human Rights Law Review*, *37*, 627.

Coleman, M. (2007). Immigration geopolitics beyond the Mexico-U.S. border. *Antipode*, *39*, 54–76.

Coonan, T. (1998). Dolphins caught in congressional fishnets: Immigration law's new aggravated felons. *Georgetown Immigration Law Journal*, *12*, 589.

Cornelius, W. A. (2004). *Controlling "unwanted" immigration: Lessons from the United States, 1993–2004.* Berkeley, CA: University of California, The Center for Comparative Immigration Studies.

Costanza-Chock, S. (2008). The immigrant rights movement on the net: Between "net 2.0" and communicacion popular. *American Quarterly*, *60*(3), 851.

Cox, A. B., & Rodriguez, C. (2009). The President and immigration law. *Yale Law Journal*, *119*.

Daniels, R. (2004). *Guarding the golden door: American immigration policy and immigrants since 1882.* New York: Hill and Wang.

Davenport, P. (2008). Arizona to deploy traffic camera web. *The Washington Times*, September 26.

Davis, T., & Waxman, H. A. (2006). *Waste, abuse, and mismanagement in department of homeland security contracts.* Washington, DC: United States House of Representatives.

de Jesus Butler, I. (2007). *Unraveling sovereignty: Human rights actors and the structure of international law*. Oxford: Intersentia.

Dean, M. (2007). *Governing societies*. Maidenhead: Open University Press.

Deepa, F. (2006). *Targeted: Homeland security and the business of immigration*. New York: Seven Stories Press.

del Bosque, M. (2008). Holes in the wall: Homeland security won't say why the border wall is bypassing the wealthy and politically connected. *The Texas Observer*, February 22.

del Bosque, M. (2009). Back to the wall. *The Texas Observer*, February 27.

DeLong, M. (2008). Obama to defer to Napolitano on border fence. *Washington Independent*, December 10.

Department of Homeland Security, & Office of Inspector General. (2006). *Detention and removal of illegal aliens: U.S. immigration and customs enforcement* (ICE No. OIG-06-033), April 14.

Devins, N. (2006). Should the supreme court fear congress? *Minnesota Law Review*, *90*, 1337.

DHS. (2003). Secretary of homeland security tom ridge announces private sector senior advisory committee members. Press Release.

DHS. (2009). Secretary Napolitano announces ARRA funding for southwest border ports of entry. Retrieved September 2, 2009, from www.dhs.gov/ynews/releases/pr_1238626069590.shtm.

Dobkin, D. (2007). Court stripping and limitations on judicial review of immigration cases. *Justice System Journal*, *28*, 104.

Donnelly, J. (2003). *Universal human rights in theory and practice* (2nd ed.). Ithaca: Cornell University.

Donner, F. J. (1981). *The age of surveillance: The aims and methods of America's Political intelligence system*. New York: Vintage Books.

Dow, M. (2004). *American gulag: Inside U.S. immigration prisons*. Los Angeles: U.C. Press.

Dunn, T. (1996). *The militarization of the U.S. Mexico border, 1978–1992: Low intensity conflict doctrine comes home*. Austin, TX: University of Texas.

Dunn, T. (2009). *Blockading the border and human rights: The el paso operation that remade immigration enforcement*. Austin, TX: University of Texas.

Durand, J., & Massey, D. (Eds.) (2006). *Crossing the border: Research from the Mexican migration project*. New York: Russell Sage.

Edelman, M. (1985). *The symbolic uses of politics*. Urbana, IL: University of Illinois.

Egelko, B. (2009). Obama administration backs telecom immunity. *San Francisco Chronicle*, February 27.

EPIC. (2008). *REAL ID implementation review: Few benefits, staggering costs*. Wasington, DC: Electronic Privacy Information Center.

EPIC. (2009). US-VISIT. Retrieved June 15, 2009, from http://epic.org/privacy/us-visit/#introduction.

Ericson, R. V. (2008). The state of preemption: Managing terrorism through counter law. In L. Amoore, & M. de Goede (Eds.), *Risk and the war on terror*. New York: Routledge..

Fahim, K. (2007). Should immigration be a police issue? *The New York Times*, April 29.

Family, J. E. (2009). *A broader view of the immigration adjudication problem* (09–02 ed.). Wilmington, DE: Widener University, Widner Law School Legal Studies Research Paper Series.

Fernandes, D. (2007). *Targeted: Homeland security and the business of immigration.* New York: Seven Stories Press.

Fiallo v Bell. (430 U.S. 787 1977).

Fisher, L. (2007). The scope of inherent powers. In G. C. Edwards, & D. S. King (Eds.), *The polarized presidency of George W. Bush.* Oxford: Oxford University.

Fisher, W. (2009). Rights-US: ACLU sues controversial sheriff. *Inter Press Service (IPS),* August 21.

Fitzpatrick, P., & Joyce, R. (2007). *Democracy's empire: Sovereignty, law, and violence.* Hoboken: Wiley.

Fong Yue Ting v. United States. (149 U.S. 1893).

Frank, T. (2008). Napolitano backs security tech. *USA Today,* December 29.

Freeman, J., & Minow, M. (2009). *Government by contract: Outsourcing and American democracy.* Cambridge, MA: Harvard University.

Galuszka, P. (2008). UT-Brownsville, feds compromise on border fence. *Diverse Issues in Higher Education,* September 18.

GAO. (2003). *Border security: Challenges facing the department of homeland security in balancing its border security and trade facilitation missions* (No. GAO-03-902T). Washington, DC: General Accountability Office (GAO).

GAO. (2006). *Border security: Continued weaknesses in screening entrants into the United States* (No. GAO-06–976T). Washington, DC: General Accountability Office (GAO).

GAO. (2008). *Employment verification: Challenges exist in implementing a mandatory electronic employment verification system* (No. GAO-08-895T). Washington, DC: General Accountability Office (GAO).

GAO. (2008). *Homeland security: U.S. visitor and immigrant status indicator technology program planning* (No. 09-96). Washington, DC: General Accountability Office (GAO).

GAO. (2008). *Secure border initiative: Observations on the importance of applying lessons learned.* Washington, DC: General Accountability Office (GAO).

Garcia, A. (2007). Court rules secretary Chertoff violating the law in building border wall. Retrieved 6/20, 2009, from www.nnirr.org/news/index.php?op=read&id=130&type=8.

Garland, D. (2001). *The culture of control.* Chicago: University of Chicago.

Gaynor, T. (2008). U.S. offers self deportation to illegal immigrants. *Reuters,* August 5.

German, M., & Stanley, J. (2007). What's wrong with fusion centers? *ACLU,* December.

Gibney, M., & Hansen, R. (2005). *Immigration and asylum: From 1900 to the present.* Cambridge: Cambridge University Press.

Gilman, D. (2008). *Obstructing human rights: The Texas–Mexico border wall.* Austin, TX: University of Texas, Rapport Center for Human Rights and Justice.

Glantz, A. (2008). Border fence raises environmental concerns. *OneWorld US,* November 3.

Gordon, S. (2008). ICE anti-gang operation nets 81. *North County Times,* July 22.

Gorman, A. (2009). U.S. to collect DNA samples of arrested immigrants. *The Los Angeles Times*, January 9.

Greenwald, G. (2009). New and worse secrecy and immunity claims from the Obama DOJ. *Salon.com*, April 6.

Grossman, Z. (2009). Iran protests: Twitter, the medium of movement. *Time Magazine*, June 17.

Guttentag, L. (2009). Obama administration takes on immigration reform. *ACLU*, April 16.

Hacker, J. S. (2006). *The great risk shift: The assault on American jobs, family, health care, and retirement—and how you can fight back*. New York: Oxford University.

Haddal, C., Kim, Y., & Garcia, M. J. (2009). *Border security: Barriers along the U.S. international border*. Washington, DC: Congressional Research Service (CRS).

Hall, L. (2004). Nomads under the tent of blue: Migrants fuel the U.S. prison industry. *Rutgers Race & the Law Review*, 6, 265.

Hamdi v Rumsfeld. (542 U.S. 557 2004).

Hamilton, A. (2006). A day without immigrants: Making a statement. *Time Magazine*, May 1.

Harisiades v Shaughnessy. (342 U.S. 580 1952).

Harper, J. (2007). Testimony of Jim Harper to the Senate Committee on the Judiciary. *Will real ID actually make us safer?* Washington, DC: CATO Institute.

Harvey, D. (2005). *A brief history of neoliberalism*. Oxford: Oxford University.

Harwood, E. (1986). *In liberty's shadow: Illegal aliens and immigration law*. Stanford, CA: Stanford University, Hoover Institution.

Hayes, S. F. (2007). *Cheney: The untold story of America's most powerful and controversial vice president*. New York: Harper Collins.

Henderson v Mayor of City of New York. (92 U.S. 259 1875).

Hernandez, C. C. G. (2008). E-Verify: Bad execution, bad idea. *Z Magazine*, July.

Higham, J. (1955). *Strangers in the land: Patterns of American nativism 1860–1925*. New Brunswick: Rutgers.

Hing, B. O. (2008). SALT and NLG statement on Postville raid. http://lawprofessors.typepad.com/immigration/2008/06/salt-and-nlg-st.html.

Hinman, K. (2007). Valley park to Mexican immigrants: Adios, illegals. *Riverfront Times*, 28 February.

Hofstadter, R. (1964). The paranoid style in American politics. *Harper's Magazine*, 77, November.

Hsu, S. (2009). Immigration priorities questioned. *The Washington Post*, February 5.

Hsu, S. (2009). Delay in immigration raids may signal policy change. *The Washington Post*, March 29.

Hsu, S. (2009). Obama revives Bush idea of using E-Verify to catch illegal contract workers. *The Washington Post*, July 8.

Hsu, S., & Sheridan, M. B. (2009). Anti drug effort at border is readied: Obama plans to send agents, equipment to aid Mexican fight. *The Washington Post*, March 22.

Huntington, C. (2008). The constitutional dimension of constitutional federalism. *Vanderbilt Law Review*, 61(3), 787.

Jackson, J. L. S. (2006). "Si se puede" means "we shall overcome". *Tribune Media Services*, May 2.

Janofsky, M. (2004). 911 panel calls policies on immigration ineffective. *The New York Times*, April 17.

Jean v. Nelson. (727 F. 2d 957 1985).

Judiciary House of Representatives. (2009). Joint hearing on the "Public safety and civil rights implications of state and local enforcement of federal immigration laws," April 2, Washington, DC: United States House of Representatives.

Kalhan, A. (2008). *Immigration enforcement and federalism after September 11, 2001.* New York: Fordham University School of Law.

Kamp, D. (2008). Grijalva condemns border fence waivers. *Green Valley News*, April 1.

Kanstroom, D. (2007). *Deportation nation: Outsiders in American history.* Cambridge: Harvard University Press.

Kanstroom, D. (2006/2007). The better part of valor: The real ID act, discretion, and the "rule" of immigration law. *New York Law School Law Review, 51,* 161.

Kenney, M. (2004). DHS announces unprecedented expansion of expedited removal to the interior. *American Immigration Law Foundation Practice Advisory*, August 13.

Kettles, G. W. (2009). Day labor markets and public space. *Mississippi College of Law Research Paper, 2009–05,* Jackson, MS: Mississippi School of Law.

Klatell, J. (2006). Preparing for immigration protests. *AP Press*, April 26.

Klein, N. (2007). *The shock doctrine.* New York: Metropolitan Books.

Klinenberg, E., & Frank, T. (2005). Looting homeland security. *Rolling Stone*, December 15.

Kobach, K. (2005). The quintessential force multiplier: The inherent authority of local police to make immigration arrests. *Albany Law Review, 69,* 179.

Kobach, K. (2006). *Courting chaos: Senate proposal undermines immigration law.* Washington, DC: Heritage Foundation.

Konvitz, M. (1953). *Civil rights in immigration.* Ithaca, NY: Cornell University.

Koslowski, R. (2005). *Real challenges for virtual borders: The implementation of US-VISIT.* Washington, DC: Migration Policy Institute.

Koulish, R. (1992). Systemic deterrence against prospective asylum seekers: A study of a South Texas immigration district. *New York University Review of Law and Social Change*, 19.

Koulish, R. (1994). U.S. immigration authorities and victims of human and civil rights abuses: The border interaction project study of South Tucson, Arizona, and South Texas. Tucson, AZ: University of Arizona.

Koulish, R. (1996). Bordering on chaos. Unpublished Ph.D., University of Wisconsin-Madison, Madison, WI.

Koulish, R. (2007). Privatizing the leviathan immigration state. *Monthly Review (Online)*, July 20.

Koulish, R. (2008). Blackwater and the privatization of immigration control. *St. Thomas Law Review, 20*(3), 462.

Kouri, J. (2006). Mexico, ACLU preparing lawsuit against US over guard deployment. Retrieved 6/20, 2009, from www.americandaily.com/article/13577.

Kravets, D. (2009). In spy case, Obama's justice department holds fast to state secrets privilege-update. *Wired*, February 13.

Krawczeniuk, B. (2008). Carney focuses on illegal immigration. *Times-Tribune*, February 20.

Kurzban, I. (2008). *Immigration law sourcebook* (11th ed.). Washington, DC: AILA.

Lacey, M. (2008). Janet Napolitano—homeland futility. *The Village Voice*, November 26.

Lakoff, G. (2004). *Don't think of an elephant: Know your values and frame the debate*. White River Junction: Chelsea Green.

Laplante, L. J. (1999). Expedited removal at U.S. borders: A world without a constitution. *New York University Review of Law and Social Change*, 25, 213.

LaVallee, A. (2007). New short story imagines google as a bad big brother. *Wall Street Journal*, September 26.

Legomsky, S. (2006). Deportation and the war on independence. *Cornell Law Review*, 91, 369.

Leiderman, A. (2006). Preserving the constitution's most important human right: Judicial review of mixed questions under the real ID act. *Columbia Law Review*, 106, 1367.

LeMay, M. C. (1987). *From open door to Dutch door: An analysis of U.S. immigration policy since 1820*. New York: Praeger.

Lemons, S. (2009). ACLU and Julio and Julian Mora Sue Joe Arpaio, Arpaio whines on twitter. *Phoenix New Times*, April 2.

Lillis, M. (2009). A border wall, at what cost? *The Washington Independent*, July 27.

Lipowicz, A. (2007). Waxman suggests SBI-net contractor Booz Allen has conflict. *GCN*, February 8.

Lipowicz, A. (2008). DOD tests contractors' ID cards. *Washington Technology*, September 17.

Lipowicz, A. (2009). SBI-net system could get UAVs. *Federal Computer Week*, March 10.

Lipowicz, A. (2009). SBI-net continues to draw fire. *Washington Technology*, June 4.

Little, C. (2009). The medical crisis in immigration detention. *Facing South*, March 26.

Lovato, R. (2008). Immigration reform trapped in political dualism. *New American Media*, December 2.

Lozano v. City of Hazleton. (496 F. Supp. 2d 477 2007).

Lucas, F. (2008). Immigration agents terrorize communities, Obama says. *CNSnews. com*, July 15.

Lupton, D. (2006). Sociology and risk. In G. Mythen, & S. Walklate (Eds.), *Beyond the risk society*. Maidenhead: Open University.

Lutheran Immigration and Refugee Service. (2007). *Locking up family values: The detention of immigrant families*. Washington, DC: LIRS.

Lyon, D. (2003). *Surveillance as social sorting*. New York: Routledge.

Lyon, D. (2007). *Surveillance studies: An overview*. London: Polity.

Mann, J. (2004). *Rise of the Vulcans: The history of Bush's war cabinet*. New York: Penguin Books.

Manns, J. (2006). Private monitoring of gatekeepers: The case of immigration enforcement. *University of Illinois Law Review*, 887.

Martin, D. (1983). Due process and membership in the national community: Political asylum and beyond. *University of Pittsburgh Law Review*, 44, 165.

Massey, D. S. (2005). *Backfire at the border: Why enforcement without legalization cannot stop illegal immigration (No. 29)*. Washington, DC: CATO Institute.

McCarter, M. (2008). Key congressman "cautiously optimistic" about future of SBInet. *HSToday*, May 14.

McCarter, M. (2009). Napolitano links border security, immigration enforcement. *HSToday*, April 8.

McCombs, B. (2007). O'odham leader vows no border fence. *Arizona Daily Star*, August 19.

McCombs, B. (2008). Report: Faulty design turned border fence into dam. *Arizona Daily Star*, August 15.

Medoff, P., & Sklar, H. (1999). *The streets of hope: The fall and rise of an urban neighborhood*. Cambridge, MA: South End Press.

Mendelson, M., Strom, S., & Wishnie, M. (2009). *Collateral damage: An examination of ICE's fugitive operations program*. Washington, DC: Migration Policy Institute.

Meyer, J., & Gorman, A. (2009). Homeland security shifts focus to employers. *The KLose Angeles Times*, March 31.

Milkman, R. (2006). *L.A. story: Immigrant workers and the future of the labor movement*. New York: Russell Sage.

Miller, T. (2005). Blurring the boundaries between immigration and crime control after September 11th. *Boston College Third World Law Journal*, 25(1), 81–124.

Miller, T. (2007). The criminalization of illegal aliens. Unpublished manuscript.

Mitchell, D. J. (2004). Protectionist politics and border security. *Heritage Foundation*, August 19.

Moeckli, D. (2006). The selective war on terror: Executive detention of foreign nationals and the principle of non-discrimination. *Brooklyn Journal of International Law*, 31(2), 495.

Moeckli, D. (2008). *Human rights and non-discrimination in the "war on terror"*. Oxford: Oxford University.

Monahan, T. (2006). The surveillance curriculum: Risk management and social control in the neoliberal school. In T. Monahan (Ed.), *Surveillance and security: Technological politics and power*. London: Routledge.

Montejano, D. (1987). *Anglos and Mexicans in the making of Texas 1836–1986*. Austin, TX: University of Texas.

Moore, S. (2009). Push on immigration crimes is said to shift. *The New York Times*, January 11.

Morse, R. (2008). Fence in the sky: Border wall cuts through native land. *The Native Press*, April 8.

Mouffe, C. (Ed.). (1999). *The challenge of Carl Schmitt*. Brooklyn, NY: Verso.

Nadesan, M. H. (2008). *Governmentality, biopower, and everyday life*. New York: Routledge.

National Network for Immigrant and Refugee Rights (NNIRR). (2008). *Over-raided, under siege: U.S. immigration laws and enforcement destroy the rights of immigrants*, January.

Nedderman, L., Dulitzky, A., & Gilman, D. (2008). *Violations on the part of the united states government of the right to property and non-discrimination held by residents of the Texas Rio Grande valley*. Austin, TX: University of Texas, University of Texas Law School Rapport Center.

Ngai, M. (2004). *Impossible subjects: Illegal aliens and the making of modern America*. Princeton: Princeton University.

Nishimura Ekiu v. United States. (142 U.S. 651 1892).

Norrell, B. (2004). Tohono O'odham: Caretakers protecting sacred mountain. *Indian Country*, March 24.

Norrell, B. (2006). Indigenous opposition to the border wall. *Counterpunch*, November 1.

Norris, N. (2008). Written testimony of the Honorable Ned Norris, Jr., Chairman. Tohono O'odham nation to the subcommittee on fisheries wildlife and oceans and subcommittee on national parks, forests, and public lands of the house committee on natural resources: House of Representatives.

Norton-Taylor, R. (2009). Evidence of torture "buried by ministers." *The Guardian*, February 5.

OIG. (2003). *The September 11 detainees: A review of the treatment of aliens held on immigration charges.* Washington, DC: OIG.

Oliveri, R. C. (2009). Between a rock and a hard place: Landlords, Latinos, anti-illegal immigrant ordinances, and housing discrimination. *Vanderbilt Law Review, 62*(1), 55.

Ong, A. (2006). *Neoliberalism as exception: Mutations in citizenship and sovereignty.* Durham, NC: Duke University.

Ong, B. (2008). Frank Sharry new E.D. at America's voice. http://lawprofessors.typepad.com/immigration/2008/03/frank-sharry-ne.html.

O'Rourke, R. (2007). *CRS report for congress: Coast guard deepwater program: Background, oversight issues, and options for congress* (No. RL33753). Washington, DC: Congressional Research Service.

Oswald, R. (2009). Obama administration defends telecom immunity in new brief. *The Raw Story*, February 26.

Panganiban, R. (2007). *Grantee profile: Study explores radio as a mobilization tool in Latino Community.* Brooklyn, NY: Social Science Research Council (SSRC) Media Research Hub.

Pape, P., & Dew, R. (2004). *No backup: A female agent's life in the FBI.* New York: Carroll & Graff.

Parenti, C. (1999). *Lockdown America: Police and prisons in the age of crisis.* New York: Verso.

Parker, A. (2007). Human rights watch testimony before the house committee on foreign affairs, 2009, from www.hrw.org/en/news/2007/08/08/human-rights-watch-testimony-house-committee-foreign-affairs-subcommittee-western-he.

Parry, J. T. (2007). *Evil, law, and the state.* Amsterdam, NY: Rodopi.

Passenger Cases. (48 U.S. 283 1849).

Penn State Center for Immigrant Rights. (2009). *NSEERS: The consequences of America's efforts to secure its borders.* White Paper.

Phillips, Z. (2007). Features vast expanse. *Government Executive.com*, April 1.

Priest, D., & Goldstein, A. (2008). System of neglect: As tighter immigration policies strain federal agencies, the detainees in their care often pay a heavy cost. *The Washington Post*, May 11.

Prize Cases, 2 Black. (635 1863).

Reno v American-Arab Anti-Discrimination Committee. (525 U.S. 471 1999).

Resnik, J. (2006). Opening the door: Court stripping, unconscionable and unconstitutional? *Slate*, February 1.

Reyes, W. C. (2003). Ten years is enough: Immigrants in San Diego organize against operation gatekeeper. Retrieved September 2, 2009, from www.afsc.org/Immigrants Rights/ht/d/ContentDetails/i/19266.

Rhoads, C., & Chao, L. (2009). Iran's web spying aided by western technology. *The Wall Street Journal*, June 22.

Riesco, M. (2007). Is Pinochet dead? *New Left Review, 47.*

Riley, K. J., Treverton, G. F., & Wilson, J. M. (2005). *Intelligence in the war on terrorism.* Washington, DC: RAND Corporation.

Roberts, A. (2008). *The collapse of fortress Bush: The crisis of authority in American government.* New York: New York University Press.

Roberts, M. (2009). U.S. can lock up immigrants for years. *Associated Press*, March 15.

Rockefeller, J. I. (2007). Partners in the war on terror. *The Washington Post*, October 31.

Rodriguez, A. J. (2008). Punting on the values of federalism in the immigration arena? Evaluating operation linebacker, a state and local law enforcement program along the U.S.–Mexico border. *Columbia Law Review, 108*, 1226.

Rodriguez, C. (2008). The significance of the local in immigration regulation. *Michigan Law Review, 106* (February), 567.

Rogin, M. (1988). *Ronald Reagan, the movie and other episodes in political demonology.* Berkeley, CA: University of California.

Rome, M., & Frickey, J. (2009). Democrats play "soft cop" on immigration reforms. www.socialistaction.org/frickey5.htm.

Rose, N. (1999). *Powers of freedom: Reframing political thought.* Cambridge: Cambridge University Press.

Rotstein, A. (2008). Feds to begin building virtual fence expected to span nearly entire Mexican border in five years. *Associated Press*, May 8.

Saito, N. (1999). Critical race theory as international human rights law. *American Society of International Law Proceedings, 93.*

Saito, N. (2003). The enduring effect of the Chinese exclusion cases: The "plenary power" justification for ongoing abuses of human rights. *Regents of the University of California Asian Law Journal, 10*(13), 12.

Saito, N. (2007). *From Chinese exclusion to Guantanamo Bay: Plenary power and the prerogative state.* Boulder, CO: University Press of Colorado.

Sarat, A., & Clarke, C. (2008). Beyond discretion: Prosecution, the logic of sovereignty, and the limits of law. *Law & Social Inquiry, 33*(2), 387.

Savage, C. (2009). Obama looks to limit impact of tactic Bush used to sidestep new laws. *The New York Times*, March 9.

Scheuerman, W. (2004). *Liberal democracy and the social acceleration of time.* Baltimore, MD: Johns Hopkins University Press.

Schiavone, M. (2008). *Unions in crisis? the future of organized labor in America.* Westport: Praeger.

Schneiderman, D. (2000). Public perspectives on privatization: Constitutional approaches to privatization: An inquiry into the magnitude of neo-liberal constitutionalism. *Law and Contemporary Problems, 63*, 83.

Schooner Exchange v. McFadden. (7 Cranch 116).

Schuerman, W., E. (1999). *The end of law.* New York: Rowman & Littlefield.

Sciacchitano, K. (2008). From NAFTA to the SPP: Here comes the security and prosperity partnership. *Dollars & Sense*, February.

Sharkey, J. (2008). Arne Duncan's privatization agenda. *Counterpunch*, December 18.

Sheridan, M. B., Hsu, S., & Fainaru, S. (2009). Plan would deploy guard near Mexico. *The Washington Post*, April 25.

Sherman, C. (2008). Judge stalls border fence at UT Brownsville. *Associated Press*, July 1.

Shorrock, T. (2008). *Spies for hire: The secret world of intelligence outsourcing.* New York: Simon & Schuster.

Sieff, K. (2008). Tamez to be awarded by Texas civil rights project. *The Brownsville Herald*, October 1.

Sieff, K. (2008). Border fence construction to begin at UTB-TSC. *The Brownsville Herald*, October 2.

Simon, J. (1997). Governing through crime. In L. Friedman, & G. Fisher (Eds.), *The crime conundrum: Essays in criminal justice.* Boulder, CO: Westview.

Simon, J. (2001). Fear and loathing in late modernity: Reflections on the cultural sources of mass imprisonment. *Punishment & Society, 2*, 213.

Singel, R. (2008). Border agents can search laptops without cause. *Wired*, April 22.

Sparke, M. (2006). A neoliberal nexus: Economy, security and the biopolitics of citizenship on the border. *Political Geography, 25*(2), 151.

Stern, R. (2008). Napolitano yanks Arpaio's immigration funding. *Phoenix News Times*, May 14.

Story, B. (2008). The people vs Michael Chertoff. *The Nation Magazine*, March 11.

Story, B. (2008). The people vs. Michael Chertoff: An elder fights back. Message posted to http://elder-abuse-cyberray.blogspot.com/2008/03/seizing-of-elders-property-is-wrong.html.

Stout, D. (2008). Justices refuse checks on border fences. *The New York Times*, June 24.

Strohm, C. (2009). Governors, Napolitano discussing changes to real ID law. *NextGov: Technology and the Business of Government*, March 3.

Stumpf, J. P. (2006). The crimmigration crisis: Immigrants, crime, and sovereign power. *American University Law Review, 56*, 367.

Suskind, R. (2006). *The one percent doctrine: Deep inside America's pursuit of its enemies since 9/11.* New York: Simon & Schuster.

Tanner, M., & Davies, H. (2006). *Effective border management through mission critical collaboration.* Annapolis: CollabraSpace Revolutionary Collaboration.

TEDBlog. (2009). Q&A with Clay Shirky on twitter and Iran. http://blog.ted.com/2009/06/qa_with_clay_sh.php.

Theimer, S. (2002). Lobbyists aim for homeland security department's millions. *The Boston Globe*, November 22.

Theimer, S. (2005). Plum job opportunities await old cabinet. *AP*, January 10.

Thompson, G. (2009). U.S. taking steps to control violence on the Mexican border. *The New York Times*, March 24.

Tillman, L. (2009). Officials present "no fence" alternative. *Brownsville Herald*, March 6.

Tirman, J. (Ed.) (2004). *The maze of fear: Security and migration after September 11th.* New York: The New Press.

Tomsic, M. (2008). Many Latinos deported, not for felonies, but for minor offenses. *IndyWeek.Com*, December 24.

TRAC.syr.edu: Transactional Records Access Clearing House. (2009). Website. Retrieved May, 2009, from http://trac.syr.edu.

Trumbull, M. (2005). For illegals, a spreading backlash. *The Christian Science Monitor*, August 12.

Turnbull, L. (2009). Workers arrested in Bellingham work-site raid freed. *Seattle Times*, March 31.

U.S. v Curtiss-Wright Export Corporation. (299 U.S. 304 1936).

United States Ex Rel. Knauff v. Shaughnessy. (338 U.S. 537 1950).

United States Ex Rel. Mezei v Shaughnessy. (345 U.S. 206 1953).

United States v. Arnold. (523 3d 941 2008).

Valenzuela Jr., A. (2006). *New immigrants and day labor: The potential for violence. Immigration and crime, ethnicity and violence.* New York: NYU Press.

Valverde, M., & Mopas, M. (2004). Insecurity and the dream of targeted governance. In W. Larner, & W. Walters (Eds.), *Global governmentality: Governing international spaces.* New York: Routledge.

Vargas, M. (2005). Immigration consequences of guilty pleas of convictions in New York courts. Unpublished manuscript.

Varsanyi, M. W. (2008). *Immigration policing through the backdoor: City ordinances, the "right to the city," and the exclusion of undocumented day laborers.* San Diego, CA: University of California, The Center for Comparative Immigration Studies.

Vogel, R. D. (2007). Transient servitude: The U.S. guest worker program for exploiting Mexican and Central American workers. *Monthly Review*, March 5.

Wald, M. (2008). Real ID rules loosened, but state still balks. *The Seattle Times*, January 12.

Walters, W. (2008). Putting the migration-security complex in its place. In L. Amoore, & M. de Goede (Eds.), *Risk and the war on terror* (p. 158). New York: Routledge.

Ward, B. (2008). Don't fence me in with eminent domain. Retrieved September 2, 2009, from www.njeminentdomain.com/national-dont-fence-me-in-with-eminent-domain.html.

The Washington Times (2008). Texas cities oppose border fence: Residents deny federal officials access to land. (2008). *The Washington Times*, February 21.

Weissman, D. (2009). *The policies and politics of local immigration enforcement law.* Chapel Hill: UNC Law School.

Welch, M. (2003). *Detained: Immigration laws and the expanding I.N.S. jail complex.* Philadelphia: Temple University.

Whitney, M. (2005). Failing upwards: The rise of Michael Chertoff. *Counterpunch*, January 22/24.

Wilson, J. G., Benavides, J., Reisinger, A., Leman, J., Hurwitz, Z., Spangler, J., et al. (2008). *An analysis of demographic disparities associated with the proposed U.S.–Mexico border fence in Cameron County, Texas.* Austin, TX: University of Texas.

Winn, P. (2008). Border fence is progressing but it's not the one congress had in mind. *CNSnews.Com*, December 18.

Witness for Peace (2009) The Change We Need for Latin America. Retrieved July 31, 2009, from http://74.125.47.132/search?q=cache:PjWA9duBZuwJ:org2.democracyinaction.org/o/5436/t/2467/petition.jsp%3Fpetition_KEY%3D163+%22"instead+of+spending+billions+in+a+failed+"supply+side"+strategy%22&cd=5&hl=en&ct=clnk&gl=us&client=safari.

Yale-Loehr, S., & Papademetriou, D. (2005). *Secure borders, open doors: Visa procedures in the post-September 11 era.* Washington, DC: Migration Policy Institute.

Yamataya v Fisher. (189 U.S. 86 1903).

Yost, P. (2009). Obama administration tries to kill email case. *Associated Press*, February 21.

Yoxall, P. (2006). The minuteman project, gone in a minute or here to stay? The origin, history and future of citizen activism on the United States–Mexico border. *The University of Miami Inter-American Law Review, 37*, 517.

Zadvydas v. Davis. (533 U.S. 678 2001).

Zimmer, M. (2007). Privacy and surveillance in web 2.0: Unintended consequences and the rise of "netaveillance". http://idtrail.org/content/view/696/42/.

Index